Seaside Interiors
Intérieurs de la côte
Häuser am Meer

Seaside

Intérieurs de la côte   Häuser am Meer

Edited by Angelika Taschen
Diane Dorrans Saeks

Interiors

TASCHEN

KÖLN LONDON MADRID NEW YORK PARIS TOKYO

Endpapers | Pages de garde | Vorsatzpapier:
Sailing in the Aegean Sea, Greece
Voguer sur la mer Egée, Grèce
Segeln in der Ägäis, Griechenland
Photo: Paul Ryan/International Interiors

Pages 2 and 3: At Knokke-Heist Beach, Flanders, Belgium
Pages 2 et 3: A la plage, Knokke-Heist en Flandres, Belgique
Seite 2 und 3: Am Strand von Knokke-Heist, Flandern, Belgien
Photo: Deidi von Schaewen

Pages 4 and 5: Living near Tangier, Northern Morocco
Pages 4 et 5: Vivre près de Tanger, Maroc du Nord
Seite 4 und 5: Bei Tanger, Nordmarokko
Photo: Deidi von Schaewen

Pages 6 and 7: Sunbathing on the coast of Chile, Los Vilos, Coquimbo Region
Pages 6 et 7: Prendre des bains de soleil sur la côte du Chili, Los Vilos, Coquimbo Region
Seite 6 und 7: Sonnenbaden in Chile, Los Vilos, Coquimbo Region
Photo: Guy Wenborne

Pages 8 and 9: Cluster of bungalows on the tidal lagoon of Hana Iti, Huahine, Tahiti
Pages 8 et 9: Un groupe de bungalows au bord du lagon à marées de Hana Iti, Huahine, Tahiti
Seite 8 und 9: Bungalows an der Tidenseite der Lagune von Hana Iti, Huahine, Tahiti
Photo: Guy Hervais & Bibi Gex

Pages 10 and 11: Morning on the Baltic Sea
Pages 10 et 11: Un matin sur une plage de la Baltique
Seite 10 und 11: Morgen an der Ostsee
Photo: Edvin Paas

Page 15: On the terrace of Catherine Feric, St. Barthélemy, Guadeloupe
Page 15: Sur la terrasse de Catherine Feric, Saint Barthélemy, Guadeloupe
Seite 15: Auf der Terrasse von Catherine Feric, St. Barthélemy, Guadeloupe
Photo: Jean-Pierre Godeaut & Philippe Seulliet/Inside

© 2000 Benedikt Taschen Verlag GmbH
Hohenzollernring 53, D–50672 Köln
www.taschen.com

© 2000 VG Bild-Kunst, Bonn, for the work
by Tamara de Lempicka

Edited by Angelika Taschen, Cologne
Text edited by Ursula Fethke, Cologne
Lithography by Ute Wachendorf, Cologne
German translation by Gabriele-Sabine Gugetzer, Hamburg
French translation by Philippe Safavi, Paris

Printed in Spain

ISBN 3-8228-6414-5
ISBN 3-8228-6159-6 (Edition with French cover)

Contents
Sommaire
Inhalt

Blue Horizons
By Diane Dorrans Saeks

Horizons bleus
De Diane Dorrans Saeks

Blaue Horizonte
Von Diane Dorrans Saeks

I spent my childhood summers in New Zealand at the beach, diving into churning waves, floating on limpid aquamarine water, and racing along the sea-slick sands, swallowing great gulps of air that tasted of sea urchins and salt and seaweed. Snorkeling for hours, I glimpsed garden-green underwater worlds of sunlight flashing and refracting on limpet shells, blanched coral branches and skittering crabs. Schools of silvery fish darted among the rocks and disappeared. Zigzagging across Diamond Harbour in the South Island in an old sailboat, I dreamed of explorers crossing oceans and seas, their hopes filling the sails and buoying their brave ships. The coast has always been a point of departure, offering up all the inspiration in the world. Golden days on the shore spun by as we gathered triangular white pipi shells in hand-woven flax baskets, built labyrinthian sandcastles decorated with seagrass and shells, and spent the last pearlescent hours of the day lying in the warm sand dunes watching the tide and feeling the cool, salty air licking sunburnt shoulders. Even when it was dark, we never wanted to go inside. The coast is an infinite world. The sea and salt air and sunshine engage all the senses, and heighten a sense of well-being. Freed of noise and complication, the seaside mind can float free, listening for the soprano sounds of the wind, the reassuring screech and squawk of seagulls. Escaping the city, sunstruck sailors follow the stars over the horizon to discover islands beyond the band of blue. In search of the perfect beach, I've headed to the shore in many other parts of the world since those glory days of picnics and tide pools and seagulls. I've beach-combed in Sri Lanka, Salvador de Bahia, the Côte d'Azur, Big Sur, Mendocino, Mykonos, Zihuatanejo in Mexico, Rio de Janeiro, Long Island, Goa, Costa Careyes, Bar Harbor on the coast of Maine, Penzance in Cornwall, Bondi Beach near Sydney, Palm Beach, New Zealand's Kare Kare, and Majorca, and Camber Sands on the south-east coast of England. I've got shells, sand in my sandals, and pockets full of memories. We would like to take you on a journey to some of the most beautiful and pure places on the globe. Skies are cerulean blue. Follow us as we set sail for distant, dreamy shores.

J'ai passé tous les étés de mon enfance sur la plage en Nouvelle-Zélande, plongeant dans les vagues, faisant la planche sur une eau limpide aigue-marine ou courant sur le sable humide, inspirant de grandes bouffées d'air frais qui sentait bon le sel, les oursins et les algues. Pendant des heures, armée de mon masque et de mon tuba, j'observais des jardins sous-marins où les rayons du soleil faisaient scintiller les berniques, les branches de corail et les crabes fuyants. Des bancs de poissons argentés fusaient entre les rochers avant de disparaître. Zigzaguant dans un vieux voilier à travers Diamond Harbour, sur l'île du Sud, je rêvais d'explorateurs traversant les océans, leurs espoirs gonflant leurs voiles et poussant en avant leurs vaisseaux intrépides. La côte a toujours été un point de départ, offrant toute l'inspiration du monde. Les jours dorés se succédaient tandis que nous recueillions des coquillages dans des paniers en lin tressés à la main, construisions des châteaux de sable labyrinthiques ornés d'algues et de coquillages, et passions les dernières heures cuivrées de la journée couchés dans les dunes, à contempler la marée et à sentir l'air frais et iodé lécher nos épaules brûlées par le soleil. Même une fois la nuit tombée, nous ne voulions pas rentrer à la maison. La côte est un monde sans fin. La mer, l'air salé et le soleil titillent tous les sens et renforcent le sentiment de bien-être. En quête de la plage parfaite, j'ai sillonné les rivages de bien des coins de la planète depuis ces jours heureux de pique-niques, de barbotage et de mouettes. J'ai passé au peigne fin les plages du Sri Lanka, de Salvador de Bahia, de la Côte d'Azur, de Big Sur, de Mendocino, de Mykonos, de Zihuatanejo au Mexique, de Rio de Janeiro, de Long Island, de Goa, de la Costa Careyes, de Bar Harbour sur la côte du Maine, de Penzance en Cornouailles, de Bondi Beach près de Sydney, de Palm Beach, de Kare Kare en Nouvelle-Zélande, de Majorque et de Camber Sands au sud-est de l'Angleterre. J'ai des coquillages et du sable dans mes sandales et des souvenirs pleins les poches. Nous aimerions vous emmener visiter certains des endroits les plus beaux et les plus purs du globe. Suivez-nous tandis que nous mettons le cap sur des rivages lointains et enchanteurs.

Während meiner Kindheit in Neuseeland verbrachte ich die Sommermonate am Strand. Ich tauchte ein in stampfende Wellen, ließ mich treiben auf glasklarem, aquamarinblauem Wasser, rannte an feuchtglitschigen Stränden entlang und sog gierig die Meerluft ein, die nach Seeigeln und Salz und Algen schmeckte. Bei stundenlangen Schnorchelausflügen entdeckte ich die grasgrün gefärbte Unterwasserwelt. Silbrig glänzende Fischschwärme tauchten pfeilschnell zwischen Felsen auf und verschwanden wieder. Auf einem Segeltörn über Diamond Harbour auf der Südinsel träumte ich in einem alten Segelboot von Entdeckern, wie sie Meere und Ozeane erkundeten, wie ihre Hoffnungen die Segel blähten und ihre Schiffe über das Wasser trieb. Goldene Tage am Strand vergingen wie im Flug, während wir dreieckige weiße »pipi shells« in handgeflochtenen Flachskörben sammelten, labyrinthische Sandburgen bauten, diese mit Strandhafer und Muscheln dekorierten und die letzten perlmuttschimmernden Stunden des Tages in den warmen Dünen verbrachten. Nie wollten wir hineingehen, selbst nachdem es schon dunkel geworden war. Die Küste ist eine unendliche Welt. Meer, salzige Luft und Sonne nehmen sämtliche Sinne gefangen. Befreit vom Lärm und allen Komplikationen kann der Geist sich am Meer unbeschwert bewegen, dem Sopran des Wir des nachhängen und dem beruhigenden Kreischen der Seemöwen. Seit jenen wunderbaren Tagen voller Picknicks und Tidenlöchern und Seemöwen bin ich auf der Suche nach dem perfekten Strand. Ich durchkämmte die Strände auf Sri Lanka und bei Salvador de Bahia, an der Côte d'Azur und in Big Sur, bei Mendocino, auf Mykonos, im mexikanischen Zihuatanejo, in Rio de Janeiro, auf Long Island und Goa, Bar Harbor an der Küste von Maine, Penzance in Cornwall, Bondi Beach bei Sydney, Palm Beach, Costa Careyes, dem neuseeländischen Kare Kare, auf Mallorca und in Camber Sands an der Südostküste von England. Von dort brachte ich Muscheln, Sand in meinen Sandalen und wunderbare Erinnerungen zurück. Wir wollen Sie an einige der schönsten und ursprünglichsten Orte dieser Welt entführen. Folgen Sie uns, wenn wir die Segel setzen und Kurs nehmen auf weit entfernt liegende Traumstrände.

Destination Europe

The allure and variety of European beaches inspire the most pleasant form of wanderlust. A dreamy traveler could begin in the north with a visit to the island of Gotland, off the coast of Sweden. There the freedom-loving wanderer can hike at will along pebbly beaches, forage in forests stocked with wild mushrooms and blackberries, and circle limestone monoliths on rocky shores. On the French Ile de Noirmoutier, damp autumn afternoons smell of clams and sea-wrack and oysters. Strolling along the beach, bundled in slick raincoats and woolly mufflers, fresh-air seekers encounter leaping dogs, skittering crabs, and stolid old horses. Seasons on the islands of Filicudi and Pantelleria, and on the deserted coasts of Portugal and Latvia, sail by with breathtaking speed, and soon seagulls hover and huddle waiting for the first signs of spring. High in the hills above the Côte d'Azur, Pierre Cardin, patron of the avant-garde, frolics with a favorite dog in his architectural playland, a tribute to 20th-century creativity. On the Greek Islands, swimmers dive naked into the glistening waters. Ulysses and his heroic sailors haunt grottoes and wave-lapped beaches.

Le charme et la variété des plages d'Europe suscitent la plus délicieuse des envies de flâner. Le voyageur rêveur peut commencer au nord par une visite sur l'île de Gotland, au large de la Suède. Là, il pourra errer librement le long des plages de galets, cueillir les champignons et les mûres dans les bois et contourner des monolithes de calcaire sur la grève rocailleuse. Sur l'île française de Noirmoutier, les après-midi humides d'automne sentent la palourde, l'algue et l'huître. En se promenant sur la plage emmitouflés dans des cirés et des cache-nez laineux, les amateurs de grand air croisent des chiens joueurs, des crabes fuyants et de bons gros chevaux. Sur les îles de Filicudi et de Pantelleria, comme sur les côtes désertes du Portugal et de la Lettonie, les saisons se succèdent à une allure étourdissante et, bientôt, les mouettes se rassemblent et ses blottissent en attendant les premiers signes du printemps. Haut perché sur les collines qui dominent la Côte d'Azur, Pierre Cardin, mécène avant-gardiste, joue avec son chien préféré sur son terrain de jeux architectural, un hommage à la créativité du 20e siècle. Sur les îles grecques, les baigneurs plongent nus dans les eaux étincelantes. Ulysse et ses marins héroïques hantent encore les grottes bleues et les plages léchées par les vagues.

Der Reiz und die Vielfalt europäischer Strände machen wanderlustig. Ein träumender Reisender könnte dieser Lust in Nordeuropa auf der Insel Gotland, vor der schwedischen Küste, frönen und dort, als freiheitsliebender Wanderer, nach Lust und Laune die Kiesstrände erkunden, in den Wäldern nach Pilzen und Brombeeren stöbern und an den Felsküsten Kalksteinmonolithen umrunden. Auf der französischen Ile de Noirmoutier riechen die feuchten Herbstnachmittage nach Muscheln und Seetang und Austern. Bei einem Strandspaziergang in dickem Ölzeug und wollenen Schals treffen Frischluftfanatiker auf umhertollende Hunde, krabbelnde Krebse und phlegmatische alte Pferde. Auf Inseln wie Filicudi und Pantelleria oder an den einsamen Küsten von Portugal und Lettland verfliegen die Jahreszeiten mit atemberaubender Geschwindigkeit. Bald warten die Seemöwen, dicht zusammengedrängt in der Luft kreisend, schon auf die ersten Vorboten des Frühlings. Hoch über der Côte d'Azur thronend vergnügt sich Pierre Cardin, Ikone der Avantgarde, mit einem Lieblingshund in seinem architektonischen Spielzeugland – einer Verbeugung vor der Kreativität des 20. Jahrhunderts. Auf den griechischen Inseln tauchen die Schwimmer nackt in glitzernde Wellen ein. In den blauen Grotten und auf den wellenumspülten Stränden weht noch immer der Geist Odysseus' und seiner heldenhaften Matrosen.

Johan Brauner

Gotland, Sweden, Baltic Sea

Gotland, la plus grande île de la mer Baltique, ne se trouve qu'à 90 kilomètres des côtes suédoises, mais sa culture, son paysage et ses formations calcaires sculptées par les vents lui donnent un air à part. Le climat y étant plus chaud en été que sur le continent, les randonnées sur ses grèves sauvages et les pique-niques sur ses plages de galets y sont des passe-temps favoris. La Suède étant l'un des rares pays où existe depuis longtemps le droit de passage sur les propriétés privées, visiteurs et riverains peuvent se promener librement partout, camper, cueillir des champignons sauvages et des baies en automne, ou simplement jouir de la beauté de la nature et du grand air sans être dérangés. Pour les jours où le vent du nord amène ses orages, l'île offre des concerts, une semaine médiévale, des danses folkloriques et un festival de cinéma. Partout, la nature triomphe. L'observation des bergeronnettes citrines, des chevaliers, des martins roselins et des bécasseaux comble les ornithologues de joie.

Gotland, the largest island in the Baltic Sea, lies just 90 kilometers off the Swedish coast, but its culture, natural landscape, and wind-sculpted limestone formations give it a distinctive air. The climate is warmer in summer than on the Swedish mainland, so hiking on miles of undeveloped beaches, and picnicking along the pebble-strewn shore are popular pastimes. Uniquely, Sweden has a long tradition of Right of Common Access, so visitors and local inhabitants may roam freely on private land to camp, gather edible wild mushrooms and pick berries in the autumn, or simply enjoy the beauties of nature and the fresh air, undisturbed. For days when rainstorms fly in from the north, the island offers music festivals, an annual medieval week, country-dancing festivals, and a film festival. And nature is triumphant. Sightings of citrine wagtails, raptors, sandpipers, rose-colored starlings, and buff-breasted snipes send birdwatchers into raptures.

Gotland ist die größte Insel in der Ostsee. Sie liegt nur 90 Kilometer von der schwedischen Küste entfernt, doch eine eigene Kultur, Landschaft und die vom Wind geschaffenen Kalksteinformationen verleihen der Insel etwas ganz Eigenes. Im Sommer ist es hier wärmer als auf dem schwedischen Festland. Deshalb erfreuen sich Wanderungen entlang kilometerlanger unerschlossener Strände und Picknicks am Küstenstreifen aus Kieselstein großer Beliebtheit. Das Jedermannsrecht hat in Schweden eine lange Tradition: Besucher und Bewohner können ungehindert auf Privatland spazieren gehen und campen, im Herbst Pilze und Beeren suchen oder einfach nur die Schönheit der Natur und die frische Luft genießen. An Tagen, an denen von Norden kommende Regenstürme die Insel überziehen, gibt es jede Menge Festivals, die der Musik, dem Mittelalter, den alten Tänzen auf dem Land und dem Film gewidmet sind. Und über allem triumphiert die Natur. Hier sieht man Zitronenstelzen, Greifvögel, Strandläufer, Rosenstare und Grasläufer, deren Anblick Vogelliebhaber in Verzückung versetzt.

Previous pages: *This charming 200-year-old house, originally the residence of people who made their living from the sea, has become the summer residence of graphic designer, Johan Brauner. Walls are painted in the old style, in cheerful, winter chill-chasing pink with a sky-blue border. Collections of scavenged stones, country crafts, and unpretentious antiques are displayed like precious objects.*
Above and left: *The small, sunny living room has pretty-in-pink walls, traditional blue-painted doors, and a harmonious collection of furniture. The cottage is not electrified, so Johan Brauner spends evenings by candlelight.*

Double page précédente: *Cette charmante maison, qui appartenait il y a 200 ans à des gens qui vivaient de la mer, est devenue la résidence de vacances du dessinateur Johan Brauner. Les murs sont peints à l'ancienne. Les joyeux pans roses qui repoussent le froid sont bordés d'une frise bleu ciel. Des collections de cailloux, d'objets artisanaux et d'antiquités sont présentées comme autant de trésors.*
Ci-dessus et à gauche: *Le petit salon ensoleillé a des murs roses, des portes peintes dans le bleu traditionnel et un ensemble harmonieux de meubles. La maison n'ayant pas l'électricité, Johan Brauner passe ses soirées à la lueur des bougies.*

Vorhergehende Doppelseite: *Dieses atmosphärische, 200 Jahre alte Haus war einst das Heim von Menschen, die ihren Lebensunterhalt dem Meer abtrotzten. Heute ist es das Sommerhaus des Grafikers Johan Brauner. Die Wände sind nach alter Art gestrichen – in einem fröhlichen Rosa mit himmelblauem Rand.*
Oben und links: *das kleine sonnige Wohnzimmer mit seinen ansprechenden, rosafarbenen Wänden, den traditionell blauen Türen und harmonisch aufeinander abgestimmtem Mobiliar. Es gibt keine Elektrizität; Johan Brauner verbringt die Abende bei Kerzenlicht.*

Gotland, Sweden, Baltic Sea 57°30'N 18°33'E   Johan Brauner

Right: Time for gardening!

Below and following pages: Johan Brauner has carefully preserved the historic style and mood of the two-room house and site. The art is to make the rooms look as if they had not been touched, even when time and weather and sunlight have faded and chipped and worn away at the wood, the old plaster walls, and the plank floors. No signs of modern life should intrude. The white-walled bedroom, with its angelic sleeping inhabitant, was furnished with an old painted country bed, a traditional seaman-crafted corner chair, slat-backed chairs, and a round pine table.

A droite: Il est temps de se mettre au travail!

Ci-dessous et double page suivante: Johan Brauner a soigneusement conservé le style et le charme historiques de ses deux pièces. Tout l'art réside à faire croire que rien n'a été touché et qu'on a laissé les années, les intempéries et le soleil faner et écailler le bois, les vieux murs en plâtre et les lattes du plancher. Aucun signe de la vie moderne ne doit apparaître. La chambre aux murs blancs, où dort un petit ange, a été meublée d'un vieux lit paysan peint, d'une chaise d'angle traditionnelle confectionnée par un marin, de chaises à dossier en barreaux et d'une table ronde en sapin.

Rechts: Die Gartenarbeit ruft!

Unten und folgende Doppelseite: Johan Brauner hat die historische Ausstrahlung und den Stil dieses Zweizimmerhauses bewahren können. Die Kunst dabei ist, die Zimmer unberührt wirken zu lassen, auch wenn der Zahn der Zeit – und des Klimas – am Holz genagt und die Gipswände und Dielen gebleicht und abgewetzt hat. Symbole des modernen Lebens mussten draußen bleiben. Das weiß gestrichene Schlafzimmer mit dem schlafenden Kind wurde mit einem alten bemalten Bett im Landhausstil, einem Eckstuhl, wie ihn traditionellerweise Matrosen fertigten, Stühlen mit Holzstäben und einem runden Tisch aus Kiefernholz eingerichtet.

Sylvia and
Edvin Paas

Gulf of Riga, Latvia

Les jours d'été sont délicieusement longs pour Sylvia et Edvin Paas lorsqu'ils se réfugient dans leur maison de vacances lettone. Nichée sur la berge du golfe de Riga, là où la Dvina occidentale se jette dans la Baltique, celle-ci leur offre le luxe de retrouver la simplicité. On puise l'eau au puits, on mange les fraises et les framboises du jardin et le brochet ou l'anguille pêchés par Edvin. «C'est comme un conte de fées», confie Edvin, chef cuisinier aux éditions Taschen. «Nous n'avons pas de voisins. Il n'y a que moi et ma famille. C'est comme si la mer nous appartenait». Construite au début du siècle pour un capitaine de la marine russe, leur maison conserve ses ornements en bois chantournés et ses vitraux artisanaux. La «Laivinieki» (maison de marin) se dresse sur un demi-hectare de terrain, avec sa grange à foin, son saloir, deux autres dépendances qui abritaient autrefois le bétail et les chevaux, et son sauna traditionnel.

Summer days are long and luscious for Sylvia and Edvin Paas when they escape to their Latvian holiday house. Nestling on the shore of the Gulf of Riga, where the Daugava River flows into the Baltic Sea, their charming turn-of-the-century cottage affords them the luxury of stepping back to simpler times. Water is drawn from a well, strawberries and raspberries are cultivated in their garden, and when fish is on the menu, Edvin himself goes out to catch pike or eels. "It's like a fairy tale," admitted Edvin, chef at Benedikt Taschen Verlag. "I have no neighbors. It's just me and my family. We feel as if the sea belongs to us." Their house was built for a captain of the Russian fleet, and it retains the original wooden fretwork ornamentation and hand-crafted stained-glass windows. Known locally as "Laivinieki" (Boatman's House) it stands on a half hectare, with a hay barn, a fish-salting room, two barns which formerly housed cattle and horses, and a traditional sauna.

Für Sylvia und Edvin Paas sind die Sommertage lang und wunderbar – wenn sie Zeit für ihr lettisches Ferienhaus finden. Eingekuschelt in den Küstenstreifen des Golfs von Riga, wo die Daugava in die Ostsee mündet, bietet ihr liebenswertes Sommerhäuschen aus der Jahrhundertwende den Luxus einer Zeitreise zurück in ein einfaches Leben. Sie pumpen ihr Wasser aus dem Brunnen, pflücken Erdbeeren und Himbeeren im Garten und wenn Fisch auf den Tisch kommt, hat ihn Edvin vorher selbst gefangen. »Fast wie aus einem Märchen«, erzählt Edvin, Chefkoch des Benedikt Taschen Verlags. »Wir haben keine Nachbarn. Hier sind nur meine Familie und ich. Und das Gefühl, als würde das Meer uns allein gehören.« Ein Kapitän der russischen Flotte baute das Haus für sich. Es weist noch die ursprünglichen Zierelemente auf: Durchbrucharbeiten aus Holz und handgearbeitete Buntglasfenster. In der Umgebung kennt man das Haus unter dem Namen »Laivinieki« (Bootsbauerhaus). Auf dem einen halben Hektar großen Grundstück stehen noch ein Heuschober, ein Raum zum Einsalzen der Fische, zwei Schober, die früher als Rinder- und Pferdeställe dienten, und eine traditionelle Sauna.

Previous pages: Sylvia and Edvin Paas, who live in Cologne, enjoy the simple country pleasures of walking, cooking, fishing, and sun-bathing. Their daughter, and her baby, Laira, revel in the delicious days of summer. In winter, the sea is frozen over and they can walk for miles on the ice.
Above and right: The air is so soothing and their bedroom is so cosy, said Edvin Paas, that they sleep like babies. Elaborate windows cast Klimt-like shadows on the walls.
Facing page: Sylvia's flowers, simply arranged, grace the dining table.

Double page précédente: Sylvia et Edvin Paas, qui vivent à Cologne, aiment les plaisirs simples de la campagne tels que les promenades, la cuisine, la pêche et les bains de soleil. Leur fille et son bébé, Laira, profitent de ces délicieux jours d'été. L'hiver, quand la mer gèle, on peut parcourir des kilomètres sur la glace.
Ci-dessus et à droite: De l'aveu même d'Edvin Paas, l'air est si pur et leur chambre si douillette qu'ils dorment comme des bébés. Les fenêtres finement ouvragées projettent des ombres à la Gustav Klimt.
Page de droite: Les bouquets de Sylvia, d'une simplicité raffinée, ornent la table de la salle à manger.

Vorhergehende Doppelseite: Sylvia und Edvin Paas leben in Köln und genießen die einfachen Landfreuden – Spazierengehen, Kochen, Fischen, Sonnenbaden. Ihre Tochter und deren Baby Laira räkeln sich wohlig im warmen Sommertag. Im Winter dagegen ist das Meer zugefroren und man kann stundenlang auf dem Eis spazierengehen.
Oben und rechts: Die Landluft ist so entspannend und ihr Schlafzimmer so kuschelig, dass sie schlafen wie die Murmeltiere, erzählt Edvin Paas. Die aufwändig gestalteten Fenster werfen Schatten an die Wand, die an Motive von Klimt erinnern.
Rechte Seite: Ein einfaches Blumenarrangement von Sylvia Paas schmückt den Esstisch.

Gulf of Riga, Latvia 57°30'N 24°20'E   Sylvia and Edvin Paas

Facing page: Preparing pickles and cooking lake-caught pike are Edvin's special delights. In late June, the countryside celebrates with traditional mid-summer bonfires, and feasting.
Above: With skill and sensitivity to the indigenous architecture, Sylvia and Edvin Paas have restored their charming century-old Latvian house. Water is drawn from a well. Sylvia and Edvin love to spend evenings on the verandah watching the sun go down over the Gulf of Riga.
Right: the sauna. "In winter we love to have a sauna, then roll in the snow. It's sauna madness," said Edvin.

Page de gauche: Préparer des pickles et cuisiner les brochets qu'il a pêchés dans le lac sont un des grands plaisirs d'Edvin. Vers la fin juin, toute la campagne célèbre le solstice d'été avec des feux de camp et des banquets.
Ci-dessus: Sylvia et Edvin Paas ont restauré leur charmante maison de marin avec habileté et le respect de l'architecture locale. L'eau est tirée du puits. Sylvia et Edvin aiment passer leurs soirées sous la véranda et regarder le soleil se coucher sur le golfe de Riga.
A droite: le sauna. «En hiver, on adore y aller, puis se rouler comme des fous dans la neige».

Linke Seite: Edvin macht Gewürzgurken ein und bereitet selbst gefangenen Hecht zu. Ende Juni feiert man überall auf dem Land das Mittsommerfest mit Freudenfeuern und üppigen Gelagen.
Oben: Mit Geschick und Sensibilität haben Sylvia und Edvin Paas ihr hübsches, 100 Jahre altes Haus in Lettland restauriert. Sie lieben es, die Abende auf der Veranda zu verbringen und die Sonnenuntergänge über dem Golf von Riga zu beobachten.
Rechts: die Sauna. »Im Winter gehen wir erst in die Sauna und wälzen uns dann im Schnee. Da leiden wir unter Saunawahn!«, erzählt Edvin Paas.

Mandy Coakley and Christopher Crooks

Rye Bay, England, Channel

La baie de Rye, qui s'ouvre sur la Manche au sud de l'Angleterre, est un paradis pour les oiseaux, en particulier pour les hirondelles de mer, les bergeronnettes flavéoles, les culs-blancs et, en hiver, les canards et les échassiers. Ses plages larges et ses dunes de sable de Camber attirent également de fougueux cavaliers, des clubs de judo, des surfeurs sur sable et des amateurs de cerfs-volants. Le cottage appartenait autrefois à un véliplanchiste qui l'a vendu à Christopher Crooks et à Mandy Coakley. Celle-ci possède une agence de coiffeurs, de maquilleurs et de stylistes dans le quartier de Notting Hill à Londres. Leur maison se dresse juste au bord de la plage. «Quand la marée est basse, on aperçoit à peine la mer sur la ligne d'horizon». Quand elle remonte, Mandy, Chris et leurs amis mettent les voiles vers le port voisin de Rye. Coakley et Crooks sont tombés sous le charme hivernal de cette côte sud de l'Angleterre. «On se promène dans les dunes, la lumière est grise et sinistre. C'est tout simplement magnifique!», déclare Mandy.

Windswept Rye Bay, in East Sussex on the English Channel, is a rich habitat for birds, including terns, yellow wagtails, wheatears, and, in winter, ducks and waders. Its broad, gusty beaches and the dunes of Camber Sands also draw lively gatherings of energetic equestrians, judo schools, sandsurfers, and kite-flyers. The local fauna included the windsurfer who sold Mandy Coakley and Christopher Crooks their South Coast house standing right on the edge of the broad, tidal sands. "When the tide is out, the sea is barely on the horizon," said Mandy, who has an agency representing hair and make-up artists, and stylists in London's chic Notting Hill. When the tide comes in, she and Chris and their friends sail to the nearby harbor town of Rye. Coakley and Crooks have fallen under the winter spell of the South Coast. "We wander along the sand dunes, the light is grey and bleak, and it's just wonderful," she said.

Die windumtoste Bucht von Rye, in East Sussex am Ärmelkanal gelegen, ist ein artenreiches Vogelhabitat. Hier gibt es Seeschwalben, Gelbe Bachstelzen, Steinschmätzer und im Winter Enten und Sumpfvögel. Allerdings zieht es zu den breiten, vom Wind verwehten Stränden und Dünen von Camber Sands auch Reiter, Judokämpfer, Sandsurfer und Leute, die Drachen steigen lassen. Zu dieser »Lokalfauna« gehörte auch der Windsurfer, der Mandy Coakley und Christopher Crooks ihr Haus an der englischen Südküste verkaufte. Es steht direkt am Rand des breiten Sandstrands. »Bei Ebbe sieht man das Meer fast gar nicht«, sagt die Agenturinhaberin aus dem Londoner In-Stadtteil Notting Hill, die sich auf Haare, Make-up und Stylisten spezialisiert hat. Doch wenn die Flut kommt, unternehmen Chris und sie mit ihren Freunden Segeltörns zum nahe gelegenen Hafenstädtchen Rye. Beide sind ganz verzaubert von den Wintern an der Südküste. »Wir laufen an den Dünen entlang, das Licht ist grau und trübe und es ist einfach wunderbar.«

Previous pages: As bright as a wind-whipped flag, Mandy Coakley and Chris Crooks' beach house dips its toes into the South Coast sands. Their dog, Simba, accompanies them on jaunts. The beach stretches for miles.
Above and right: Coakley and Crooks have kept the interior design comfortable and cosy. Most of the easy-going furnishings were brought down from London. "We warm the house with fires in our old iron stove in winter," said Coakley.
Facing page: A friend crafted the driftwood coat rack and shelves from flotsam and jetsam brought in with the tides.

Double page précédente: Pimpante comme un drapeau claquant au vent, la maison de plage de Mandy Coakley et de Chris Crooks plonge ses orteils dans les sables de la côte sud. Leur chien Simba les accompagne lors de promenades sur la plage qui s'étire sur des kilomètres.
Ci-dessus et à droite: L'intérieur du cottage de Coakley et de Crooks est confortable et cosy. La plupart des meubles simples ont été apportés de Londres. «En hiver, on réchauffe la maison en faisant du feu dans notre vieux poêle en fonte», déclare Coakley.
Page de droite: Un ami a fabriqué le portemanteau et les étagères avec du bois d'épave rejeté par la mer.

Vorhergehende Doppelseite: Leuchtend wie eine Flagge im Wind bohrt das Strandhaus von Mandy Coakley und Chris Crooks seine Zehen in den Sand der englischen Küste. Begleitet wird das Pärchen auf seinen kilometerweiten Strandwanderungen von Hund Simba.
Oben und rechts: Das Innere des Hauses ist bewusst bequem und gemütlich gehalten. Der Großteil des lässigen Mobiliars wurde aus London hierher transportiert. Im Winter sorgt ein alter gusseiserner Ofen im Haus für Wärme.
Rechte Seite: Ein Freund baute die Garderobe und die Regale aus Treibholz, das von der Flut angespült wurde.

Below: The interior of the house is essentially one large open room, so it's a two-person house with a little extra room for weekend guests. The windows are double-glazed, and the interior and exterior timbers are mahogany. The sleeping loft is accessible by the steep, ship-like stairs with their sturdy handrail. There's night storage heating, as the house is not on the main gas supply, and the wood stove, so the house stays warm in spite of the vast expanses of glass facing the open sea. In summer, Chris, who is an award-winning club promoter, likes to head out on the water in a small but nimble boat.

Ci-dessous: L'intérieur de la maison est essentiellement une grande pièce ouverte, une maison pour deux avec un peu d'espace supplémentaire pour les visiteurs du week-end. Les fenêtres sont équipées d'un double vitrage et toutes les boiseries intérieures et extérieures sont en acajou. On accède à la mezzanine par une échelle de bateau bien raide, heureusement pourvue d'une rampe robuste. Comme il n'y a pas de chauffage central, la chaleur est stockée pendant la nuit, en plus du poêle à charbon, et il fait toujours bon en dépit des grandes fenêtres qui font face à la mer. L'été, Chris, qui est aussi un promoteur de clubs primé, aime partir en mer dans son petit bateau.

Unten: Das innere des Zwei-Personen-Hauses besteht eigentlich nur aus einem großen Raum. Wochenendgäste werden in einem kleinen, zusätzlichen Zimmer untergebracht. Die Fenster sind doppelt verglast; verarbeitet wurde innen und außen Mahagoni. Den Schlafloft erreicht man über eine steile Treppe mit solidem Geländer, wie man sie auch auf Schiffen findet. Da das Haus nicht an die zentrale Gasversorgung angeschlossen ist, gibt es eine Nachtspeicherheizung und einen Holzofen, die das Haus schön warm halten, obwohl die riesige verglaste Fensterfront direkt auf das offene Meer blickt. Im Sommer fährt Chris, ein mit mehreren Preisen ausgezeichneter Club-Promoter, gerne mit seinem kleinen Boot aufs Meer hinaus.

Facing page: The small, shipshape kitchen is tucked beneath the sleeping loft. It was layered with driftwood slats in front of the bar and counter. "We've had to stop ourselves from displaying too much sea-themed stuff," said Mandy Coakley.
Above: Masks collected at holiday destinations are displayed on their study wall. The desk was made by the previous owner, who also built the house. The chair that sits with the desk was made by Alan Zoeftig. Coakley and Crooks' house is in demand as a location for photographic shots.

Page de gauche: La petite cuisine proprette est nichée sous la mezzanine où l'on dort. Le devant du bar-comptoir a été tapissé de planches en bois d'épave brut. «Il a fallu qu'on se maîtrise pour ne pas mettre trop de choses liées à la mer», confie Mandy.
Ci-dessus: Des masques collectionnés au fil des voyages sont exposés sur le mur du bureau. La table de travail a été fabriquée par le propriétaire précédent, qui a également construit la maison. La chaise devant la table a été réalisée par Alan Zoeftig. Le cottage de Coakley et de Crooks est souvent demandé par des photographes qui veulent le louer pour des prises de vues.

Linke Seite: Die winzige Küche liegt unter dem Schlafloft. Bar und Arbeitsplatte wurden mit Treibholzplanken verkleidet. »Wir mussten unsere Begeisterung für nautische Dekostücke etwas im Zaum halten«, sagt Mandy Coakley.
Oben: Die Masken, die die beiden aus dem Urlaub mitgebracht haben, haben an der Wand des Arbeitszimmers ihre Bleibe gefunden. Der Schreibtisch stammt vom früheren Hausbesitzer, der auch das Haus selbst erbaute. Der Schreibtischstuhl wurde von Alan Zoeftig gefertigt. Es verwundert nicht, dass dieses Haus gern als Location für Fototermine verwendet wird.

A Family Farmhouse

Ile de Noirmoutier, Vendée, France

Imaginez des mimosas en fleurs en plein cœur de l'hiver et des champs de lavande et de romarin au début du printemps. Non, nous ne sommes pas au bord de la Méditerranée mais sur la toute petite île de Noirmoutier, à la sortie de la baie brumeuse de Bourgneuf. Noirmoutier, située 85 kilomètres à l'ouest du port historique de Nantes, jouit d'un climat clément similaire à celui de Majorque. On y vient en famille pour se détendre, se promener le long des larges plages de l'Atlantique, faire de la voile ou pêcher. Le week-end, on passe généralement quelques heures à chiner dans des boutiques d'antiquités à moitié cachées, cherchant des trésors nautiques tels que de vieux compas, des flotteurs en verre, des télescopes en laiton ou des maquettes de bateau peintes à la main. Tout au long de l'année, les visiteurs peuvent faire de la bicyclette sur des routes de campagne bordées de champs de pommes de terre. Dans le vieux quartier de Noirmoutier-en-l'Ile, le port principal, se trouve cette vieille ferme en pierres datant du 18ᵉ siècle. Lorsqu'on y pénètre, l'accueil est chaleureux et tout rend hommage à la mer.

Imagine mimosa flowers in bloom in the heart of winter and fields of lavender and rosemary in early spring. No, this is not the Mediterranean, it's the tiny island of Noirmoutier, off the coast of France in the fog-prone Bay of Bourgneuf. Noirmoutier, 85 kilometers west of the historic port of Nantes, has a similar sunny outlook to that of Majorca. Families come here to relax, stroll along the broad Atlantic beaches, and go sailing or fishing. Weekends usually include a few hours of antiquing in old hidden-away shops, looking for antique nautical treasures such as old compasses, glass buoys, brass telescopes, and hand-painted toy boats. Throughout the year, visitors bicycle along country roads bordered by fields of potatoes. In the old quarter of Noirmoutier-en-l'Ile, the port capital, stands this old stone farm dating from the 18th century. Indoors, the welcome is warm and everything pays homage to the sea.

Mimosen, die mitten im Winter blühen, Lavendel und Rosmarin, die sich im Frühjahr über ganze Felder erstrecken – nein, das ist nicht das Mittelmeer. Das ist das Inselchen Noirmoutier in der oft nebelverhangenen Bucht von Bourgneuf vor der Küste Frankreichs, 85 Kilometer westlich der alten Hafenstadt Nantes gelegen, aber ähnlich sonnenverwöhnt wie Mallorca. Familien kommen hierher, um auszuspannen, am breiten Atlantikstrand spazieren zu gehen oder um zu segeln und zu fischen. Am Wochenende legt man noch gern ein paar Stöberstunden in alten und versteckt liegenden Antiquitätenläden ein und sucht nach nautischen Schätzen wie alten Kompassen, Glasbojen, Teleskopen aus Messing und handbemalten Spielzeugschiffen. Das ganze Jahr hindurch befahren die Besucher mit dem Fahrrad die Landstraßen, die zu beiden Seiten von Kartoffeläckern gerahmt werden. In der Altstadt von Noirmoutier-en-l'Ile, dem Haupthafen, steht dieses alte Bauernhaus aus Stein, das aus dem 18. Jahrhundert stammt. Das Innere strahlt Wärme und Herzlichkeit aus und ist eine Hommage an das Meer.

Previous pages: low tide on the Ile de Noirmoutier on the edge of the Atlantic Ocean. Residents and visitors alike enjoy the balmy summer days, and play a little with the marine decor theme. Sailor's headgear and a shark-shaped letter box show a sense of humor. Whitewashed house exteriors trimmed with indigo are a tradition on Noirmoutier. *Above, right and facing page:* Restored flea-market treasures in the brick-floored salon and dining room include a Louis Quinze-style sofa and marquetry table, a bronze barometer, an antique Louis Vuitton trunk, and ornithological prints.

Doubles pages précédentes: marée basse sur l'île de Noirmoutier. Les propriétaires des lieux, comme leurs invités, aiment les douces journées d'été et jouent un peu avec le décor marin. Le béret à pompon de marin et la boîte aux lettres en forme de requin témoignent de leur sens de l'humour. Les façades blanchies à la chaux et bordées d'indigo sont une tradition sur Noirmoutier. *Ci-dessus, à droite et page de droite:* Dans le salon et la salle à manger pavés de briques, les trésors chinés dans des marchés aux puces incluent un sofa de style Louis Quinze, une table en marqueterie, un baromètre en bronze, une malle ancienne Louis Vuitton et des gravures d'ornithologie.

Vorhergehende Doppelseiten: Ebbe auf der Ile de Noirmoutier am Rand des Atlantiks. Anwohner und Besucher lieben die linden Sommertage und den spielerischen Umgang mit dem Marinethema, wie man an der Matrosenmütze und dem Briefkasten in Form eines Hais sehen kann. Weiß und Indigoblau sind typisch für Noirmoutier. *Oben, rechts und rechte Seite:* In Salon und Esszimmer mit ihren Backsteinböden finden sich aufgearbeitete Schätze vom Flohmarkt, darunter ein Sofa und ein mit Einlegearbeiten verzierter Tisch im Louis-Quinze-Stil, ein Barometer aus Bronze, ein alter Louis-Vuitton-Schrankkoffer und Drucke mit ornithologischen Motiven.

Ile de Noirmoutier, Vendée, France 47°01'N 2°15'W   A Family Farmhouse

Tami and Anders Christiansen

Cadaqués, Costa Brava, Spain

Le petit port de pêche de Cadaqués est niché au creux du Cabo de Creus, à un jet de pierre de la frontière française et à une heure de route au nord de Barcelone. C'est dans ce village ancestral qu'Anders Christiansen et sa femme Tami, lui danois et elle américaine, ont aperçu un jour un panneau «A vendre» devant une vieille maison de pêcheur. Habitant en France, les Christiansen étaient tombés amoureux des façades blanchies à la chaux et des rues pavées de Cadaqués pendant leurs vacances. Après avoir lorgné sur la maison de leurs rêves pendant une semaine, ils décidèrent de l'acheter. Restaurateurs expérimentés, ils limitèrent les travaux au strict minimum afin de conserver le caractère de l'architecture traditionnelle du village. Ils réparèrent le toit, rénovèrent l'électricité et la tuyauterie et remirent les pièces à neuf sans toucher à la structure. «Nous avons surtout cherché à créer une impression de luminosité, d'air et de fantaisie», explique Tami.

The small Spanish fishing port of Cadaqués circles the coast near the Cabo de Creus, a stone's throw from the French border and an hour north of Barcelona. It was in the centuries-old village that Danish-born Anders Christiansen and his American-born wife, Tami, discovered a "For Sale" sign hanging on an old fisherman's cottage. The Christiansens were living in France, but fell in love with the whitewashed houses and cobblestone streets of Cadaqués while on holiday. Within a week of spying their dream house, they agreed to buy it. Experienced remodelers, they decided to make minimal changes to the interiors to maintain the traditional character of the village architecture. They repaired the roof, updated the electricity and plumbing, and refurbished the rooms, but made no structural alterations. "We decorated to give the impression of light and air and fantasy," said Tami.

Das kleine spanische Fischerdörfchen Cadaqués umzieht die Küste nahe Cabo de Creus, nur einen Steinwurf von der französischen Grenze entfernt und eine Stunde nördlich von Barcelona gelegen. In diesem jahrhundertealten Dorf entdeckten der gebürtige Däne Anders Christiansen und seine amerikanische Frau Tami ein »For-Sale«-Schild an einem alten Fischerhaus. Zu diesem Zeitpunkt lebte das Ehepaar in Frankreich und hatte sich während eines Urlaubs in die weiß getünchten Häuser und kopfsteingepflasterten Straßen von Cadaqués verliebt. Eine Woche nach der Entdeckung ihres Traumhauses entschlossen sie sich zum Kauf. Aufgrund ihrer Erfahrung mit Umbauten und Modernisierungen wollten sie nur wenige Erneuerungen im Innern des Hauses vornehmen, um den traditionellen Charakter des Dorfs nicht zu beeinträchtigen. Das Dach wurde instand gesetzt, Elektrizität und Sanitäranlagen modernisiert und die Zimmer renoviert, doch es wurden keine strukturellen Veränderungen vorgenommen. »Bei der Ausstattung der Zimmer ging es uns darum, einen Eindruck von Licht, Luft und Fantasie zu vermitteln«, sagt Tami.

Previous pages: *Tami and Anders Christiansen walking down a cobblestone lane in Cadaqués. Most of the houses are painted white, in the traditional manner, and the couple love the unpretentious, timeless streets and house exteriors.*
Above and right: *the old kitchen and adjacent dining room. The petite and formerly rather utilitarian rooms have little light, and were crammed at the back of the house, which was carved into the rocky hillside. The stone sink and rock walls are craggy and full of character.*

Double page précédente: *Tami et Anders Christiansen descendant une ruelle pavée de Cadaqués. La plupart des maisons sont peintes dans le blanc traditionnel. Le couple adore ces rues et ces façades humbles et hors du temps.*
Ci-dessus et à droite: *la vieille cuisine et la salle à manger adjacente. Ces petites pièces, autrefois surtout utilitaires, étaient sombres et groupées à l'arrière de la maison, qui est creusée dans la falaise. Un évier en pierre et des murs bruts et crevassés sont pleins de caractère.*

Vorhergehende Doppelseite: *Tami und Anders Christiansen schlendern durch ein mit Steinen gepflastertes Gässchen in Cadaqués. Die meisten Häuser sind in traditionellem Weiß gestrichen und in den einfachen Straßen scheint die Zeit stehen geblieben zu sein.*
Oben und rechts: *die alte Küche und das sich anschließende Esszimmer. Die kleinen Zimmer, früher vorrangig zweckgebunden, waren recht dunkel und lagen im rückwärtigen Teil des Hauses, das sich in die felsige Hügellandschaft schmiegt. Das steinerne Spülbecken und die Felswände strahlen viel Charakter aus.*

Cadaqués, Costa Brava, Spain 42°17'N 3°17'E   Tami and Anders Christiansen

The joys of simplicity are evident in the cool, crisp sitting rooms. The Christiansens found their friendly mix of unpretentious old furniture throughout Europe. The white-painted iron daybed – given the cotton-ticking-mattress-and-pillows treatment – and the Louis-Seize-style chair, are French. The couple's mastery of the art of illusion is evident in their multi-layered plaster wall treatment. They washed and bleached decades of paint jobs ... but cleverly left the evidence of years.

La fraîcheur des petits salons atteste des joies de la simplicité. Les Christiansen ont glané leurs charmants meubles anciens aux quatre coins d'Europe. Le lit de repos en fer tapissé de toile à matelas et peint en blanc, ainsi que le fauteuil de style Louis Seize, sont français. Le couple est passé maître en l'art de l'illusion, comme en témoignent les murs revêtus de plusieurs couches d'enduit au plâtre. Ils ont lessivé et décoloré des décennies de peintures en laissant astucieusement transparaître la patine du temps.

Freude am Einfachen – das drückt sich in den beiden kühl-frischen Wohnräumen aus. Die freundliche Mischung einfacher alter Möbel fanden die Christiansens in ganz Europa: Das weiß gestrichene Tagesbett aus Eisen – ausgestattet auf die übliche Weise, nämlich mit gestreiften Baumwollkissen und -matratzen – und der Stuhl im Louis-Seize-Stil stammen beispielsweise aus Frankreich. Wie gut das Ehepaar die Kunst der Illusion beherrscht, sieht man an dem vergipsten Mauerwerk, das aus verschiedenen Schichten besteht. Unzählige Farbanstriche wurden abgewaschen und gebleicht, doch die Patina blieb erhalten.

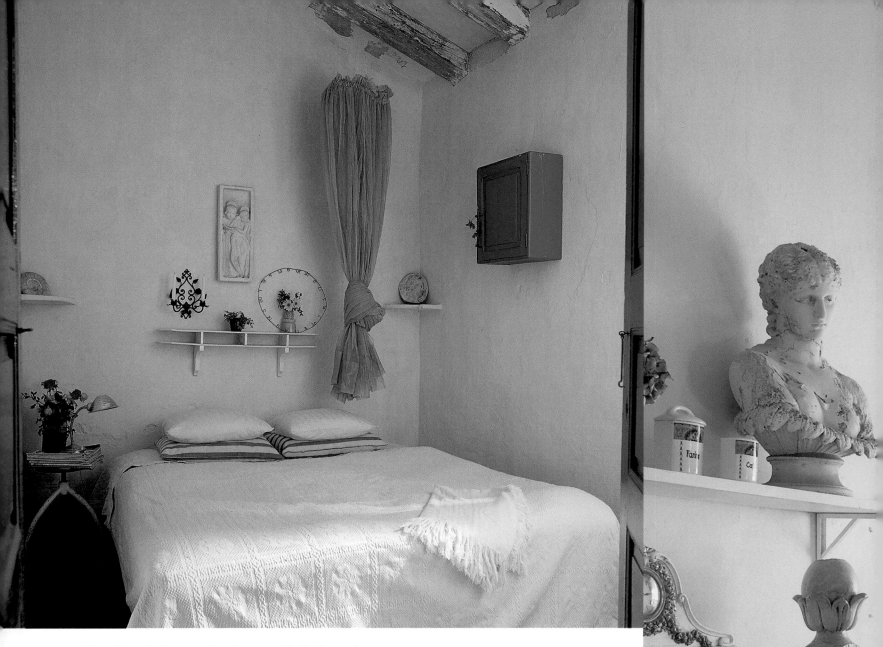

Above: *The tiny bedroom is a place for repose and a few favorite flea-market treasures. The Christiansens used a mostly-white palette to lighten and brighten the minuscule room.*
Right: *To maintain the charm and unpretentious style of the house, the Christiansens left the ceiling beams chipped and time-worn. "Signs of life make a house," noted Tami. The old round table is the perfect perch for morning coffee, afternoon newspaper reading, and even twilight cocktails.*

Ci-dessus: *La minuscule chambre est consacrée au repos et à quelques trésors chinés dans des marchés aux puces. Pour éclairer et égayer cette toute petite pièce, les Christiansen ont utilisé une palette où domine le blanc.*
A droite: *Pour conserver le charme sans prétention de leur maison, les Christiansen ont laissé telle quelle la peinture écaillée des poutres apparentes rongées par le temps. «Ce sont les signes du vécu qui font une maison», déclare Tami. La vieille table ronde est idéale pour prendre son café le matin, lire son journal ou boire l'apéritif à la tombée du soir.*

Oben: *Das winzige Schlafzimmer ist ein Ort der Entspannung und bringt einige Flohmarktschätze gut zur Geltung. Durch die auf Weiß ausgerichtete Farbpalette wirkt der winzige Raum heller und größer.*
Rechts: *Um den schlichten Charme des Hauses zu bewahren, beschlossen die Christiansens, die Altersspuren an den Deckenbalken nicht zu beseitigen, denn »solche Lebenszeichen sind es, die ein Haus erst ausmachen«, findet Tami. Der runde Tisch ist das perfekte Fleckchen für den Frühstückskaffee, das nachmittägliche Blättern in der Zeitung und für Cocktails in der Dämmerung.*

Cadaqués, Costa Brava, Spain 42°17'N 3°17'E   Tami and Anders Christiansen

Caroline and Hans Neuendorf

Majorca, Spain

Ceux qui ont séjourné à Majorque pendant un de ces étés qui fleurent bon le miel connaissent la douce et langoureuse indolence de ses longs après-midi dorés et le pâle scintillement gris vert de ses étendues d'oliviers. On peut passer des matinées entières à contempler les ombres dansantes de la paroi nacrée du Puig Mayor qui domine la côte. Les villas somnolent, bercées par les cigales, et l'on ne s'extirpe de sa torpeur que pour piquer une tête dans la piscine ou ajouter quelques glaçons dans son verre de limonade. C'est dans ce décor enchanteur et hors du temps qu'un marchand d'art allemand et son épouse ont commandé une maison de vacances aux architectes Claudio Silvestrin et John Pawson, basés à Londres. Fidèles à la devise «Moins il y en a, mieux c'est», ils ont conçu une villa aux lignes simples, modernes et dépouillées. La maison est ouverte aux brises marines et sa silhouette cubiste rappelle la noble histoire de l'architecture provinciale majorquine.

Those who visit Majorca in honey-scented summer know the sweet, dizzy indolence of long, golden afternoons, and the pale gray-green shimmering of countless olive trees. The ivory rock-face of Puig Mayor rears up from the coast, and one may spend mornings doing nothing more than watching its shadows shift and dance. Quiet villas doze, cicadas sing, and there is little motivation to move except to splash in a pool or add some more ice to a cool glass of lemonade. It was for this timeless, seductive setting that a German art dealer and his wife commissioned London-based architects Claudio Silvestrin and John Pawson to design a holiday house. "Less is more" is the architects' credo. The lines of the villa are uncompromisingly simple, modern and unembellished. The house opens to catch sea breezes. And its cubist silhouettes recall the noble history of Majorcan country architecture.

Wer Mallorca im Sommer besucht, wenn die Insel nach Honig duftet, der erlebt die süße, leicht schwindlige Trägheit langer, goldfarbener Nachmittage und den Glanz der blassen, graugrünen Blätter der unzähligen Olivenbäume. Die elfenbeinfarbene Felswand von Puig Mayor erhebt sich an der Küste und man kann ganze Vormittage nur damit verbringen, den Tanz und die Bewegungen zu beobachten, die die Schatten auf ihr vollführen. Stille Villen dösen vor sich hin, Zikaden zirpen und man fühlt sich zu wenig mehr berufen, als sich im Pool abzukühlen oder noch einige Eiswürfel ins Limonadenglas zu geben. Genau dieses zeitlose, verführerische Umfeld war es, das einen deutschen Kunsthändler und seine Frau dazu bewog, die Londoner Architekten Claudio Silvestrin und John Pawson mit dem Entwurf für ein Ferienhaus zu beauftragen. »Weniger ist mehr« ist das Credo der beiden Architekten. Die Linienführung des Villenentwurfs ist kompromisslos einfach, modern und schmucklos. Das Haus öffnet sich der Meeresbrise. Und seine kubistische Silhouette erinnert an die stattliche und klare Optik der mallorquinischen ländlichen Architektur.

The Majorca holiday house of Caroline and Hans Neuendorf stands like an ancient fort among the old olive and almond trees. The golden-ocher color of the exterior stucco was taken directly from the land surrounding the house. Architects John Pawson and Claudio Silvestrin elided the borders between indoors and outdoors. From the deeply recessed porch one gazes over the lap pool, and imagines the possibility of swimming to the horizon.

La villa majorquine de Caroline et Hans Neuendorf se dresse tel un vieux fort parmi les vieux oliviers et amandiers. L'ocre doré de ses façades provient directement de la terre environnante. Les architectes John Pawson et Claudio Silvestrin ont effacé les frontières entre l'intérieur et l'extérieur. Depuis le porche profondément enchâssé dans la façade, le regard se porte instinctivement au-delà de la longue piscine et on se prend à rêver de rejoindre la ligne d'horizon à la nage.

Das Ferienhaus von Caroline und Hans Neuendorf steht wie eine uralte Festung zwischen den alten Oliven- und Mandelbäumen. Der Goldockerton der verputzten Außenfassade entspricht genau dem Farbton des Bodens, auf dem das Haus steht. Die Architekten John Pawson und Claudio Silvestrin verzichteten auf eine Trennung zwischen Innen und Außen. Von der tief eingelassenen Veranda lässt man den Blick über den Pool schweifen und stellt sich vor, bis zum Horizont zu schwimmen.

Facing page: The stucco face of the house has become mottled and rock-like over time, and now seems part of the arid landscape.
Above and following pages: Long, low benches around the swimming pool were crafted locally from Santanyi stone, quarried in Majorca. The cubist terrace provides a shady spot from which to view the cool water and miles of uninterrupted olive groves.
Right: Narrow slits in the walls provide glimpses of cactus, olive trees and natural landscape.

Page de gauche: Au fil du temps, l'enduit de la façade s'est bigarré pour revêtir des teintes rocheuses, s'intégrant parfaitement dans le paysage aride qui l'entoure.
Ci-dessus et double page suivante: Les longs bancs bas qui bordent la piscine ont été réalisés dans la région dans de la «santanyi», une pierre extraite des carrières de Majorque. La terrasse cubiste offre un coin ombragé d'où l'on peut contempler l'eau fraîche et les oliveraies qui s'étendent sur des kilomètres.
A droite: A travers les meurtrières, on aperçoit les cactus, les oliviers et la nature environnante.

Linke Seite: Die mörtelverputzte Fassade des Hauses ähnelt mit ihren im Lauf der Zeit entstandenen Flecken Felsengestein und wirkt fast wie ein Bestandteil der Wüstenlandschaft.
Oben und folgende Doppelseite: Die schmalen, lang gestreckten Bänke am Pool wurden auf Mallorca hergestellt. Grundmaterial ist Stein aus dem inseleigenen Steinbruch Santanyi. Die kubistische Terrasse liefert ein schattiges Plätzchen, von dem aus man das kühle Wasser und die sich kilometerweit erstreckenden Olivenhaine betrachten kann.
Rechts: Schmale Schlitze im Mauerwerk gewähren einen Blick auf Kakteen, Olivenbäume und Naturlandschaft.

Above: The interior of the house has been crafted so that heat and light can be modified throughout the seasons. In summer, when heat stays constant and rain seldom cools the day, the inner courtyard stays open to catch passing breezes.
Right: Rooms take on a monastic simplicity, and invite repose and quietness. The rigorous simplicity of the interiors requires in turn that all craftsmanship and materials must be perfect.
Facing page: The versatile "Y" chair, used throughout the house, was limned by Danish furniture designer Hans J. Wegner in 1950.

Ci-dessus: L'intérieur de la villa a été conçu pour pouvoir contrôler la lumière et la chaleur au fil des saisons. L'été, lorsque la chaleur est constante et que la pluie vient rarement rafraîchir les journées, la cour intérieure reste ouverte aux brises qui passent.
A droite: D'une simplicité monacale, les pièces invitent au repos et au silence. La simplicité rigoureuse des intérieurs requiert que les matières et les moindres détails de la construction soient parfaits.
Page de droite: Les chaises au dossier en Y, que l'on retrouve dans toute la villa, ont été dessinées en 1950 par le designer danois Hans J. Wegner.

Oben: Das Innere des Hauses wurde so entworfen, dass Temperatur und Licht jeder Jahreszeit angepasst werden können. Im Sommer, wenn die Temperaturen konstant hoch sind und die Tage nur selten durch Regen abgekühlt werden, bleibt der innere Hof geöffnet, um jeden sich regenden Luftzug einzufangen.
Rechts: Die Räume strahlen eine Einfachheit aus, die an Klosterzellen erinnert, und laden zur inneren und äußeren Ruhe ein. Die strenge Schlichtheit der Interieurs erfordert ein Höchstmaß an Handwerkskunst und beste Qualität der Materialien.
Rechte Seite: Den vielseitigen »Y«-Stuhl, der überall im Haus Einsatz findet, entwarf Hans J. Wegner im Jahr 1950.

Majorca, Spain 39°30'N 3°00'E   Caroline and Hans Neuendorf

Victor Esposito

Ses Salines, Ibiza, Spain

*Pour une petite île, Ibiza est capable des contrastes les plus surpre-
nants. On y vient du monde entier pour s'adonner à des joies tonitruantes, frénétiques et tape-à-l'œil. Pourtant, dans ses collines et le
long de ses côtes désertes se cachent des habitants des plus discrets
ainsi qu'une clique internationale d'artistes. C'est cet aspect calme
ainsi que le style si manifeste de la région qui ont attiré ici Victor Esposito, ancien restaurateur et fondateur à Ibiza de la boutique Pan
con Tomate. Esposito avait acheté 5 000 mètres carrés de terrain dans
les collines qui dominent la baie de Ses Salines il y a 14 ans, mais il
a longuement attendu avant d'y construire une maison entièrement
issue de son imagination, inspirée par l'architecture cubiste typique
des pays chauds tels que le Nouveau-Mexique ou le Mexique de Luis
Barragàn. L'extraordinaire esthétique monochrome et disciplinée
d'Esposito est tout en retenue, entièrement tournée vers la beauté
environnante.*

For a small island, Ibiza produces some wonderfully contradictory
images. It's been an international destination of frantic flash, cash
and chic ... and yet in the hills and along deserted coastlines live
some of the most private, low-key residents and an international
coterie of artists who come to hide out. It was this quiet side of
Ibiza, along with the style so demonstrably there, that drew Victor
Esposito, a former restaurateur and founder of the Ibizan boutique Pan con Tomate. Esposito first acquired 5 000 square meters of land in the hills overlooking the bay of Ses Salines more
than 14 years ago. Finally, he built the house of his imagination,
inspired by archetypal cubist architecture of warm climates like
New Mexico and the Mexico of Luis Barragán. Esposito's extraor-
dinarily disciplined monochromatic aesthetic calls for restraint,
and rewards with its enveloping beauty.

*Obwohl die Insel klein ist, findet man auf Ibiza doch ganz wunderbar
kontrastierende Elemente. Die Insel ist ein internationaler Anzie-
hungspunkt für Geldadel und Partyfans ... und doch leben in den Bergen und entlang der wenig bewohnten Küstenstreifen neben einer in-
ternationalen Künstlerclique auch andere Menschen, die viel Wert auf
ihre Privatsphäre legen oder ein ganz einfaches Leben führen wollen.
Diese stille Seite und der für sie typische Stil waren es, die den ehema-
ligen Restaurantbesitzer und Gründer der ibizenkischen Boutique
»Pan con Tomate«, Victor Esposito, hierher führten. Bereits vor 14
Jahren erwarb er ein 5 000 Quadratmeter großes Grundstück in den
Hügeln über der Bucht von Ses Salines. Später baute er darauf sein
Traumhaus, inspiriert von der archetypischen, an kubischen Formen
orientierten Architektur warmer Klimazonen wie New Mexico und der
mexikanischen Architektur von Luis Barragán. Espositos außerordent-
lich disziplinierte monochromatische Ästhetik verlangt nach Be-
schränkung und belohnt diese mit einer alles umhüllenden Schönheit.*

Previous pages: Life at the house of Victor Esposito revolves around the terraces and the swimming pool. Across the cool blue water is a rustic pool house, its open-air hut style inspired by primitive tropical structures around the world.
Left and above: It would be a mistake to see Esposito's interior design as plain and unembellished. In fact, it is highly evolved and superbly detailed. Stonework around the doors and windows is boldly delineated. Concrete floors in a chalky hue were given a buffed hand finish.

Double page précédente: La vie domestique est centrée autour des terrasses et de la piscine. De l'autre côté du plan d'eau, une «pool house» rustique et ouverte aux éléments, inspirée des habitations primitives tropicales.
A gauche et ci-dessus: Faussement simple et dépouillée, l'architecture d'intérieur d'Esposito est en fait très sophistiquée et riche en détails soignés. La maçonnerie autour des portes et des fenêtres est habilement soulignée. Les sols en béton d'un ton crayeux ont été polis à la main.

Vorhergehende Doppelseite: Das Leben in Victor Espositos Haus findet auf den Terrassen und am Pool statt. Am anderen Ende des Pools liegt ein Haus, dessen offene Hüttenbauweise an die einfache Bauweise in den Tropen erinnert.
Links und oben: Es wäre ein Fehler, Espositos Innenarchitektur schlicht und schmucklos zu nennen, denn sie ist hoch entwickelt und äußerst detailreich. Kühn betont Mauerwerk Türen und Fenster. Die Betonböden wurden nach ihrer Kalkfärbung von Hand poliert.

Clockwise from top left: *An antique Egyptian ibis perches on an old workbench, now a dining table; the fireplace, its crisply functional shape by Argentinean designer Emiliano Policastro is framed by gnarled driftwood branches; the cabinet adds instant "architecture" to the pared-down room; a pair of nail-head studded doors.*

Du haut à gauche, dans le sens des aiguilles d'une montre: *Un ibis égyptien antique est perché sur un vieil établi en bois reconverti en table; la cheminée, pratique et originale, dessinée par le designer argentin Emiliano Policastro, est encadrée de branches noueuses reje-*

tées par la mer; le petit placard ajoute une note «architecturale» à cette pièce dépouillée; la double porte cloutée.

Im Uhrzeigersinn von links oben: *Ein ägyptischer Ibis sitzt auf einer alten Arbeitsbank, die mittlerweile als Tisch dient; verwittert-verzogenes Treibholz betont den Kamin, von dem argentinischen Designer Emiliano Policastro klar und funktional gestaltet; der Schrank verleiht dem sehr zurückgenommenen Raum einen architektonischen Zug; eine zweiflüglige, mit Nägeln beschlagene Tür.*

Ses Salines, Ibiza, Spain 39°20'N 3°30'E

Victor Esposito

Clockwise from top left: The kitchen sink is carved from recycled timber; like a bathroom carved from a rock face, this one has a rustic basin; the chair's arabesques of forged iron offer a lacy contrast to a rough wood armoire; in the kitchen, a village bench has the look of flotsam and jetsam.

Du haut à gauche, dans le sens des aiguilles d'une montre: L'évier de la cuisine a été taillé dans un tronc d'arbre; avec sa vasque rustique, la salle de bains semble avoir été creusée dans la roche; les arabesques d'une chaise en fer forgé forment une dentelle qui contraste avec le bois brut de l'armoire; dans la cuisine, le banc de village semble avoir été rejeté par la mer.

Im Uhrzeigersinn von links oben: Die Spüle in der Küche besteht aus wiederverwertetem Holz; das Badezimmer mit dem schlichten Waschbecken wirkt, als sei es aus einer Felswand gehauen; die an Spitze erinnernden Arabesken des schmiedeeisernen Stuhls bilden einen reizvollen Gegensatz zu dem Schrank aus grob bearbeitetem Holz; auch die einfache Dorfbank in der Küche gleicht Strandgut.

Above: The beauty of bare wood from around the world is exposed in Esposito's Ibizan kitchen. In one corner, a useful cabinet was crafted from found off-cuts of pine, left plain. Shelves, an old wine barrel, and a village-made pine chair, all enhance the timeless scene.
Facing page: A chunky green concrete counter and stove-surround spans one wall, giving the room heft and a bold sense of scale. A wall cabinet, a mellow old bench, and a trio of buckets all seem sea-wracked, as if they had washed in on the tide.

Ci-dessus: La cuisine d'Esposito rend hommage à la beauté de bois bruts rapportés des quatre coins du monde. Dans un coin, un petit placard très pratique a été fabriqué avec des rejets de sapin, laissés bruts. Les étagères, le vieux fût, une chaise en sapin fabriquée dans un village, tous contribuent à créer cette atmosphère atemporelle.
A droite: Un plan de travail massif en béton vert, dans lequel un four est encastré, occupe tout un mur, donnant à la pièce du volume et un sens audacieux de l'échelle. Le vaisselier, le vieux banc usé et les trois seaux semblent avoir été rejetés ici par la mer.

Oben: Die Schönheit, die nacktes Holz besitzen kann, kommt in der Küche zum Ausdruck. In einer Ecke steht ein äußerst praktischer Küchenschrank, der aus gefundenem Schnittabfall von Pinienhölzern gearbeitet wurde. Ein Regal, ein altes Weinfass und der im Dorf gefertigte Stuhl aus Kiefernholz betonen die Zeitlosigkeit des Ensembles.
Rechts: Eine klobige grüne Arbeitsfläche aus Beton und ein eingebauter Herd nehmen die gesamte Länge der Wand ein: Sie verleihen dem Raum Gewicht und geben ihm ein mutiges Größenverhältnis. Ein Wandschrank, eine lässig wirkende Bank und ein Trio aus Eimern sehen aus, als hätte sie das Meer direkt in den Raum gespült.

Ses Salines, Ibiza, Spain 39°20'N 3°30'E   Victor Esposito

Left: Esposito calls this guest bedroom "Babel", and he has indeed brought together many voices ... but here in harmony. A door from Fez disguises a cabinet. A carved Balinese head, a candle-holding column carved by Emiliano Policastro, and a series of African bronzes and Mexican pots round out the cosmopolitan collection.
Above: The Robinson Crusoe aesthetic was carried out with total focus and a great love of simplicity. The floor of the bathroom is local stone.

A gauche: Esposito a baptisé sa chambre d'ami «Babel». De fait, il a marié de nombreuses voix... en une polyphonie harmonieuse. Une porte de Fès cache un placard. La tête sculptée vient de Bali. La colonne torchère est signée Emiliano Policastro. Des bronzes africains et des poteries mexicaines complètent cette collection cosmopolite.
Ci-dessus: L'esthétique à la Robinson Crusoë a été poussée jusqu'au bout avec un grand amour de la simplicité. Le sol de la salle de bains est en pierre de la région.

Links: Sein Gästeschlafzimmer nennt Esposito »Babel«. Hier hat er viele Stimmen zu einem harmonischen Ganzen vereint. Ein Schrank versteckt sich hinter einer Tür aus Fes. Ein Kopf aus Bali, eine Kerzensäule, die Emiliano Policastro geschnitzt hat, und eine Reihe afrikanischer Bronzen und Töpfe aus Mexiko vervollständigen die kosmopolitische Sammlung.
Oben: Die Robinson-Crusoe-Ästhetik wurde mit höchster Konzentration und Liebe zur Einfachheit umgesetzt. Der Boden im Badezimmer ist aus Steinen gearbeitet, die vor Ort gefunden wurden.

French fashion designer Pierre Cardin demonstrates the comforts and loopy curves of his Côte d'Azur funhouse, the Palais Bulles. Unlike many avant-garde structures which challenge the architectural establishment, this residence was crafted like an extravagant palace, using the finest woods for patterned floors, and luxurious fabrics on quirky custom-crafted chairs and sofas. A glorious retro-throwback to the 70s, the house is all curves and bubbles, even on the pink and caramel-colored igloo-like exterior modules. The swimming pools and garden are created in the round.

Le couturier français Pierre Cardin démontre les conforts loufoques de sa résidence de la Côte d'Azur, le Palais Bulles. Contrairement à de nombreuses architectures d'avant-garde qui défient l'establishment, elle a été conçue comme un palais extravagant, avec des sols marquetés en bois précieux et d'excentriques meubles réalisés sur mesure et tapissés des étoffes les plus luxueuses. Glorieux retour aux années 70, la maison est tout en courbes et en bulles, y compris les igloos extérieurs rose et caramel. Mêmes les piscines et les jardins sont ronds.

Der französische Modedesigner Pierre Cardin führt sein »funhouse« an der Côte d'Azur vor, das verrückt gekurvte Palais Bulles. Im Gegensatz zu vielen Avantgardebauten, die als Provokation für das architektonische Establishment gedacht sind, wurde dieses Anwesen wie ein extravaganter Palast entworfen. So wurden nur die edelsten Hölzer für die Täfelung verwendet, ebenso edle Stoffe als Bezüge für die speziell angefertigten, verspielten Sessel und Sofas. Hinreißend ist die »Besinnung« auf den Schick der 70er Jahre: Das Haus ist eine einzige Kette von Kurven und Kuppeln, selbst die in Rosa und Karamell gehaltenen äußeren Module des Hauses, die an ein Iglu erinnern. Auch in Schwimmbad und Garten dominieren die gerundeten Formen.

Cannes, Côte d'Azur, France 43°34'N 7°10'E   Pierre Cardin

Pierre Cardin

Cannes, Côte d'Azur, France

Le couturier français Pierre Cardin, avec des centaines de boutiques franchisées de par le monde qui vendent des produits allant des articles de sport, aux bagages et aux parfums, a toujours été un joyeux outsider et un visionnaire de la mode. Dans les années 50, quand les grandes maisons parisiennes dépensaient toute leur énergie créative dans la haute couture, il commercialisait le prêt-à-porter et les accessoires, ce que feront toutes les maisons de mode par la suite. Qui d'autre, dans les années 60 et pendant les folles années 70, dessinait des robes aux formes graphiques et des cuissardes en plastique, quand tous les autres couturiers vénéraient la soie et le cuir? Mais cet enfant terrible qui vit à cent à l'heure ne s'est pas arrêté là. Sa nouvelle obsession: l'architecture. Sur la Côte d'Azur, il a enfanté une folie baptisée Palais Bulles, dessinée par l'architecte hongrois Antti Lovag. Haut perchée au-dessus de la Méditerranée, près de Cannes, on dirait une créature amicale surgie des profondeurs marines. Elle est à la fois grandiose et drôle.

French designer Pierre Cardin, with hundreds of worldwide licensees for products ranging from sportswear to luggage and fragrances, has always been a fashion visionary and a cheerful fashion-system outsider. In the 50s, when Paris fashion houses were throwing all their creative energy into couture, Cardin began his first "diffusion" lines, marketing ready-to-wear collections and licensed accessories that would become "de rigueur" for all other houses. Who else in the 60s and the mad 70s cheerfully designed couture dresses in graphic shapes and hipster boots from plastic, when all other couturiers worshiped silks and fine leather? Pierre Cardin's fast-forward fashion frolics continue. Architecture is a new obsession. On the Côte d'Azur, he has parented an architectural folly, dubbed Palais Bulles, by Hungarian architect Antti Lovag. Situated high above the Mediterranean near Cannes, it looks like a friendly creature that arose from the depths of the sea. It's both a grand and funny place.

Der französische Designer Pierre Cardin war schon immer Mode-Visionär und fröhlicher Außenseiter in der Modewelt. Hunderte von weltweit vertriebenen Marken und Lizenzen, von Sportkleidung über Reisegepäck bis zu Düften, tragen seinen Namen. In den 50er Jahren, als die Pariser Modehäuser ihre ganze kreative Energie auf die Haute Couture richteten, lancierte Cardin bereits seine »diffusion«-Kollektionen, etablierte damit die Konfektion von der Stange und vergab Lizenzen für die Vermarktung von Accessoires. Und in den 60er und verrückten 70er Jahren war er es natürlich, der Couture-Kleidern grafische Linien verlieh und coole Stiefel aus Plastik fertigte, während alle anderen Modezaren Seide und feinstes Leder anbeteten. Auch jetzt noch feuert das Enfant terrible im gewohnt rasanten Tempo Modeverrücktheiten ab. Architektur ist seine neue Obsession. An der Côte d'Azur stand Cardin Pate bei einer architektonischen Exzentrizität des ungarischen Architekten Antti Lovag: Palais Bulles, hoch über Cannes, erinnert an eine friedliche Kreatur, die sich aus den Tiefen des Mittelmeers erhoben hat – eindrucksvoll und gleichzeitig witzig.

Previous pages: *The living room is a celebration of futuristic cartoon-style decor, down to the round television, rocking chairs, kinetic sculptures, and out-in-the-galaxy pod-like chairs.*
Left and below: *Cardin has carried his curve-and-circle, cartoon-futuristic theme through consistently into each room. A fitted module-like doorway and intergalactic porthole add a jocular space-exploration air to the kitchen. Does Cardin dine on space rations? In the living room, low-slung sofas, accompanied by a fine collection of 70s metal sculptures, afford a fine view of the Côte d'Azur.*

Double page précédente: *Le salon est une célébration du décor futuriste inspiré des bandes dessinées, jusqu'à la télévision ronde, aux fauteuils à bascule, aux sculptures cinétiques et aux sièges qui ressemblent à des engins extra-terrestres.*
A gauche et ci-dessous: *Cardin a poursuivi le thème de la bande dessinée futuriste dans toutes les pièces. Une porte ovoïde de LEM et des hublots intergalactiques donnent à la cuisine un air de vaisseau spatial. On s'attend presque à dîner de rations de la NASA. Les canapés bas du salon, accompagnés d'une belle collection de sculptures en métal des années 70, offrent une vue imprenable sur la Côte d'Azur.*

Vorhergehende Doppelseite: *Das Wohnzimmer ist eine Hommage an futuristisches, dem Cartoon entlehntes Design – bis hin zum runden Fernseher, den Schaukelstühlen, kinetischen Skulpturen und galaktisch anmutenden »Schoten«-Sesseln.*
Links und unten: *Die Motti »Bogen und Kreis« und »Futurismus und Cartoon« hat Cardin in jedem Zimmer konsequent fortgeführt. Eine Tür wie aus einem Raumschiff und ein intergalaktisches Bullauge verleihen der Küche ihren witzigen Charme. Ob der Hausherr wohl auch Astronautennahrung serviert? Von den niedrigen Sofas des Wohnzimmers, inmitten einer bemerkenswerten Sammlung von Metallskulpturen aus den 70er Jahren, hat man einen wunderbaren Blick auf die Côte d'Azur.*

Above: Cardin commissioned all new furniture for the circular bedroom. The circular bed on a carpeted dais is dressed in a quilted lipstick-red cover in homage to 60s Hollywood film sets. The room took on a more ornamental stance with custom-crafted petal-shaped chairs.
Right: Perhaps Cardin's greatest achievement in the Palais Bulles is that he has followed the original retro-futuristic vision for the house in every detail, down to the hand-crafted accessories, mirrors, light fixtures, carpets, materials and built-in furniture.

Ci-dessus: Cardin a fait faire tous les meubles de la chambre à coucher circulaire. Le lit rond juché sur une estrade tapissée de moquette est recouvert d'un dessus-de-lit matelassé couleur rouge «baiser» en hommage aux plateaux de cinéma hollywoodiens des années 60. Avec ses fauteuils en pétales, la pièce a tout d'une chambre d'apparat.
A droite: La plus grande prouesse de Cardin dans son Palais Bulles est sans doute d'avoir su peaufiner les moindres détails de sa vision rétro-futuriste, jusqu'aux accessoires faits à la main, aux miroirs, aux appliques, aux tapis, aux matériaux et aux meubles encastrés.

Oben: Für das kreisförmige Schlafzimmer ließ Cardin sämtliches Mobiliar neu bauen. Das auf einem teppichbezogenen Podium stehende kreisrunde Bett ist mit einer lippenstiftrot eingefärbten Steppdecke bezogen, die als Hommage an das Hollywood der 60er gedacht ist. Damit erhielt das Zimmer einen repräsentativen Charakter, verstärkt durch die eigens gefertigten, an Blütenkelche erinnernden Stühle.
Rechts: Cardins vielleicht größte Leistung im Palais Bulles ist es, dass er die retro-futuristischen Visionen, nach denen das Haus ursprünglich errichtet wurde, konsequent auch im Detail umgesetzt hat bis hin zu den von Hand gearbeiteten Accessoires, den Spiegeln, der Beleuchtung, Teppichen, Einbaumöbeln und Materialien.

Wolfgang Joop

Monte Carlo, Monaco

Le styliste allemand Wolfgang Joop déclarait récemment: «La mode la plus vivante et intéressante se nourrit de contrastes, de folie et de transgression.» Il parlait de la création de vêtements et d'accessoires de mode masculins et féminins, mais il aurait aussi bien pu être en train de décrire sa conception de la décoration d'intérieur, et notamment du décor de son appartement à Monte-Carlo. «L'avant-garde est vite récupérée», poursuit-il, lui qui a peint le sol lustré et les murs de son appartement d'un rouge cramoisi sans concession. «Les classiques et la tradition ne font plus autorité. Le Hip-hop, les raves, le Rap et la Techno influencent considérablement la mode. Les tendances se juxtaposent. Le modernisme flirte avec le futurisme, le minimalisme avec le maximalisme, le constructivisme avec le déconstructivisme».Mais avant tout, conclut-il, il ne faut pas avoir peur de suivre ses fantasmes et d'exprimer sa propre personnalité.

In a recent statement on fashion, German fashion designer Wolfgang Joop commented that "The liveliest and most interesting fashion lives from contrasts, borderline cases, and violating taboos." While he was remarking on the creation of men's and women's apparel and accessories, he could equally have been describing his approach to interior design, and in particular the decor of his Monte Carlo apartment. "Avant-gardism is quickly becoming mainstream," said Joop, who painted the glossy floor and walls of his flat in uncompromising crimson. "The classics and tradition have lost their authority," he continued. "Hip-hop, Rave, Rap and Techno are all having a great influence on style. Trends are juxtaposed, for example, Modernism with Futurism, Minimalism with Maximalism, and Constructivism with Deconstructivism." But, above all, said Joop, it is important to be brave, follow your fantasies, and make a personal statement.

Erst kürzlich ließ der Modedesigner Wolfgang Joop verlauten, dass »die interessanteste und lebendigste Mode von Kontrasten und Grenzbereichen lebt und Tabus verletzt.« Obwohl sich diese Aussage auf Mode für Männer und Frauen sowie Accessoires bezog, beschreibt sie gleichzeitig auch sein Verhältnis zum Interior-Design und vor allem dessen Umsetzung in seinem Apartment in Monte Carlo. »Die Avantgarde wird schnell zum gesellschaftlich anerkannten Mainstream«, sagt Joop, der die Böden und Wände seiner Wohnung in kompromisslosem, glänzenden Purpur anstreichen ließ. »Klassiker und Tradition haben ihre Autorität eingebüßt. HipHop, Rave, Rap und Technomusik haben mittlerweile einen großen Einfluss auf die Innenarchitektur. Trends werden oft gegeneinander gekehrt und beispielsweise Futurismus mit der Moderne, Minimalismus mit Maximalismus oder Konstruktivismus mit Dekonstruktivismus kombiniert.« Doch für Wolfgang Joop ist es am wichtigsten, Mut zu haben, den eigenen Vorstellungen zu folgen und auf diese Weise einen wirklich persönlichen und einzigartigen Weg zu finden.

Previous page: German fashion designer Wolfgang Joop, who divides his professional time between his design office in Hamburg, a new boutique in Miami, and an office and apartment in New York. His colorful apartment in Monaco provides both escape and visual stimulation. On his sunny terrace, curvy 30s-style chairs provide comfort and a modicum of shade.
Above and right: For Wolfgang Joop, Monte Carlo style means furniture with modern geometries and bold color, snapped with sculptural collections of ethnic art, and a witty combination of animal prints.

Page précédente: Le styliste allemand Joop, qui partage sa carrière entre son bureau de style à Hambourg, sa nouvelle boutique de Miami, son autre bureau et son appartement à New York, vient se ressourcer et chercher une stimulation visuelle dans son appartement coloré de Monaco. Sur sa terrasse ensoleillée, des fauteuils ovoïdes des années 30 offrent confort et un minimum d'ombre.
Ci-dessus et à droite: Pour Wolfgang Joop le style monégasque se traduit par des meubles modernes aux lignes géométriques et des couleurs vives, le tout parsemé de sculptures ethniques et rehaussé d'une amusante combinaison d'imprimés aux motifs animaliers.

Vorhergehende Seite: Der deutsche Modedesigner Wolfgang Joop hat ein Designbüro in Hamburg, eine Boutique in Miami sowie ein Büro und ein Apartment in New York. Er zieht sich aber gerne in sein farbenfrohes Apartment in Monaco zurück. Auf der Terrasse spenden bequeme, gebogene Sessel im Stil der 30er Jahre Schatten.
Oben und rechts: Für Wolfgang Joop vereint der Stil von Monte Carlo moderne, geometrische Formen mit kühnen Farben sowie ethnische Skulpturen mit witzigen Stoffmustern.

Monte Carlo, Monaco 43°44'N 7°25'E   Wolfgang Joop

Left: Wolfgang Joop, whose 23-year-old international company sells 17 design collections ranging from eyewear to shoes and children's wear, comes to Monte Carlo to recharge his batteries. Uncompromising red, in Mondrianesque blocks with white linens, signifies that he is on the Mediterranean coast – but without its attendant design clichés.
Above: The crisp coolness of blue walls is given a jolt of glamor with a gilt-framed mirror and a collection of Venetian glass.

A gauche: Wolfgang Joop, dont la société fondée il y a 23 ans commercialise 17 collections de mode allant des montures de lunettes aux chaussures en passant par les vêtements pour enfants, vient à Monte-Carlo pour recharger ses batteries. Le rouge vif, appliqué en carrés à la Mondrian et accompagné de linge blanc, lui rappelle qu'il se trouve au bord de la Méditerranée, mais sans tomber dans les clichés de décoration qui caractérisent la Côte d'Azur.
Ci-dessus: Un miroir doré et une collection de verreries vénitiennes ajoutent une note «glamour» au bleu pimpant des murs.

Links: Wolfgang Joops mittlerweile 23 Jahre altes Firmenimperium verkauft in seinen 17 Design-Kollektionen alles von der Sonnenbrille über Schuhe bis zur Kinderkleidung. In Monte Carlo kann er sich erholen und seine Batterien aufladen. Das kompromisslose Rot, das sich mondrianartig von dem Weiß der Bettwäsche abhebt, zeigt, dass man sich hier an der Mittelmeerküste befindet – doch ohne die üblichen Designklischees.
Oben: Das kühle Blau der Wände bekommt durch einen Spiegel mit Goldrahmen und eine Sammlung venezianischen Glases einen Schuss Glamour.

Franco Menna

Filicudi, Aeolian Islands, Italy

Ah, la légende des vents! Les îles éoliennes doivent leur nom à Eole, le dieu des vents qui, après avoir capturé les brises, les aurait emprisonnées dans une grotte perdue de la région. Poussé par des vents favorables, le mythique Ulysse a navigué parmi ces îles volcaniques qui semblent elles-mêmes avoir été éparpillées çà et là dans la mer Tyrrhénienne au gré des bourrasques. Situées au nord de la Sicile, elles furent colonisées par les Grecs en 580 avant notre ère. Aujourd'hui, on y arrive en avion, ferry ou hydroptère. C'est sur Filicudi, l'une des plus petites d'entre elles, que le Milanais Franco Menna, producteur de cinéma et architecte d'intérieur, a installé la maison de ses rêves. Débarquant sur l'île il y a douze ans, il a aménagé sa demeure avec des meubles simples rapportés d'Inde et d'autres pays d'Asie, la transformant en un lieu des plus hospitaliers. On comprend que ses amis de passage ne veulent plus jamais repartir.

Ah, the legend of the winds. The Aeolian Islands were named for Aeolus, God of the Winds, who is said to have captured the breezes and kept them in a remote grotto here. Mythical Ulysses sailed among these scattered islands, propelled by favorable winds. And the rocky islands themselves seem to have been blown hither and thither into the Tyrrhenian Sea just north of Sicily. The colonizing Greeks first came this way in 580 BC, and travelers now arrive on these volcanic islands by plane, ferry, and hydrofoil. It's on Filicudi, one of the smallest islands, that Franco Menna, a Milanese film producer and interior designer, has his dream house. Menna first came here more than a dozen years ago. Furnishing the house with casual furniture he found in India and other parts of Asia, he has turned this into a most hospitable spot. Understandably, friends who fly in never wish to leave.

Hier spürt man die Legenden der Winde. Denn die Liparischen Inseln, auch Äolische Inseln genannt, erhielten ihren Namen von Äolus, dem griechischen Windgott, der sich die Winde untertan machte und sie in einer entlegenen Grotte versteckt hielt. Auf seiner Fahrt entlang der verstreut liegenden Inseln konnte sich Odysseus auf günstige Winde verlassen. Und auch die felsigen Inseln scheinen selbst im Tyrrhenischen Meer nördlich von Sizilien hin und her geworfen worden zu sein. Die Griechen kamen schon im Jahr 580 v. Chr. hierher: heute sind es die Touristen, die per Flugzeug, Fähre und Tragflügelboot auf den Vulkaninseln einfallen. Auf Filicudi, einer der kleinsten von ihnen, liegt das Traumhaus von Franco Menna, einem Filmproduzenten und Innenarchitekten aus Mailand. Vor über zwölf Jahren kam Menna das erste Mal hierher. Mittlerweile hat er das Haus auf eher ungezwungene Weise mit Stücken eingerichtet, die er in Indien und anderen Teilen Asiens fand, und daraus ein äußerst gemütliches Heim gemacht. Verständlich, dass die Freunde, die ihn hier besuchen, gar nicht wieder fahren wollen ...

Previous pages: Making landfall on the steep side of the volcanic island of Filicudi, Franco Menna has crafted a dreamscape of a house. Blue-tiled pathways become privileged observatories from which to watch the intense summer light vibrating across the surface of the sea, sunrises and sunsets, and the migration of birds. The garden is luxuriant with bougainvillea, geraniums, aloe, succulents, and vines.
Above, right and facing page: Menna, a generous host, sets breakfasts and lunches on the shaded terrace where the island's brisk breezes cool the air. The hand-loomed tablecloth is Indian.

Double page précédente: Franco Menna a conçu sa maison dans un paysage onirique perché sur la côte escarpée de l'île volcanique de Filicudi. Les allées en carreaux bleus deviennent des observatoires privilégiés d'où l'on contemple les reflets dansants du soleil sur les vagues, les couchers et levers de soleil et les oiseaux migrateurs. Le jardin déborde de bougainvilliers, de géraniums, d'aloès, de plantes grasses et grimpantes.
Ci-dessus, à droite et page de droite: Menna, en hôte généreux, sert les petits déjeuners et les déjeuners sur la terrasse couverte où filtrent des brises rafraîchissantes. La nappe tissée à la main est indienne.

Vorhergehende Doppelseite: An einem steil abfallenden Hang der Vulkaninsel Filicudi baute Franco Menna ein Haus mit traumhaftem Ausblick. Blau gefliese Wege wurden zu Ausgucken, von denen man Sonnenauf- und -untergänge, den Zug der Vögel und das gleißende Sommerlicht beobachten kann, das über dem Wasser flirrt. Der Garten ist üppig mit Bougainvillea, Geranien, Aloepalmen, Kakteen und Efeu bestanden.
Oben, rechts und rechte Seite: Menna, ein großzügiger Gastgeber, bewirtet seine Freunde zum Frühstück und Mittagessen auf der geschützten Terrasse, die von den frischen Winden der Insel gekühlt wird. Das handgewebte Tischtuch stammt aus Indien.

Filicudi, Aeolian Islands, Italy 38°34'N 14°34'E   Franco Menna

Left and facing page: *To update the old house, Franco Menna tiled the floors and terraces with glossy blue tiles. Their cerulean hue mirrors the colors of the sky and ocean, and on warm afternoons the house feels ethereal and light, as if it is about to float out to sea. Schiapparelli-pink draperies float in the doorways as a witty counterpoint to the traditional pared-down aesthetic. Menna hung a painting by his friend, artist Thomas Kuhn, who painted in a studio on the property.*

A gauche et page de droite: *Pour donner un coup de jeune à la vieille bâtisse, Franco Menna a fait daller les sols et les terrasses de carreaux bleus brillants, dont les tons céruléens reflètent ceux du ciel et de la mer. Par les chauds après-midi d'été, la maison semble faite d'air et de lumière, flottant au-dessus des vagues. Des draperies rose Schiaparelli encadrent les portes, clin d'œil espiègle à l'esthétique traditionnelle de l'île. Menna a accroché une toile de son ami, l'artiste Thomas Kuhn, qui peint dans un atelier sur la propriété.*

Links und rechte Seite: *Um dem alten Haus ein modernes Gefühl zu geben, wählte Franco Menna als Bodenbelag für Flure und Terrassen glänzende blaue Kacheln aus, deren intensiver Farbton an Meer und Himmel erinnert. An warmen Nachmittagen wirkt das Haus leicht und fast ätherisch – so als wolle es jeden Moment selbst in See stechen. Vorhänge in Schiaparelli-Pink bewegen sich sanft fächelnd in Türeingängen – ein geistreicher Gegensatz zur traditionellen schlichten Ästhetik. An der Wand hängt ein Bild von einem Freund, dem Maler Thomas Kuhn, der auf dem Anwesen sein eigenes Atelier hatte.*

Right: *The antique four-poster bed, swathed in cool white cotton muslin, was brought back from India. The bed is alluring, but Menna says that during the full moon he loves to sleep on the terrace. "It feels like sleeping on the deck of a ship," he reports.*

A droite: *Le vieux lit à baldaquin, drapé dans une fraîche mousseline en coton blanc, a été rapporté d'Inde. Même si le lit est accueillant, les nuits de pleine lune, Menna préfère coucher sur la terrasse. «J'ai l'impression de dormir sur le pont d'un navire», affirme-t-il.*

Rechts: *Das alte Himmelbett mit Vorhängen aus weißem Baumwollmusselin wurde von einer Indienreise mitgebracht. So schön es auch ist – bei Vollmond zieht der Hausherr doch die Terrasse für die Nachtruhe vor: »Man hat das Gefühl, an Deck eines Schiffs zu schlafen.«*

Filicudi, Aeolian Islands, Italy 38°34'N 14°34'E

Paolo Deganello

Filicudi, Aeolian Islands, Italy

Les îles Eoliennes sont connues pour leurs vents qui balayent la mer Tyrrhénienne. Mais ce sont des volcans, la plupart éteints, certains somnolents, et une poignée qui crachotent encore, qui ont formé ces îles aux silhouettes spectaculaires. Filicudi, un rocher en goutte de pluie de 9,5 kilomètres de long (et pas un mètre carré de plat!), est l'une des plus tranquilles. Ses maisons sont perchées sur des terrasses ou à flanc de colline. Mais les dieux destructeurs savent aussi se montrer généreux: les versants vertigineux, un défi pour ceux qui manquent de souffle, sont autant de points de vue somptueux d'où admirer la mer calme percée au loin par e Stromboli, qui se réveille de temps à autre, Alicudi, Vulcano et, plus près, Lipari. Juchée au-dessus de la petite ville de Valdichiesa, la maison de Paolo Deganello est étroitement enlacée par la roche volcanique. A l'arrivée du printemps, on reconstruit le toit de la pergola avec de nouvelles branches.

The Aeolian Islands are noted for the winds which sweep across the Tyrrhenian Sea. But it's the volcanoes – some extinct, others dormant and one or two perhaps just snoozing – which have formed this grab-bag of islands and given them their dramatic profiles. Filicudi, shaped like a raindrop and just 9.5 square kilometers long, is one of the quietest islands. With little (no!) flat land, its houses perch on terraces and lava-rock hillsides. But the gods take away, and they give, and the vertiginous mountainsides, challenging to the unathletic, are also the most superb vantage points from which to see somewhat-active Mount Stromboli across the flat sea, and Alicudi, Vulcano, and Lipari nearby. Above the small town of Val di Chiesa on Filicudi, Paolo Deganello's house stands in the rocky embrace of the volcano's earthbound sculpture. Come spring, it's time to craft the roof of the pergola with fresh branches.

Die Liparischen Inseln sind bekannt für die Winde, die über das Tyrrhenische Meer fegen. Geformt wurde die Inselgruppe mit dem dramatischen Profil, eine Art Wundertüte großer und kleiner Inseln, allerdings durch Vulkane – einige mittlerweile erloschen, andere untätig, einige vielleicht nur faul. Filicudi hat die Form eines Regentropfens, ist nur 9,5 Quadratkilometer groß und gehört zu den ruhigsten Liparischen Inseln. Hier gibt es wenig – eher kein – Flachland, und die Häuser schmiegen sich an Terrassen und Berghänge aus Lavagestein. Doch die Götter nehmen nicht nur, sie geben auch: Die Schwindel erregenden Berghänge, die für Ungeübte eine ziemliche Herausforderung darstellen, bieten gleichzeitig eine hervorragende Aussicht über das flache Meer auf den mehr oder weniger aktiven Stromboli und die nahe gelegenen Inseln Alicudi, Vulcano und Lipari. Über dem Städtchen Val di Chiesa ruht das Haus von Paolo Deganello in der felsigen Umarmung des Vulkans. Wenn der Frühling kommt, ist es an der Zeit, das Dach der Pergola wieder mit neuen Zweigen zu bekrönen.

Previous pages: The stones of the 1930 house have acquired a rustic appearance over the years and now add a relaxed air to the 25-meter-long pergola. Paolo Deganello, who was an architect before opening a furniture and lighting design studio, restored his delightful holiday home himself in 1970.
Above: Drawings by Dario Passi adorn the walls of the bedroom.
Right: the traditional tiled kitchen.
Facing page: The architect kept all signs of age and time, and employed locally crafted chairs and a ladder as instant sculpture.

Doubles pages précédentes: Au fil des ans, les pierres de la maison construite en 1930 ont pris une patine rustique qui sied à l'atmosphère décontractée de la pergola longue de 25 mètres. Les travaux de restoration de la maison de vacances furent entrepris en 1970 par Paolo Deganello en personne. Après des études d'architecture, il a ouvert un studio de design spécialisé en mobilier et lampes.
Ci-dessus: Des dessins de Dario Passi ornent les murs de la chambre.
A droite: la cuisine au carrelage traditionnel.
Page de droite: L'architecte a préservé les traces d'usure et du temps, utilisant des chaises fabriquées dans la région et une échelle en guise de sculpture instantanée.

Vorhergehende Doppelseiten: Die Steine des Hauses, das von 1930 stammt, haben mit der Zeit ein rustikales Äußeres angenommen und verleihen der 25 Meter langen Pergola eine gewisse Lässigkeit. Im Jahr 1970 restaurierte Paolo Deganello selbst sein Ferienhaus - schließlich war er Architekt, bevor er ein Designstudio für Möbel und Leuchten gründete.
Oben: Zeichnungen von Dario Passi schmücken das Schlafzimmer.
Rechts: die traditionell gekachelte Küche.
Rechte Seite: Der Architekt beließ alle Altersspuren und verwendete auf der Insel gefertigte Stühle sowie eine Leiter als skulpturale Elemente.

Filicudi, Aeolian Islands, Italy 38°34'N 14°34'E   Paolo Deganello

Flavio Albanese

Pantelleria, Italy, Strait of Sicily

L'île de Pantelleria volette à mi-chemin entre la Sicile et la Tunisie, tel un insecte projeté par le gros orteil de la botte italienne. C'est son isolement et son paysage austère de rocailles qui ont attiré l'architecte Flavio Albanese dans les années 70. Ce dernier avant-poste de l'Europe, balayé en permanence par les vents capricieux de la Méditerranée, a vu se succéder au cours des millénaires les Grecs, les Phéniciens, les Vandales, les Angevins, les Souabes, les Bourbons et les Maures. En deux décennies, l'architecte Flavio Albanese a transformé un groupe de «dammusi», des habitations anciennes construites avec les roches volcaniques de l'île, en une élégante résidence d'été. Respectant la structure des bâtisses originales, il a construit plusieurs chambres voûtées pour les amis, une cuisine superbement équipée avec une cuisinière en acier à dix brûleurs, une somptueuse chambre meublée d'ottomans en velours de soie et un bureau égayé d'une collection de photos modernes.

The island of Pantelleria hovers halfway between Sicily and Tunisia, like an insect flicked off the toe of Italy's boot. It was the remoteness and the rock-strewn starkness of the landscape that drew architect Flavio Albanese to this last outpost of Europe. Greeks, Phoenicians, Vandals, Angevins, Swabians, Bourbons and Moors had all set foot here, and the wild Mediterranean winds still sweep across the island. The architect Flavio Albanese first discovered the volcanic island in the 70s, and over the last two decades he has transformed a cluster of "dammusi" – ancient dwellings crafted from indigenous volcanic rocks – into a chic summer residence. Taking his cue from the centuries-old structures, he has carved out a group of vaulted guest rooms, a superbly equipped kitchen with a ten-burner steel stove, a glamorous bedroom with silk-velvet ottomans, and a study enlivened with a collection of contemporary photographs.

Pantelleria scheint im Mittelmeer zwischen Sizilien und Tunesien fast zu schweben – wie ein Insekt, das von der Stiefelspitze Italiens weggeschnippt wurde. Die entlegene Lage und die von Felsen übersäte, karge Landschaft waren es, die den Architekten Flavio Albanese zu diesem letzten Außenposten Europas zogen, wo bereits Griechen, Phönizier, Vandalen, das Königshaus von Anjou, Schwaben, Bourbonen und Mauren gesiedelt hatten und wo der wilde Mittelmeerwind über die Insel fegt. In den 70er Jahren entdeckte auch der Architekt Flavio Albanese diese Insel vulkanischen Ursprungs für sich. Während der letzten zwei Jahrzehnte formte er eine Ansiedlung von »dammusi«, traditionellen Bauten aus dem heimischen Vulkanstein, um zu einer eleganten Sommerresidenz. Dabei ließ er sich von der Atmosphäre der jahrhundertealten Bauten anregen. So gestaltete er mehrere gewölbte Gästeräume, eine perfekt eingerichtete Küche inklusive eines Profi-Gasherds aus Stahl mit zehn Flammen, einen äußerst luxuriösen Schlafraum mit samtbezogenen Hockern und ein Arbeitszimmer, das durch zeitgenössische Fotografien belebt wird.

Previous page: Terraces and a pool interconnect the guest rooms and living quarters, and provide a vantage point for viewing the sunlight flickering across the sea, and the distant coast of Africa.
Left: Flavio Albanese created a retreat among terraces of olives, grapevines, and breezy palm trees. The cupola-shaped roofs allow gusts of rain to drain easily. Precious water is then collected in a series of cisterns, and recycled in the gardens.
Below: Palm-shaded terraces are furnished with Moroccan tables, and benches dressed in graphic African cottons.

Page précédente: Les chambres d'amis sont reliées au corps principal du bâtiment par des terrasses et une piscine, qui sont autant de points de vue d'où admirer les reflets dansants du soleil sur la mer et la côte lointaine de l'Afrique.
A gauche: Flavio Albanese s'est créé un refuge à l'abri des vents parmi les terrasses d'oliveraies, de vignobles et de palmeraies. L'eau de pluie précieuse s'écoule facilement sur les toits en coupole puis est recueillie dans une série de citernes avant d'irriguer les jardins.
Ci-dessous: Sur les terrasses, des tables marocaines et des bancs couverts de cotonnades africaines aux motifs graphiques.

Vorhergehende Seite: Terrassen und ein Pool verbinden die Gästeräume mit dem Wohnbereich und bieten gleichzeitig eine herrliche Aussicht auf die ferne Küste Afrikas und das über dem Meer gleißende Sonnenlicht.
Links: Flavio Albanese schuf eine luftige Oase zwischen Terrassen mit Olivenbäumen, Weinstöcken und Palmen. Die kuppelförmigen Dächer lassen Regengüsse leicht abfließen. Das kostbare Nass wird in Zisternen aufgefangen und als Gießwasser für den Garten verwendet.
Unten: Auf den Terrassen bedecken afrikanische Baumwollstoffe marokkanische Tische und Sitzbänke.

Above: On Pantelleria, Albanese has learned to improvise shade and soft harbors of relaxation. On seaview terraces he used swaying swags of cotton to cover a metal-framed bed, and thatched a dining loggia with palm fronds. When the winds and heat are especially oppressive, most of the living is conducted within, embraced by ancient walls that measure as much as two meters thick.
Right: The house and its outbuildings nestle in the rocks as if they had somehow grown there over the centuries. Albanese calls his vacation home "Gelkhammar" (the crescent moon).

Ci-dessus: Ici et là, Albanese a improvisé de petits havres de paix ombragés. Sur une des terrasses qui dominent la mer, un lit en métal est protégé par de grands voiles de coton légers et la loggia où l'on dîne le soir par un dais en feuilles de palmier. Lorsque les vents et la chaleur se font particulièrement oppressants, on se retranche à l'intérieur, derrière de vieux murs faisant près de deux mètres d'épaisseur.
A droite: La maison et ses dépendances, qu'Albanese a baptisées «Gelkhammar» (croissant lunaire), sont nichées entre les rochers comme si elles s'y étaient développées peu à peu au fil des siècles.

Oben: Auf Pantelleria hat Flavio Albanese gelernt, schattige Plätze und Oasen der Entspannung zu improvisieren. Auf Terrassen mit Meerblick wehen Stoffbahnen aus Baumwolle an einem Eisenbett, während eine als Essplatz dienende Loggia von Palmwedeln beschattet wird. Wenn der Wind und die Hitze besonders drückend sind, findet das Leben zum großen Teil im Hausinneren statt, geschützt durch uralte Mauern, die bis zu zwei Meter dick sein können.
Rechts: Das Haus und seine Nebengebäude schmiegen sich in die Felsen ein, als seien sie auf wundersame Weise über Jahrhunderte hinweg dort gewachsen. Der Architekt nennt sein Ferienhaus »Gelkhammar« (Mondsichel).

Facing page: *Bold mud-colored African fabrics form crossword puzzles on the banquettes and cushions of the study. The rattan chair was designed by Borek Sípek for Driade. Albanese has allowed the original architecture to be expressed fully within his reworking of the rooms. Traditionally the buildings had small or no windows, and narrow doorways that could be secured against the howling winds. On a narrow metal shelf, Albanese displays a series of masterworks by photographers including Richard Avedon, Robert Mapplethorpe, and Karl Lagerfeld.*

Page de droite: *Dans le bureau, les tissus africains aux couleurs de terre qui recouvrent banquettes et coussins semblent former un message à décrypter. Le fauteuil en rotin a été dessiné par Borek Sípek pour Driade. Lors de l'aménagement des pièces, Albanese a laissé la structure d'origine s'exprimer librement. Traditionnellement, les bâtiments n'avaient que de petites fenêtres, voire aucune, et des portes étroites que l'on gardait fermées pour se protéger des vents violents. Sur une mince étagère métallique, Albanese a exposé sa collection de chefs-d'œuvre photographiques signés Richard Avedon, Robert Mapplethorpe ou encore Karl Lagerfeld.*

Rechte Seite: *Kräftig gemusterte afrikanische Stoffe in Erdtönen fügen sich wie in einem Kreuzworträtsel auf den Sitzbänken und Kissen im Arbeitszimmer aneinander. Der Rattanstuhl ist ein Entwurf von Borek Sípek für Driade. Der ursprünglichen Architektur der Räume ließ Albanese bei der Umgestaltung vollen Ausdrucksspielraum. So hatten die traditionellen Bauten nur kleine oder gar keine Fenster und verfügten über schmale Gänge, die sich leicht gegen den heulenden Wind verschließen ließen. Auf einem schmalen Metallregal stehen Fotografien aus Albaneses Sammlung, darunter Arbeiten von Richard Avedon, Robert Mapplethorpe und Karl Lagerfeld.*

Above and right: *A series of interlocking passages and arched rooms have been turned into gracious galleries and uncomplicated places of shade and respite from summer's glare. In perfect harmony with the cross-cultural fables of this floating history book of an island, Albanese has furnished his interiors with an artful gathering of antique Moroccan tables, Bedouin tents, Mali cottons, Italian furniture limned by contemporary French and Italian designers, Indian tables, and elaborate Sicilian silver candelabra.*

Ci-dessus et à droite: *Une série de couloirs s'entrecroisant et de pièces voûtées ont été convertis en d'élégantes galeries dépouillées et fraîches où se réfugier de la lumière aveuglante de l'été. Fidèle aux légendes de Pantelleria, véritable carrefour de cultures et livre d'images flottant, Albanese a rassemblé avec art tables marocaines anciennes, tentes bédouines, cotonnades maliennes, meubles italiens signés par des designers contemporains français et italiens, tables indiennes et d'élégants chandeliers siciliens en argent.*

Oben und rechts: *Miteinander verbundene Passagen und gewölbte Räume wurden zu anmutigen Galerien und schlichten Rückzugsorten gegen die gleißende Hitze des Sommers umgewandelt. In perfekter Harmonie mit den Sagen der Insel, die man fast als schwimmendes Geschichtsbuch verschiedener Kulturen beschreiben könnte, bestückte Flavio Albanese die Innenräume seines Anwesens mit einer kunstvollen Sammlung antiker Tische aus Marokko, Beduinenzelten, Baumwollstoffen aus Mali, zeitgenössischem französischen und italienischen Design, Tischen aus Indien und kunstvoll verzierten, sizilianischen Kandelabern.*

Pantelleria, Italy, Strait of Sicily 36°45'N 12°10'E

Facing page: In a small cell-like guest room, Albanese has combined a simple cotton-draped bed, contemporary lamps, and a swoop of cool hand-woven cotton to soften the hard outlines of the stone walls.
Above: Most of the rooms open to the outdoors and views of the wide-open sea and the rocky shore. Albanese's door pivots to allow easy access to the great outdoors.
Right: Reflecting the North-African aspect of its nature, this cool corner of the house is simply furnished with Saharan rugs, a cotton ceiling banner, and Moroccan lanterns.

Page de gauche: Dans cette petite chambre d'ami monacale, Albanese a marié un simple dessus-de-lit en coton, des lampes modernes et une cascade de cotonnades tissées à la main dont les couleurs fraîches adoucissent la texture brute des murs en pierres.
Ci-dessus: La plupart des chambres donnent directement sur l'extérieur, avec des vues sur le grand large et la rive rocailleuse. Les portes pivotent pour accéder plus facilement à la nature.
A droite: Ce coin frais de la maison est décoré simplement avec des tapis sahariens, une tenture en coton suspendue au plafond et des lanternes marocaines.

Linke Seite: In einem Gästezimmer, das an eine Klosterzelle erinnert, kombinierte Albanese ein einfaches, mit Baumwollstoffen bedecktes Bett mit modernen Lampen und einer kühnen Drapierung aus handgewebten Baumwollstoffen, die die harten Konturen der Steinmauern mildern.
Oben: Die meisten Räume bieten einen herrlichen Blick auf das offene Meer und die felsige Küste. Als Übergang vom Haus zur Natur hat Albanese eine Drehtür gewählt.
Rechts: In dieser kühlen Ecke wird der nordafrikanische Charakter durch schlichte Teppiche aus der Sahara, eine Wandbespannung aus Baumwolle und marokkanische Lampen betont.

Facing page: Luxury is its own reward in this windswept outpost. Albanese revels in the sensual colors and silken textures of tufted velvet ottomans, a raspberry-colored velvet daybed piped in a contrasting pink, and a chrome-yellow painted chest. Friends gather, nestling in a rainbow of cushions, and sip chilled mint tea from traditional Moroccan goblets.

Page de droite: Cet avant-poste balayé par les vents est aussi un havre de luxe et de volupté. Albanese aime se perdre dans les couleurs sensuelles et les textures soyeuses de ses ottomans moelleux. Le lit de repos est tapissé de velours framboise et galonné d'un rose contrastant. Le coffre est peint en jaune chrome. Affalés dans un arc-en-ciel de coussins, les amis se rassemblent ici pour déguster du thé à la menthe dans des verres traditionnels marocains.

Rechte Seite: Auf diesem windumtosten Außenposten belohnt man sich mit Luxus. Albanese schwelgt in den sinnlichen Farben und seidig weichen Oberflächen der mit Samt bezogenen Hocker, des mit himbeerfarbenem Samt bezogenen Tagesbetts mit kontrastierenden pinkfarbenen Akzenten und der in Parisergelb gestrichenen Kiste. Hier versammeln sich Freunde, lagern auf einem wahren Regenbogen aus Kissen und schlürfen Pfefferminztee aus marokkanischen Trinkbechern.

Above: A collection of traditional Moroccan lanterns stands at the ready in a cool hallway. Lanterns may be taken outside for evening festivities, or used when electricity fails. Walls in this structure have been enlivened with brightly pigmented plaster, in homage to Moroccan interiors.
Right: Life on Pantelleria is not all indolence. Albanese likes to draw and paint, and his lively mind creates architectural sketches and colorful models.

Ci-dessus: une collection de lanternes marocaines au garde à vous dans un couloir frais. Elles éclairent les terrasses lors de festivités nocturnes ou sont mises à contribution quand l'électricité tombe en panne. Les murs ont été égayés par un plâtre aux couleurs vives, hommage aux intérieurs marocains.
A droite: La vie sur Pantelleria n'est pas qu'indolence. Toujours alerte, Albanese aime peindre et dessiner des motifs architecturaux et des sujets pittoresques.

Oben: Eine Sammlung traditioneller marokkanischer Lampen steht griffbereit in einem kühlen Flur. Sie werden als festliche Außenbeleuchtung verwendet, aber auch, wenn die Elektrizität ausfällt. Die Mauern wurden mit Gips in leuchtender Pigmentierung belebt – eine Hommage an marokkanische Interieurs.
Rechts: Das Leben auf Pantelleria ist nicht nur vom Müßiggang geprägt. Flavio Albanese zeichnet und malt und in seinem nimmermüden kreativen Kopf entstehen Architekturentwürfe und farbenfrohe Modelle.

Pantelleria, Italy, Strait of Sicily 36°45'N 12°10'E

On top of
Mosquito Mountain

Mykonos, Cyclades Islands, Greece

Voguer sur la mer Egée parmi les îles ensoleillées des Cyclades est une expérience si envoûtante qu'on ne peut s'empêcher de se croire revenu aux temps d'Ulysse et de ses voyages. Le paysage n'a sans doute guère changé depuis et les journées passées sur l'eau s'écoulent dans un climat d'optimisme. Le poète grec Constantin Cavafy (1863–1933) a écrit des errances d'Ulysse: «Souhaite que ton voyage soit long, que nombreux soient les matins d'été, où – avec quels délices! – tu pénétreras dans des ports vus pour la première fois.» Les capricieux vents éoliens poussent les embarcations du minuscule port de Mykonos à Naxos et à Santorin, et des jetées de Paros et d'Adros vers la poétique Delos. Les beautés et les particularités de ces îles fabuleuses invitent à prolonger son séjour. Les rythmes anciens des mélodies grecques résonnent encore dans le creux des vagues et les silhouettes cubistes des chapelles et des maisons blanches se détachent sur les collines volcaniques.

Sailing in the Aegean Sea among the sun-bright Cyclades Islands is so soporific that the imagination soon floats away to the time of Ulysses and his mythical journeys. The seascape seems little changed, and days on water drift along optimistically. The Greek poet Constantine P. Cavafi (1863–1933) wrote of Ulysses and his wanderings: "Hope that the voyage is a long one, that the summer mornings are many, and that you will enter ports for the first time, with such pleasure and such joy!" The whims of the Aeolian winds blow boats from the tiny harbor of Mykonos to Naxos and Santorini, and from the docks of Paros and Andros to poetic Delos. The beauties and idiosyncrasies of these fabled islands invite longer stays. The ancient rhythms of Greek music still echo across the sea, and the white cubist forms of chapels and stone houses stand in relief against the volcanic hillsides.

Wenn man auf dem Ägäischen Meer zwischen den in der Sonne leuchtenden Kykladeninseln hindurchsegelt, stiehlt sich die Vorstellungskraft bald in Richtung des Helden Odysseus und dessen mythische Reisen davon. Die Landschaft des Meeres verändert sich kaum und die Tage auf dem Wasser gleiten in froher Erwartung vorbei. Der griechische Dichter Konstantinos P. Kavafis (1863–1933) schrieb über Odysseus und dessen Irrfahrten: »Hoffe, dass die Reise eine lange sein, es viele Sommermorgen geben wird und dass du zum ersten Mal Häfen mit diesem Hochgefühl der Freude anlaufen wirst!« Die launischen äolischen Winde pusten die Boote aus dem winzigen Hafen von Mykonos nach Naxos und Santorini und von den Docks von Paros und Andros zur idyllischen Insel Delos. Die vielen Schönheiten und Besonderheiten dieser berühmten Inseln laden zum Verweilen ein. Heute noch wirft der Rhythmus der griechischen Musik des Altertums sein Echo über das Meer und die kubistischen weißen Formen von Kapellen und Häusern aus Stein stehen wie Reliefs vor der vulkanischen Hügellandschaft.

Previous pages: American interior designer Deborah French, Greek photographer Vangelis Tsangaris, and their son, Ilias, on Mykonos.
Above: The dining room was at first an open, brick-floored terrace. The skylight and a wall of windows were added later, when the couple discovered that incessant summer winds – known locally as "Meltemi" – made dining al fresco too breezy.
Right: The house was built on Kounoupas ("mosquito") mountain.
Facing page: The living room is furnished simply with an ancient Greek urn, and with finds from the flea market in Piraeus.

Double page précédente: la décoratrice américaine, Deborah French, le photographe grec, Vangelis Tsangaris, et leur fils Ilias.
Ci-dessus: A l'origine, la salle à manger était une terrasse ouverte avec un sol en briques. La verrière et les baies vitrées furent ajoutées plus tard, lorsque le couple s'est rendu compte que les vents d'été incessants, appelés «Meltemi» dans la région, perturbaient leurs dîners à la belle étoile.
A droite: La maison est construite sur le mont Kounoupas (mont «moustique»).
Page de droite: Le salon est meublé simplement avec une urne grecque et des trouvailles chinées sur le marché aux puces du Pirée.

Vorhergehende Doppelseite: die amerikanische Interior-Designerin Deborah French, der griechische Fotograf Vangelis Tsangaris und der gemeinsame Sohn Ilias auf Mykonos.
Oben: Das Esszimmer war ursprünglich eine offene Terrasse mit Ziegelfußboden. Das Oberlicht und die Fensterwand kamen später dazu, weil die Sommerwinde – auf der Insel als »Meltemi« bekannt – das Essen unter freiem Himmel unmöglich machten.
Rechts: das Haus auf dem Berg Kounoupas, dem »Mückenberg«.
Rechte Seite: Das Wohnzimmer wurde einfach eingerichtet: mit einer alten Amphore und Fundstücken vom Trödelmarkt in Piräus.

Mykonos, Cyclades Islands, Greece 37°28'N 25°23'E   On top of Mosquito Mountain

For this bedroom, as with other rooms of the house, French encouraged the builders not to use plumb lines. "I wanted them to work in a very naive manner, and to let their eyes and experience be their guides, rather then making it all perfectly straight," said French, who has an interior design studio in New York. Before the house was built, she and Tsangaris climbed their hill at sunset, and decided where all the rooms should be placed. French decorated the rooms very simply with American Indian baskets, hand-crafted Greek-island textiles, and vintage furniture.

Pour construire cette chambre et d'autres pièces, French, qui possède un bureau de décoration d'intérieur à New York, a encouragé les maçons à ne pas utiliser de fil à plomb. «Je tenais à ce qu'ils travaillent d'une manière très naïve, qu'ils laissent leurs yeux et leur expérience leur servir de guides plutôt que faire tout parfaitement droit». Avant le début des travaux, Tsangaris et French grimpèrent sur la colline au coucher du soleil et décidèrent de l'emplacement de chaque pièce. Deborah French a décoré les pièces très simplement avec des paniers amérindiens, des tissus des îles grecques tissés à la main et des meubles anciens.

Bei diesem Schlafzimmer, wie auch bei den anderen Räumen des Hauses, ermutigte Deborah French die Maurer, auf das Lot zu verzichten. »Ich wollte, dass sie auf fast naive Weise an ihre Arbeit herangehen und sich dabei von ihren Augen und ihrer Erfahrung leiten lassen, anstatt perfekt ausgelotete Wände zu schaffen«, erklärt French, die in New York ein Büro für Interior-Design besitzt. Bevor das Haus gebaut wurde, kletterten Deborah French und Vangelis Tsangaris bei Sonnenuntergang auf »ihren« Hügel und entschieden, wo die Räume sich befinden sollten. Die Räume wurden von Deborah mit indianischen Körben, handgefertigten Stoffen von den griechischen Inseln und alten Möbeln einfach eingerichtet.

Pedro Espirito Santo

Bay of Setúbal, Portugal

Au sud de Lisbonne, au-delà de la baie de Setúbal, une longue plage isolée fait front à l'Atlantique. Par miracle, la fièvre immobilière qui sévit dans les régions côtières a oublié ce charmant coin de terre balayé par les vagues. Un jour qu'il campait par là avec deux jeunes cousins, le décorateur portugais, Pedro Espirito Santo, aperçut trois petits points blancs au loin sur le sable. Après une longue marche, ils tombèrent sur trois humbles maisons de pêcheurs abandonnées. Espirito Santo, qui a voyagé et vécu un peu partout dans le monde, est immédiatement tombé amoureux de leurs lignes simples qui les font ressembler à des dessins d'enfants: une petite porte, une fenêtre à peine esquissée, le tout peint dans des bleus et des blancs joyeux. Espirito Santo et ses cousins les ont achetées et restaurées soigneusement. Elles avaient été à la merci des intempéries pendant des années et ils ont pris soin de ne pas détruire leur charme ensoleillé.

South of Lisbon and beyond the Bay of Setúbal is a remote stretch of beach facing full-on to the Atlantic Ocean. Somehow, in the rush to develop coastal regions, this lovely, wave-washed area has remained untouched. It was here that Portuguese interior designer, Pedro Espirito Santo, discovered a trio of simple fishermen's cottages. He and two young cousins had gone off on a camping trip, and saw the huts in the distance — like tiny white dots on the sand. After a long walk, they came upon the three cottages, lonely and deserted. Espirito Santo, who has traveled and lived around the world, immediately loved their uncomplicated lines, each as simple as a young child's drawing of a house. There is the little door, a mere sketch of a window, all painted in cheerful blue and white. The houses had been neglected and weather-damaged over the years. Espirito Santo and his cousins acquired them and renovated them without destroying their sun-bleached charm.

Südlich von Lissabon und unterhalb der Bucht von Setúbal gibt es einen entlegenen Strand direkt am Atlantik. Irgendwie hatte man bei der Erschließung der Küstenregionen dieses wunderbare und von Wellen umrauschte Kleinod übersehen. Hier entdeckte der portugiesische Innenausstatter Pedro Espirito Santo bei einem Campingausflug mit zwei jüngeren Cousins ein Trio aus schlichten Fischerhütten. Aus der Entfernung hatten sie noch wie kleine weiße Punkte auf dem Sand gewirkt, aber nach einem langen Fußmarsch stellten sie sich als drei einsam gelegene, verlassene Hütten heraus. Espirito Santo, der schon in allen Weltregionen gelebt und gearbeitet hat, verliebte sich sofort in ihre einfache Linienführung. Jedes Haus könnte auch von einer Kinderzeichnung stammen: Es gibt eine kleine Tür, eben noch ein Fenster und alles ist in fröhliches Weißblau getaucht. Die Häuschen waren durch die Wettereinwirkung vieler Jahre heruntergekommen. Espirito Santo und seine Cousins kauften sie und renovierten sie sorgfältig, ohne ihren sonnengegerbten Charme zu zerstören.

Left and below: The designer and his cousins set out to clean and repair the houses. Making a careful restoration, they painted the old concrete floors with bright blue paint in the traditional manner. But the water-splotched woodwork was merely washed lightly to remove dust and cobwebs, and left in all its glory. The kitchen and indoor dining area were furnished with a table and checkered cloth, a china cabinet, and an old carved teak bench.

A gauche et ci-dessous: Pedro Espirito Santo et ses cousins ont entrepris de retaper les maisons. Ils ont peint les vieux sols en béton dans le bleu et blanc traditionnels. Les boiseries striées de taches d'humidité ont simplement été lessivées pour en ôter la poussière et les toiles d'araignées, retrouvant ainsi leur beauté patinée d'origine. La cuisine et le coin repas intérieur sont meublés avec une table couverte d'une nappe à carreaux, un cabinet chinois et un vieux banc en teck sculpté.

Links und unten: *Pedro Espirito Santo und seine Cousins renovierten die Häuschen und strichen die alten Betonfußböden in traditioneller Manier mit leuchtend blauer Farbe. Die wasserfleckigen Holzeinbauten wurden von Staub und Spinnweben gereinigt und die Farbe nur dünn aufgetragen, um die Holzstruktur zu erhalten. Die Küche und der Essbereich wurden mit einem Tisch mit einer gewürfelten Tischdecke, einem Geschirrschränkchen und einer alten geschnitzten Teakholzbank eingerichtet.*

Previous pages: The unpretentious houses found by Pedro Espirito Santo and his family make a virtue of simplicity. Walls were given fresh coats of whitewash, one exterior wall was striped with blue and white, then paired with a daybed dressed in Brazilian fabrics.
Facing page: Espirito Santo goes to his cottage to get away from the cares of the city, and has assiduously avoided tricking up his little hideaway with decor. He improvised shade for the dining terrace with an awning of branches. Tables and benches are old painted pieces he found locally.

Double page précédente: Ces maisons sans prétention font de la simplicité une vertu. Les murs ont été reblanchis à la chaux. Une façade a été peinte avec des rayures bleues et blanches puis parée d'un lit de repos drapé de tissus brésiliens.
Page de gauche: Espirito Santo vient se réfugier dans son cabanon pour échapper aux soucis de la ville. Il n'était donc pas question de surcharger le décor. La terrasse où l'on prend ses repas est abritée sous un dais de branchages improvisé. Les tables et les bancs sont de vieux meubles dénichés sur place.

Vorhergehende Doppelseite: *Die Häuser, die Pedro Espirito Santo mit seiner Familie entdeckte, machen aus der Einfachheit eine Tugend. Die Wände erhielten einen frischen Kalkanstrich, eine Außenwand wurde in blauweißen Streifen gestrichen und davor wurde ein Tagesbett gestellt, bezogen mit einem brasilianischen Stoff.*
Linke Seite: *In seinem Häuschen entflieht Espirito Santo der Großstadt. Deshalb hat er auch ein Übermaß an Dekoration vermieden. So improvisierte er aus Zweigen ein Schatten spendendes Dach für den Essplatz auf der Terrasse. Die alten bemalten Tische und Bänke fand er in der Umgebung.*

Below: The art of "fixing up" an old coastal cottage is to respect the original use and intent of the dwelling and not to try to modernize it or subvert its appeal. A plain gas stove and sinks were brought in, the walls were painted white, and the kitchen still has the charm of the original. The less time they have to spend cleaning the house, say the owners, the more time they have to enjoy the great outdoors.
Facing page: The bedroom is still essentially as it was, with the addition of a new shower behind the blue-painted lathe partition, and a new ceramic washbasin.

Ci-dessous: L'art de «retaper» une vieille maison en bord de mer consiste à respecter sa fonction initiale sans essayer de la moderniser ni de détourner son attrait. La cuisine a conservé son charme d'origine, elle a simplement été équipée d'une gazinière et d'éviers. Les murs ont été peints en blanc. Les propriétaires partent du principe que moins ils passent de temps à faire le ménage, plus il leur en reste pour profiter de la nature environnante.
Page de droite: La chambre est restée pratiquement telle quelle, on y a simplement ajouté une douche derrière la cloison aux lattes peintes en bleu et un lavabo en céramique.

Unten: Die Kunst, eine alte Hütte am Meer stilgerecht zu renovieren, besteht darin, den ursprünglichen Zweck des Hauses zu respektieren. Ein einfacher Gasherd und ein Spülbecken wurden eingebaut, die Wände weiß gestrichen – so hat die Küche ihren ursprünglichen Charme behalten. Je weniger Zeit sie für das Putzen benötigen, so die Inhaber, desto mehr Zeit bleibt ihnen für das tolle Angebot draußen vor der Tür.
Rechte Seite: Das Schlafzimmer blieb im Wesentlichen unverändert. Nur eine neue Dusche hinter der blau gestrichenen Trennwand und ein neues Keramikwaschbecken wurden eingebaut.

Above: Pedro Espirito Santo's house has been renovated for summer living, and a good mosquito net is essential. Most of the activity – swimming, hiking, boating, reading – takes place beyond the residence, so furniture was kept to a comfortable minimum. In the little bedroom, an antique painted iron bed is covered with a hand-woven cotton spread.

Ci-dessus: Pedro Espirito Santo ayant aménagé sa maison pour y passer l'été, de bonnes moustiquaires étaient indispensables. La plupart des activités, la natation, la randonnée, le bateau, la lecture, se déroulant à l'extérieur, l'ameublement est réduit à un minimum confortable. Dans la petite chambre à coucher, le vieux lit en fer peint est recouvert d'une cotonnade tissée à la main.

Oben: Pedro Espirito Santos Haus wurde so umgestaltet, dass man hier während des Sommers leben kann. Ein gutes Moskitonetz ist dafür unerlässlich. Die meisten Aktivitäten wie Schwimmen, Wandern, Bootfahren oder Lesen finden außerhalb des kleinen Anwesens statt; deshalb wurde es auch nur sparsam möbliert. Im kleinen Schlafzimmer bedeckt ein handgewebter Überwurf aus Baumwolle das alte, gestrichene Eisenbett.

Bay of Setúbal, Portugal 38°32'N 8°54'E

Exploring Africa

It's mid-afternoon, and a sweet torpor hangs over Casablanca and Tangier and Dakar. The fresh tang of oranges and jasmine mingles in the salty air along with cloves and fresh bread and cinnamon. Heat wraps around the unwary like a warm, damp blanket. There's nothing to do but give in to this languor, and disappear indoors for cool mint tea, a sly game of cards, sweet oblivion, or a sea-haunted siesta. Somewhere, a dog barks. A soft guitar thrums. But the brain has slowed and the heat mutes reactions. A shady bedroom with Portuguese tiles and drifting gauze draperies offers quiet sanctuary from the shimmering heat of Gorée Island. It's a place haunted with history's sad truths, but now merry with the laughter of children playing in the shadows of narrow, winding streets. Doorways are closed, and windows shuttered against the white sunlight. Further South, Cape Town beaches are churning, splashed wide awake by the cold, powerful waves of the southern Atlantic. Sometimes, it seems that these high-rollers have fast-tracked directly from Antarctic waters, with no time to thaw. The Seychelles Islands hover on the Indian Ocean. Stingrays and clownfish twist and dart through sapphire waters, and a lone fisherman paddles his dugout canoe in search of lunch. He picks mangoes and papayas for desert. Nature is bountiful there. On the coral coast of Kenya, a happy couple open their doors to guests and friends, and frisky dogs. Afternoon rain plays on the tin roof like a xylophone, and then washes dust from dancing palm trees.

C'est le milieu de l'après-midi et une douce torpeur plane au-dessus de Casablanca, Tanger et Dakar. De fraîches senteurs d'oranges et de jasmin se mêlent à l'odeur iodée de l'air et aux parfums de clous de girofle, de pain frais et de cannelle. La chaleur s'enroule autour des corps comme une couverture chaude et moite. Il n'y a rien d'autre à faire qu'à succomber à cette langueur et disparaître à l'intérieur siroter du thé à la menthe, jouer aux cartes, rêvasser ou sombrer dans une sieste hantée par des visions de mer. Quelque part, un chien aboie. Quelqu'un gratte doucement une guitare. Mais notre cerveau fonctionne au ralenti et la chaleur nous engourdit. Une chambre sombre, ornée de carrelage portugais et de draperies de gaze, offre un refuge tranquille à l'abri de la chaleur torride de l'île de Gorée. Ce lieu hanté par l'histoire résonne aujourd'hui des rires joyeux des enfants qui jouent à l'ombre des ruelles sinueuses. Les portes restent closes et les volets fermés protègent de la lumière aveuglante. Plus au sud, les plages de Cape Town, réveillées par la gifle glacée des vagues puissantes de l'Atlantique sud, bouillonnent de vie. Parfois, on croirait que ces hauts rouleaux, réservés aux amateurs de sensations fortes, arrivent droit de l'Antarctique sans avoir eu le temps de dégeler. Les Seychelles planent au-dessus de l'Océan Indien. Les pastenagues et les poissons-clowns fusent dans des eaux céruléennes. Un pêcheur solitaire part dans sa pirogue taillée à la main en quête de son repas. Pour son dessert, il n'aura qu'à cueillir des mangues et des papayes. Ici, la nature est généreuse. Sur la côte corallienne du Kenya, un couple heureux ouvre ses portes à ses invités et ses amis, ainsi qu'à une joyeuse meute de chiens. Les pluies de l'après-midi jouent du xylophone sur le toit en tôle puis lavent la poussière des palmiers dansants.

Mitten am Nachmittag. Eine süße Trägheit hängt über Casablanca, Tanger und Dakar. Der frische Duft von Orangen und Jasmin mischt sich in der salzigen Luft mit dem von Gewürznelken und frischem Brot und Zimt. Den Unbesonnenen umfängt die Hitze schnell wie eine warme feuchte Decke. Es bleibt einem nur, sich dieser Mattigkeit hinzugeben und im Inneren des Hauses erfrischenden Pfefferminztee zu trinken, Karten zu spielen und sich süßem Vergessen oder einer vom Meeresrauschen getragenen Siesta hinzugeben. Irgendwo kläfft ein Hund. Dann ein paar Gitarrenklänge. Doch das Gehirn arbeitet langsamer und die Hitze dämpft alle Reaktionen. Ein schattiges Schlafzimmer mit portugiesischen Fliesen und wehenden, fließenden Vorhängen bietet auf der Insel Gorée Schutz vor der flimmernden Hitze. Hier spürt man die Geister einer traurigen Vergangenheit und doch hallt das Lachen der spielenden Kinder durch die Schatten der engen, verwinkelten Straßen. Türen und Fensterläden bleiben zum Schutz vor dem gleißenden Licht der Sonne geschlossen. Weiter südlich stampfen die kalten kraftvollen Wellen des Südatlantiks an die Strände bei Kapstadt und reißen sie aus ihren Träumen. Manche Brecher scheinen direkt aus der Antarktis zu kommen und hatten auf ihrer rasend schnellen Reise kaum Zeit um aufzutauen. Im Indischen Ozean schweben kleine Inseltupfen, die Seychellen. Stachelrochen und Orange-Ringelfische winden sich sprintend durch das azurblaue Wasser. Auf der Jagd nach einem Mittagessen steuert ein einsamer Fischer seinen Einbaum durch das Meer. Zum Nachtisch pflückt er Mangos und Papayas. Die Natur bietet alles im Überfluss. Vor der Küste Kenias mit ihren Korallenriffen öffnet ein freundliches Paar seinen Gästen und Freunden – und verspielten Hunden – Tür und Tor. Am Nachmittag spielt der Regen auf dem Blechdach wie auf einem Xylophon und wäscht den Staub von tanzenden Palmwedeln.

A Romantic Retreat

North Morocco, Atlantic Coast

Le Maroc, avec son sens sublime de la couleur, sa chaleur hypnotique, sa musique envoûtante, est un lieu de villégiature privilégié des Européens depuis le 15e siècle. Casablanca, Fès, Marrakech, Rabat, la région du Rif et des villes haut perchées de l'Atlas sont devenues des haltes de choix pour les voyageurs en quête d'architecture traditionnelle, d'artisanat marocain devenu soudain branché et d'élégantes soieries chatoyantes. C'est un petit village, au sud de Tanger, qui a séduit la propriétaire d'une boutique de décoration à Paris et son mari, un architecte. Ils sont tombés en arrêt devant ses bâtiments en forme de morceaux de sucre, sa médina tranquille et parfaitement conservée, le grondement des vagues qui déferlent sur sa grève. Les propriétaires ont restauré et aménagé une vieille maison en terre enchâssée dans les remparts qui dominent l'Atlantique.

Morocco, with its heightened sense of color, trance-inducing heat, and mesmeric music, has been a favored rest stop for Europeans since the 15th century. Casablanca, Fez, Marrakech, Rabat, the region of Rif, and towns high in the Atlas Mountains have become alluring caravanserai for travelers in search of traditional architecture, suddenly-fashionable Moroccan furniture and antiques, and chic jewel-colored silks. It was a small village just south of Tangier that seduced a French style consultant, owner of a decor store in Paris, and her husband, an architect. Transfixed by the sugar-cube shaped buildings, the onrush of the Atlantic shore, and the quiet and perfectly preserved medina of the old quarter, they restored and refurbished an old mud house set into the coastal ramparts.

Seit dem 15. Jahrhundert ist Marokko wegen seiner intensiven Farbpalette, seiner in Trance versetzenden Hitze und seiner hypnotisierenden Musik für Europäer ein beliebtes Reiseziel. Casablanca, Fes, Marrakesch, Rabat, das Gebiet des Rif und die hoch im Atlas liegenden Städtchen gleichen Karawansereien für Reisende, die auf der Suche nach traditioneller Architektur, den über Nacht modern gewordenen marokkanischen Möbeln und Antiquitäten sowie den eleganten leuchtenden Seidenstoffen sind. Eine französische Stylistin und Beraterin, die in Paris einen Interior-Design-Shop besitzt, und ihr Mann, ein Architekt, konnten sich dem Charme eines kleinen Dorfs südlich von Tanger nicht entziehen. Sie waren fasziniert von den wie Zuckerwürfel aussehenden Häusern, dem laut rauschenden Atlantik und der ruhigen, perfekt erhaltenen Medina und kauften ein altes, in den Küstenschutzwall eingelassenes Lehmhaus, das sie restaurierten und neu einrichteten.

Previous pages: The house was built just inside the 1.80-meter-thick ramparts of the town. The versatile sitting room-salon-bedroom benefits from a controlled approach to decor, with simple Moroccan striped cotton fabrics picked up in the souks.
Facing page: The nearby villages are full of talented artisans with looms and paints and carving tools, so the owners set off on their decorating journey with luscious textiles and village-crafted chairs and tables from neighborhood shops and stalls in the medina.
Above and right: Sun-flecked waves beckon from every terrace.

Double page précédente: La maison est construite en partie à l'intérieur des remparts, épais de 1,80 mètre. Le salon-salle de séjour-chambre à coucher est sobrement décoré de cotonnades rayées.
Page de gauche: Les villages voisins regorgent d'artisans talentueux équipés de métiers à tisser, de peintures et d'outils de sculpteur. Les propriétaires n'ont donc qu'à se promener dans les boutiques du coin et entre les étals de la médina pour trouver des étoffes voluptueuses, des chaises et des tables fabriquées sur place.
Ci-dessus et à droite: Les vagues ourlées d'argent semblent vous appeler depuis chaque terrasse.

Vorhergehende Doppelseite: Das Haus wurde direkt in die 1,80 Meter dicke Stadtmauer eingelassen. Das Wohnzimmer, das auch als Salon und Schlafzimmer dient, profitiert von dem zurückhaltenden Dekor, der nur aus einfachen gestreiften Baumwollstoffen besteht, die aus den Souks stammen.
Linke Seite: In den benachbarten Dörfern finden sich viele sehr gute Kunsthandwerker mit ihren Webstühlen, Farben und Schnitzwerkzeugen. So erstaunt es nicht, dass die Besitzer von ihren Stöberreisen prächtige Stoffe sowie handgearbeitete Stühle und Tische mitbringen, die in den kleinen Läden der Medina gefertigt wurden.
Oben und rechts: Von jeder Terrasse locken glänzende Wellen.

Left: *The design approach is pragmatic and poetic. The owners insisted that furnishings should all come from the immediate region of the village: the hand-crafted bathroom tiles are in the colorful Moroccan style, window and door frames are painted vibrant blue and turquoise in the local vernacular.*
Below: *The house was built not only to withstand summer heat and the unrelenting sun, but also to handle the Atlantic's howling winter storms. Rather than air-conditioning, the houses have infinitely adjustable French doors and gauze draperies.*

A gauche: *La conception de la décoration est pragmatique et poétique. Les propriétaires tenaient à ce que tout, dans la maison, vienne des alentours du village. Les carreaux de la salle de bains, faits à la main, sont dans le style coloré marocain, les chambranles des portes et des fenêtres sont peints dans le bleu et le turquoise vibrants de la région.*
Ci-dessous: *La maison a été construite pour supporter la chaleur et le soleil impitoyable de l'été mais aussi pour résister aux tempêtes hurlantes de l'hiver. Plutôt que de l'air conditionné, les maisons ont des baies vitrées qui s'ajustent à l'infini et des draperies en gaze.*

Links: *Das Designkonzept verbindet Pragmatismus und Poesie. Bedingung war, dass alle Einrichtungsgegenstände aus der Umgebung des Dorfs stammen sollten. So sind die von Hand gefertigten Badezimmerfliesen im farbenfrohen marokkanischen Stil gehalten und Fenster- und Türrahmen wurden, wie hier üblich, in leuchtenden Blau- und Türkistönen gestrichen.*
Unten: *Das Haus sollte nicht nur der Sommerhitze und der unbarmherzigen Sonne trotzen, sondern auch den heulenden Winterstürmen. Anstelle einer Klimaanlage gibt es hier verstellbare Verandatüren und luftige Gazestoffe.*

Softening the furnishings and rejecting clichéd bric-à-brac, the owners
kept the colors calm and collected. From the outset they eschewed the
hot colors often associated with Morocco (think pink!), and began
with whitewashed walls, then added stripes with a light hand. Reflecting the inarguable fact that heat leads to languor and that it is wise
to retire to cool rooms, most of the interiors have built-in sofas and
beds eased with overstuffed cushions and bolsters. Wicker chairs and
stools are a practical and decorative design solution, and can migrate
from room to room.

*Pour adoucir le décor et éviter le bric-à-brac habituel, les propriétaires
ont choisi des couleurs calmes et retenues. D'emblée, ils ont rejeté les
tons chauds souvent associés au Maroc – Pensez: rose! Ils ont blanchi
les murs à la chaux puis ont rajouté des rayures légères. Conformé-
ment au fait indiscutable que la chaleur alanguit et qu'il est plus sage
de rester au frais, la plupart des pièces ont des sofas et des lits encastrés couverts d'oreillers et de traversins. Les chaises et les tabourets en
osier sont aussi pratiques que décoratifs et peuvent voyager de pièce
en pièce.*

*Die Möbel bekamen einen weichen Touch und auf typischen
»Nippes« wurde verzichtet. So gelang es den Besitzern, die Farbpalette ruhig zu halten. Intensive Farben, wie sie oft mit Marokko asso-
ziiert werden – man denke nur an Pink! –, wurden von Anfang an
vermieden. Stattdessen erhielten die Wände einen Kalkanstrich. Da
die Hitze den Menschen bekanntlich träge macht und es daher ange-
bracht ist, sich in kühlen Räumen aufzuhalten, besitzen fast alle
Räume eingebaute Sofas und Betten, die mit vielen Kissen und Pols-
tern eine weiche Ruhestätte bieten. Korbstühle und Hocker stellen
eine praktische und dekorative Lösung dar und lassen sich zudem von
Raum zu Raum transportieren.*

Views like this mesmerizing scene over Tangier can entertain for hours. The old port is still active, and the ferries arrive daily from Gibraltar and Ceuta. Moroccans are infinitely hospitable, and cool drinks – often served with refreshing mint – are an essential part of any visit.

On peut rester des heures à contempler le spectacle fascinant qu'offre Tanger. Le vieux port est encore actif et les transbordeurs venant de Gibraltar et de Ceuta y débarquent tous les jours leur cargaison de passagers. Les Marocains sont connus pour leur grande hospitalité. Les boissons fraîches, généralement accompagnées de feuilles de menthe, sont un élément indispensable de toute visite.

Dieser faszinierende Ausblick auf Tanger wird über Stunden hinweg nicht langweilig. Der alte Hafen ist noch heute belebt: Täglich landen hier Fähren aus Gibraltar und Ceuta. Marokkaner sind sehr gastfreundlich und bieten Besuchern stets kühle Getränke an, oft mit erfrischender Minze.

Tangier, Morocco 35°47'N 5°49'W   The Moroccan Experience

The Moroccan Experience

Tangier, Morocco

Depuis plus d'un siècle, des écrivains aussi différents que Gertrude Stein, Pierre Loti et Jack Kerouac, ainsi que des poètes hallucinés, des beatniks, des rockers et des aventuriers romantiques venus du monde entier se sont laissés séduire par le vieux port de Tanger. Les murs blancs incandescents, trait d'union entre la péninsule ibérique et la côte nord de l'Afrique, renforcent encore son allure de songe. Dans son autobiographie «Mémoires d'un nomade», le romancier américain Paul Bowles, dont le nom est devenu synonyme de l'expérience marocaine, a écrit que la topographie tangéroise abondait en prototypes de scènes oniriques. Dans son œuvre, il fait souvent allusion aux anciennes galeries, aux falaises, aux tunnels, aux ruines, aux escarpements et aux remparts. La chaleur intensifiait ses rêveries. «Le climat était violent et langoureux tout à la fois. Le vent d'août sifflait dans les palmiers et agitait les eucalyptus».

Writers as diverse as Gertrude Stein, Pierre Loti, and Jack Kerouac, along with wild-eyed poets, beatniks, rock musicians, and romantic adventurers from all over the world have been attracted to the ancient port of Tangier for more than a century. The incandescent white-walled setting, poised between the Iberian Peninsula and the northernmost regions of Africa, intensifies its dreamy allure. The American novelist, Paul Bowles, whose name has become synonymous with the Moroccan experience there, has written in his autobiography, "Without Stopping", that Tangier's topography is rich in prototypical dream scenes. He often refers to the ancient passageways, cliffs, tunnels, ruins, escarpments, and ramparts in his writing. And the heat intensified his reverie. "The climate was both violent and languorous," wrote Bowles. "The August wind hissed in the palms and rocked the eucalyptus trees."

So unterschiedliche Schriftsteller wie Gertrude Stein, Pierre Loti und Jack Kerouac, aber auch Poeten, Beatniks, Rockmusiker und romantische Abenteurer aus der ganzen Welt fühlen sich seit über einem Jahrhundert von der alten Hafenstadt Tanger angezogen. Das leuchtend weiße Mauerwerk dieser Stadt zwischen der iberischen Halbinsel und dem nördlichsten Teil Afrikas verstärkt diese träumerische Anziehungskraft. Der amerikanische Autor Paul Bowles, dessen Name zu einem Synonym für die »Moroccan experience« geworden ist, schreibt in seiner Autobiografie »Rastlos«, dass die Topografie der Stadt reich an prototypischen Traumszenen ist. Oft bezieht er sich in seinen Dichtungen auf die jahrhundertealten Pfade, Klippen, Tunnel, Ruinen, Steilhänge und Stadtmauern. Die Hitze tat ein Übriges, um seine Träumereien noch zu intensivieren. »Das Klima ist gewalttätig und träge zugleich«, schrieb Bowles. »Der Augustwind pfiff in den Palmen und ließ die Eukalyptusbäume schwanken.«

Left: a rooftop view of the port of Tangier.
Below: Blue walls in the hallway are as cooling in the Moroccan summer as a cold shower.

A gauche: le port de Tanger vu de la terrasse.
Ci-dessous: Pendant l'été marocain, les murs bleus de l'entrée sont aussi rafraîchissants qu'une douche froide.

Links: ein Blick über die Dächer auf den Hafen von Tanger.
Unten: Die blau gestrichenen Flurwände wirken in der marokkanischen Sommerhitze so erfrischend wie eine kühle Dusche.

Facing page: It's little wonder that pale indigo and white are "de rigueur" for the interiors of Moroccan houses. They're calming and uncomplicated. Interior designer Yves Taralon had the walls of this small sleeping corner painted chalky blue. The cotton gauze drapery turns the alcove into a private place for dreaming.

Page de gauche: Il ne faut pas s'étonner que l'indigo et le blanc soient de rigueur dans les intérieurs marocains. Ils sont simples et apaisants. Le designer Yves Taralon a peint les murs de ce petit coin de chambre à coucher d'un bleu crayeux. Des voilages en coton transforment l'alcôve en un lieu intime où il fait bon rêver.

Linke Seite: Blasses Indigoblau und Weiß – das sind die vorherrschenden Farben in marokkanischen Innenräumen. Aus gutem Grund: Sie wirken beruhigend und sind unkompliziert. Interior-Designer Yves Taralon hielt die Wände dieser kleinen Schlafkuschelecke in einem kalkigen Blauton. Die locker gehängten Vorhänge aus Baumwollgaze machen den Alkoven zu einer intimen Traumstätte.

Gian Paolo Barbieri

Mahé, Seychelles

L'archipel des Seychelles est formé d'une grappe de 115 minuscules points verts sur l'océan Indien, au nord de Madagascar. Sur ces îles s'épanouissent les casuarinas, les banians, les cocotiers de mer et les arbres tortue. Les récifs de corail offrent un spectacle psychédélique de scalaires, de tortues de Madagascar, de mérous aux rayures dorées, ainsi qu'un ballet aquatique de poissons lions, de poissons anémones, de poissons boxeurs mouchetés et de poissons squelettes. C'est ici que le photographe italien Gian Paolo Barbieri réalise ses superbes clichés noir et blanc et se repose dans sa maison au toit en feuilles de palmier, perchée sur un promontoire rocheux. Barbieri, qui habite à Milan, a créé ici son petit coin de paradis avec ses piscines en bord de plage, ses terrasses ensoleillées et ses pièces qui embaument la fleur de frangipanier. Les Seychelles sont également le cadre sensuel de son livre «Equator», qui célèbre ses plantes exotiques, ses poissons dansants, ses plages immaculées et son peuple léger qu'il admire tant.

The Seychelles archipelago is a cluster of 115 infinitely small green dots floating in the Indian Ocean, just north of Madagascar. On the islands flourish nature's most luscious casuarinas, banyans, coco de mer palms, and tortoise trees. Coral reefs are choreographed by psychedelic angelfish, hawkbill turtles, golden-striped groupers, and an aqua-ballet of lionfish, anenomefish, spotted boxfish, and bonefish. It is here that Italian photographer Gian Paolo Barbieri heads to work on his superb black-and-white photography and to relax in his palm-thatched house, nestling on a rocky point. Barbieri, whose home base is in bustling Milan, has created a dreamy world of beach-side swimming pools, sun-filled terraces, and frangipani-scented rooms. Seychelles is also the sensual setting for Barbieri's book "Equator", which celebrates the exotic plants, dancing fish, pristine beaches and lithe people he so admires.

Das Seychellen-Archipel besteht aus 115 winzigen grünen Tupfen, die vor der Nordküste von Madagaskar im Indischen Ozean schwimmen. Auf diesen Inseln gedeihen die üppigsten Casuarinabäume, Bengalischen Feigen und Cocos de Mer. In den Korallenriffen führen Engelshaie, Echte Karettschildkröten und Goldstreifenbarsche ein psychedelisches Ballett auf und unternehmen Unterwassertanzschritte mit Rotfeuerfischen, Sergeantenfischen, Weißpunkt-Kofferfischen und Demoiselles. In dieser Welt schafft der italienische Fotograf Gian Paolo Barbieri viele seiner herausragenden Schwarzweißfotografien und entspannt sich in seinem mit Palmwedeln gedeckten Haus, das sich an einen Felsen schmiegt. Barbieris eigentliches Zuhause ist das geschäftige Mailand; aber hier auf den Seychellen hat er eine Traumwelt aus sonnigen Terrassen, Strandpools und nach Frangipani duftenden Räumen geschaffen. Die Inseln bieten auch den sinnlichen Hintergrund für sein Buch »Equator«, eine Hommage an die exotischen Pflanzen, tanzenden Fische, unberührten Strände und geschmeidigen Menschen, denen seine ganze Bewunderung gilt.

Previous pages: *Gian Paolo Barbieri's house stands on a palm-shaded point, overlooking two private beaches. In his large, open foyer and living room a hand-crafted screen designed by Barbieri is adorned with a crocodile, a trophy from his travels in Madagascar.*
Right: *A reflecting pool has a cooling effect on the verandah.*
Below: *Barbieri designed all of his large-scale furniture and had it made of indigenous woods by skilled local craftsmen. He delights in fishing for the catch of the day – and serves the pineapples, bananas, breadfruit, mangoes, jackfruit and papayas that grow on his property.*

Doubles pages précédentes: *La maison de Gian Paolo Barbieri se dresse sur un promontoire rocheux protégé par les palmiers, surplombant deux plages privées. Dans le grand foyer-salle de séjour ouvert aux éléments, un paravent créé par Barbieri est orné d'une dépouille de crocodile, trophée rapporté d'un de ses séjours à Madagascar.*
A droite: *Les reflets du bassin ont un effet rafraîchissant sur la véranda.*
Ci-dessous: *Barbieri a dessiné lui-même tous les grands meubles de la maison, qu'il a fait réaliser dans des bois indigènes par d'excellents artisans locaux. Il adore aller pêcher lui-même le poisson du jour et sert des ananas, des bananes, des fruits de l'arbre à pain, des mangues, des jaques et des papayes qui poussent sur sa propriété.*

Vorhergehende Doppelseiten: *Das palmenumstandene Haus von Gian Paolo Barbieri liegt oberhalb von zwei Privatstränden. In der großen offenen Eingangshalle, die auch als Wohnzimmer dient, steht eine von Barbieri gefertigte Trennwand, die mit einem Krokodil geschmückt ist – einer Trophäe von seinen Madagaskar-Reisen.*
Rechts: *Ein spiegelndes Becken kühlt die Veranda.*
Unten: *Die großzügig geschnittenen Möbel sind alle Eigenentwürfe, die von örtlichen Handwerkern aus heimischen Hölzern gefertigt wurden. Doch Barbieri findet genauso viel Freude am Fischen – und serviert seine Tagesbeute mit Ananas, Bananen, Brotfrucht, Mangos, Jackfruit und Papayas aus eigenem Besitz.*

Above: Ravishing nature, glorious light, velvety darkness, and the caresses of salty air are savored here.
Right and following pages: the living room. When darkness falls, Barbieri rolls down a white movie screen. Friends gather on the capacious built-in sofa. "I love to show classic black-and-white movies," said the Cinecittà-trained photographer. "One night I showed 'The Hurricane', a 30s film with Dorothy Lamour and Mary Astor," recalled Barbieri. "We looked outside and saw the same landscape, palm trees, full moon, and open sea – but, thankfully, no hurricane."

Ci-dessus: Ici, on savoure une nature belle à couper le souffle, une lumière somptueuse, des nuits de velours et les caresses de l'air marin.
A droite et double page suivante: le salon. A la tombée du soir, Barbieri déroule un écran de cinéma blanc et ses amis se rassemblent sur le spacieux canapé encastré. «J'adore montrer de vieux films en noir et blanc», déclare le photographe formé à Cinecittà. «Un soir, j'ai projeté ‹L'Ouragan›, un film des années 30 avec Dorothy Lamour et Mary Astor. On a ensuite regardé au-dehors et on a vu exactement le même paysage avec ses palmiers, sa pleine lune et son grand large, mais heureusement, pas d'ouragan».

Oben: die atemberaubende Natur, wunderbares Licht, samtige Dunkelheit und salzige Luft, die einen sanft streichelt ...
Rechts und folgende Doppelseite: das Wohnzimmer. Abends lässt Barbieri eine weiße Leinwand herab und die Freunde versammeln sich auf dem eingebauten Sofa. »Am liebsten zeige ich Schwarzweißklassiker«, erklärt der in Cinecittà ausgebildete Fotograf. »Eines Abends sahen wir uns ›Dann kam der Orkan‹ an, einen Film aus den 30er Jahren mit Dorothy Lamour und Mary Astor. Dann blickten wir nach draußen und sahen vor der Tür die gleiche Szenerie mit Palmen, Vollmond und dem offenen Meer – Gott sei Dank ohne Orkan!«

Left: When Gian Paolo Barbieri is not out scuba-diving, his favorite tropical treat, he and his guests can cool down on low-slung chairs, and stretch out on endless sofas.
Below: "My bedroom is completely open to the sea," noted Barbieri. "The sound, as I drift off to sleep, is fantastic. On my island of Mahé, we are just four degrees south of the equator, so it is never cold." Floors throughout the house are concrete. Barbieri's painstaking method: he burnishes the freshly set concrete with coconut shells, then buffs them with wax. The surface is soft, infinitely smooth, and sensual for bare feet, he said.

A gauche: Lorsque Gian Paolo Barbieri n'est pas en train de faire de la plongée, son passe-temps tropical favori, il se prélasse avec ses amis dans des fauteuils bas ou s'allonge sur d'interminables sofas.
Ci-dessous: «Ma chambre est complètement ouverte vers la mer», confie Barbieri. «J'adore entendre ses bruits quand je m'endors. Sur mon île de Mahé, nous sommes juste quatre degrés au sud de l'équateur. Il n'y fait jamais froid.» Dans toute la maison, les sols sont en béton laborieusement patiné par Barbieri: il brunit le béton encore frais avec des coques de noix de coco avant de le lustrer à la cire. Le résultat est une surface douce et lisse, un vrai délice pour marcher pieds nus.

Links: Wenn er nicht gerade taucht – seine Lieblingsbeschäftigung in den Tropen – dann entspannt Gian Paolo Barbieri sich mit seinen Gästen in niedrigen Sesseln oder auf endlos wirkenden Sofas.
Unten: »Mein Schlafzimmer ist zur Meeresseite hin völlig offen. Im Halbschlaf höre ich nachts fantastische Geräusche. Hier auf Mahé sind wir nur vier Grad vom Äquator entfernt. Deshalb wird es nie kalt«, sagt der Hausherr. Die Böden sind durchgängig aus Beton gefertigt, den Barbieri mit einer arbeitsaufwändigen Methode »verfeinert« hat: Sobald der Guss fest geworden ist, wird er mit Kokosschalen abgerieben und mit Wachs poliert. So entsteht eine unvergleichlich glatte Oberfläche und ein sinnliches Erlebnis für bloße Füße.

Above: In a corner of his bedroom, Barbieri has stage-directed a
bureau and library with rattan-lashed shelves and a free-form desk.
The photographer, who creates memorable images for fashion houses
such as Valentino, Armani, Versace and Ferré, designed the ethnic-in-
spired stools, along with the hardwood screens.
Right: Sibilant sounds of the sea echo off the hard surfaces of the
hand-plastered walls and waxed floors of the house. There are no windows, so light and air are tamed somewhat by shutters, overhanging
palm-thatched roofs, and timbered ceilings.

Ci-dessus: Dans un coin de sa chambre, Barbieri a mis en scène un
bureau aux lignes souples et une bibliothèque en lattes de rotin. Le
photographe, qui crée des images mémorables pour des maisons de
mode telles que Valentino, Armani, Versace et Ferré, a dessiné les tabourets d'inspiration ethnique ainsi que les paravents en bois durs.
A droite: Le grondement des vagues se répercute sur les murs enduits
de plâtre et les sols cirés de la maison. Comme il n'y a pas de vitres,
l'air et la lumière sont à peine domptés par les volets, les avant-toits
en feuilles de palmiers et les poutres du plafond.

Oben: In seinem Schlafzimmer hat Barbieri eine bühnenreife
Büroecke inszeniert: mit einer Bibliothek aus rattanverknüpften
Regalen und einem scheinbar keiner Form gehorchenden Schreibtisch. Die ethnisch inspirierten Hocker und die aus Hartholz geferti-
gen Trennwände entwarf der Fotograf selbst, der für seine denk-
würdigen Modefotografien für Modehäuser wie Valentino, Armani,
Versace und Ferré berühmt ist.
Rechts: Die harten Oberflächen der handverputzten Wände und
gewachsten Böden werfen das Zischen des Meeres als Echo zurück. Es
gibt keine Fenster. Blenden, Palmwedel, die vom Dach herabhängen,
und Holzdecken halten Licht und Luft im Zaum.

Facing page: Barbieri's bathroom is simple, sculptural, and functional.
Above: A sailfish, freshly caught outside the bay, graces the kitchen. "We eat simply here," said Barbieri. "I cook fresh vegetables, experiment with Moroccan dishes, and serve fresh fruit, fish, and rice. It's so healthy, it's like going to a clinic."
Right: A volute shell, washed up on his shore, pirouettes on the solid stage of a hardwood table.

Page de gauche: La salle de bains de Barbieri est simple, sculpturale et fonctionnelle.
Ci-dessus: dans la cuisine, un poisson voile fraîchement pêché dans la baie. «Ici, on se nourrit simplement», déclare Barbieri. «Je cuisine des légumes frais, j'essaie des plats marocains, on mange des fruits, du poisson et du riz. C'est très sain, on se croirait dans une clinique.»
A droite: Une volute, échouée sur la plage, décrit une pirouette sur une table en bois dur.

Linke Seite: Barbieris Bad ist einfach und funktionell gehalten.
Oben: Ein frisch gefangener Fächerfisch ziert die Küche. »Hier essen wir sehr einfach. Ich koche frisches Gemüse, experimentiere mit marokkanischen Gerichten und verwende frisches Obst, Fisch und Reis. Es ist so gesund, dass man meinen könnte, in einem Sanatorium zu sein«, erzählt Barbieri.
Rechts: Eine spiralförmig gewundene Muschel, die an seinem Strand angespült wurde, dreht ihre Pirouetten auf einem Hartholztisch.

Marie-José Crespin

Gorée Island, Cape Verde Peninsula, Senegal

L'île de Gorée, un grand rocher surgissant de l'Atlantique à quatre ki-lomètres de la côte sénégalaise, près de Dakar, a connu une histoire mouvementée. Aujourd'hui, les enfants jouent dans les ruelles étroites, des merles chantent et volettent et d'élégantes maisons aux fenêtres à volets offrent leurs façades silencieuses sur de vieilles rues si-nueuses. Au cours des 500 dernières années, tous les aventuriers venus des quatre coins du monde sont passés par cette île, la plus à l'ouest de l'Afrique. Des marchands anglais, hollandais, portugais et français venaient y chercher de l'ivoire, de l'or, du coton et, plus tard, des esclaves. Le nom de l'île vient du hollandais «Goede reede» («Bon port»). En 1817, l'île devint une riche colonie française. Les capitaines et les administrateurs se firent construire de belles demeures. Elles étaient françaises par leur architecture classique mais dans un style nettement islamique. La maison de Marie-José Crespin figurait déjà sur les cartes en 1885. Elle a été soigneusement préservée dans la meilleure tradition coloniale française.

Gorée Island, a rocky spot in the Atlantic Ocean four kilometers off the coast of Senegal near Dakar, has had a chequered history. Today, children play in narrow alleys, black birds squawk and hover, and elegant, quiet houses with shuttered facades present their private faces to the ancient, winding streets. In the last 500 years, every adventurer under the sun has passed by this western-most point of Africa. English, Dutch, Portuguese, and French traders sailed into the port in search of ivory, gold, cotton and later, slaves. The name of the island comes from the Dutch, "goede reede" (good harbor). In 1817, the island became a rich French colony. Handsome houses were built for sea captains and administrators. They were French in their classic architecture but with a distinctly Islamic style. The house of Marie-José Crespin was built before 1885, and has been thoughtfully preserved in the best French colonial tradition.

Vier Kilometer vor der senegalesischen Küste, nahe der Hauptstadt Dakar, ragt die felsige Insel Gorée aus dem Atlantik. Sie hat eine be-wegte Vergangenheit. Heute spielen in den engen Straßen Kinder, schwarze Vögel kreisen kreischend in der Luft und ruhige Häuser säu-men mit ihren eleganten Fassaden und verschlossenen Fensterläden die alten verwinkelten Gassen. Doch in den letzten 500 Jahren war fast jeder Abenteurer unter der Sonne irgendwann einmal hier, am westlichsten Punkt Afrikas. Kap Verde war Anlaufhafen für englische, holländische, portugiesische und französische Händler, die auf der Su-che nach Elfenbein, Gold, Baumwolle und später Sklaven hier anleg-ten. Der Name der Insel stammt aus dem Holländischen: »goede reede« (guter Hafen). 1817 wurde die Insel eine reiche französische Kolonie. Für die Kapitäne zur See und die Verwaltungsbeamten wur-den stattliche Häuser im Stil des französischen Klassizismus erbaut, die aber einen deutlich islamischen Touch hatten. Das Haus von Marie-José Crespin wurde bereits 1885 errichtet und in bester franzö-sischer Kolonialtradition sorgfältig erhalten.

This house on tiny Gorée Island was designed to have both a private, inward mien, and sociable rooms and terraces open to the sun and the sea. Situated near the Tropic of Capricorn, it was also planned to allow for both shade and repose from the heat, and shuttered shelter from Atlantic Ocean storms. From the open terrace, guests who have taken the ferry "La Chaloupe" across from Dakar, may gaze over the bay, sip tea, relax. Textiles and furnishings were collected all over Africa. Locally made batiks adorn the terrace table.

Cette maison sur la minuscule île de Gorée fut conçue pour être à la fois intime et retirée, et les pièces et les terrasses accueillantes sont ouvertes au soleil et à la mer. Située près du tropique du Capricorne, elle a également été conçue pour protéger de la chaleur et des tempêtes de l'Atlantique. Les invités arrivés de Dakar par le ferry «La Chaloupe», peuvent contempler la baie depuis la terrasse, boire du thé et se détendre. Les tissus et les meubles viennent d'un peu partout en Afrique. La table de la terrasse est recouverte de batiks tissés dans la région.

Dieses Haus auf der winzigen Insel Gorée hat zwei Gesichter: Der private Bereich befindet sich im Inneren des Gebäudes, während sich Gesellschaftsräume und Terrassen dem Meer und der Sonne öffnen. Hier, nahe am Wendekreis des Steinbocks, plante man Räume, die vor der Hitze, aber auch vor den Stürmen des Atlantiks schützen. Auf der offenen Terrasse lassen die Gäste, die mit der Fähre »La Chaloupe« aus Dakar kommen, den Blick über die Bucht schweifen, trinken Tee und entspannen sich – auf Möbeln und Stoffen, die aus ganz Afrika stammen. Auf Gorée hergestellte Batiken schmücken den Terrassentisch.

Above: *A garden, fragrant with mangoes, lilies, and trumpet vines, is almost hidden from view by high walls and lush growth.*
Right and facing page: *Handcrafted masks, contemporary paintings, tribal furniture and quirky antiques in the house all have fascinating provenances: they were crafted in Ghana, Benin, Morocco, Mauritania, Senegal, Costa Rica, even New Guinea, and by many African tribes, including the Yoruba.*

Ci-dessus: *Le jardin, qui sent bon la mangue, le lys et le lys trompette, est caché derrière de hauts murs et une végétation luxuriante.*
A droite et page de droite: *Les masques artisanaux, les peintures contemporaines, les meubles tribaux et les antiquités excentriques de la maison ont tous des provenances fascinantes: Ghana, Bénin, Maroc, Mauritanie, Sénégal, Costa Rica et même Nouvelle-Guinée. La plupart ont été réalisés par des tribus africaines, y compris des Yorubas. Le sol carrelé du salon est d'origine. Les tissus viennent du Sénégal.*

Oben: *Der Garten, üppig wuchernd und erfüllt vom Duft der Mangos, Lilien und Trompetenblumen, ist hinter den hohen Mauern kaum auszumachen.*
Rechts und rechte Seite: *Die handgemachten Masken, zeitgenössische Malerei, traditionellen afrikanischen Möbel und verrückten Antiquitäten stammen alle aus den faszinierendsten Gegenden – aus Ghana, Benin, Marokko, Mauretanien, Senegal, Costa Rica, sogar aus Neu-Guinea. Viele Stücke wurden von afrikanischen Stämmen gefertigt, unter anderem von den Yoruba. Der gefliese Fußboden des Salons gehört noch zur Originalausstattung. Die Stoffe kommen aus dem Senegal.*

Gorée Island, Cape Verde Peninsula, Senegal 14°39'N 17°28'W   Marie-José Crespin

Takaungu House was sad and deserted when Charlie and Philip Mason found it, near the old town of Takaungu. The Masons, shown at the open-air beach bar of Philip's boatyard in Kilifi, enjoy the company of their friends and guests as well as a roaming band of friendly dogs, one of which is named "Dish Cloth". The verandah is supported by poles of indigenous wood in a style typical of the region. Furniture was custom-made by local craftspeople. From the limpid pool, swimmers and sunbathers may gaze out over the Indian Ocean.

Quand Charlie et Philip Mason l'ont découverte, près du port de Takaungu, Takaungu House était triste et abandonnée. Les Mason, ici au bar de la plage du hangar à bateaux de Philip à Kilifi, aiment la compagnie de leurs amis, des visiteurs de passage et d'une joyeuse meute de chiens errants dont l'un a été baptisé «serpillière». La véranda est soutenue par des poutres en bois indigène dans un style typique de la région. Tous les meubles ont été fabriqués sur mesure par des artisans locaux. Dans la piscine limpide, on peut nager ou se dorer au soleil en admirant l'océan Indien.

Als Charlie und Philip Mason nahe der alten Stadt Takaungu auf Takaungu House stießen, war es ein trister, verlassener Ort. Die Masons, hier an Philips »Open-Air«-Strandbar an seinem Anleger in Kilifi, haben gerne ihre Freunde und Gäste um sich – ebenso wie eine Bande herumstreunender freundlicher Hunde, von denen einer »dish cloth«, Geschirrtuch, heißt. Das Verandadach ruht auf Pfählen, die aus heimischem Holz auf traditionelle Weise verarbeitet wurden. Auch das Mobiliar wurde von hier ansässigen Handwerkern gefertigt. Vom glasklaren Pool aus können die Schwimmer und Sonnenanbeter ihren Blick über den Indischen Ozean schweifen lassen.

Takaungu, Kenya 3°41'S 39°51'E   Charlie and Philip Mason

Charlie and Philip Mason

Takaungu, Kenya

Ceux qui ont voyagé jusqu'à Mombasa, sur la côte sud du Kenya, savent qu'on n'échappe pas à l'histoire en Afrique orientale. Après avoir flâné dans la vieille ville arabe, s'être perdu dans le dédale de ruelles près de Dhow Harbour, médité dans les anciens temples hindous, le voyageur la retrouve à Fort Jésus, construit en 1592 par Mateus de Vascancelo. L'Afrique, l'Arabie, l'Europe et l'Asie se sont rejointes dans cet avant-poste écrasé par la chaleur. Au nord, les plages en sucre glace s'allongent sur des kilomètres. Au-delà des mangroves s'étirent les plantations d'anacardiers, de canne à sucre et de sisal. Plus loin encore, les pêcheurs vous font traverser en pirogue les eaux peu profondes. Encore quelques kilomètres et on arrive à Takaungu, un village de culture swahili. Là, le voyageur épuisé se doit de faire une pause à Takaungu House, une maison d'hôtes en claie consolidée de terre, tenue par Charlie et Philip Mason. Ici, les portes arabes ornées de laiton sont toujours ouvertes.

History lingers on in East Africa. Ask anyone who travels as far as Mombasa on the western edge of the Indian Ocean. After visits to the Old Arab Town, walks along spice-fragrant mazes of lanes near the Dhow Harbor, meditation in centuries-old Hindu temples, history reappears at Fort Jesus, which was built in 1592 by Mateus de Vascancelo as a defense post. Africa, Europe, Asia, and Arabia come together in this heat-infused outpost. Inevitably, the intrepid venture north along miles of icing sugar-white beaches. Beyond tangles of mangrove forests, plantations of cashew nuts, sugar cane, and sisal, a lazy day takes in fishermen propeling their dugout canoes through the shallows. A few more kilometers along the road is Takaungu, a Swahili Arab village, and it is here that the weary and style-conscious will want to rest at Takaungu House, a wattle-and-daub guest house run by Charlie and Philip Mason. Brass-studded Arab doors stay open to welcome ocean gusts.

In Ostafrika ist Geschichte lebendig. Das wird einem jeder bestätigen, der schon mal bis nach Mombasa am westlichen Rand des Indischen Ozeans gekommen ist. Nach Besuchen in der arabischen Altstadt, Spaziergängen durch die nach Gewürzen duftenden Gassenlabyrinthe am Dhau-Hafen, nach Meditationen in jahrhundertealten Hindu-tempeln wird Geschichte erlebbar – in der Form von Fort Jesus, das 1592 von Mateus de Vascancelo errichtet wurde. Afrika, Europa, Asien und Arabien treffen hier in diesem heißen Außenposten der Zivilisation zusammen. Natürlich machen sich Abenteurer von hier aus gen Norden auf, entlang der kilometerlangen, schneeweißen, puderzuckrigen Strände. Jenseits der Mangrovenwälder, Cashewnuss-, Zuckerrohr- und Sisalplantagen staken Fischer ihre Einbäume durch das seichte Wasser. Noch einige Kilometer weiter entlang der Straße liegt das Suaheli-Dorf Takaungu. Und hier legen erschöpfte und stilbewusste Menschen gerne eine Rast in Takaungu House ein, dem Gasthaus von Charlie und Philip Mason, das in der »wattle-and-daub«-Technik aus verputztem Flechtwerk errichtet wurde. Messingbeschlagene arabische Türen lassen die Meeresbrise herein.

Right: When the Masons first encountered their house, on the perimeter of an old African village and surrounded by frangipani and thorns, it had no electricity. Even today, they have kept the kitchen simple and manageable. There is no air-conditioning, in spite of tropical heat. The floor is black-painted concrete, the ceiling practical and rain-acoustic corrugated metal. Windows, with no glass, are covered in the local Swahili manner, with split shutters.

Below: One of the reasons guests and friends feel so comfortable at Takaungu House is that Charlie – short for Charlotte – and Philip Mason prefer furnishings that are comfortable but not fussed over.

A droite: Lorsque les Mason on trouvé cette maison, à la lisière d'un vieux village africain encerclé par les ronces et les frangipaniers, elle n'avait pas l'électricité. Encore aujourd'hui, la cuisine est simple et facile à vivre. Il n'y a pas d'air conditionné, en dépit de la chaleur tropicale. Le sol en béton est peint en noir. Le plafond en tôle ondulée offre de délicieux concerts par temps de pluie. Les fenêtres sans vitre sont protégées par des volets à double battant.

Ci-dessous: Une des raisons pour lesquelles les invités et copains se sentent si bien à Takaungu House, c'est que Charlie, abréviation de Charlotte, et Philip Mason préfèrent les meuble simples et confortables qui ne craignent rien.

Rechts: Als die Masons ihr Haus zum ersten Mal sahen, am Rande eines alten afrikanischen Dorfs gelegen und von Frangipani und Dornen überwuchert, verfügte es nicht über Elektrizität. Bis heute ist die Küche einfach und überschaubar geblieben. Trotz der tropischen Hitze gibt es keine Klimaanlage. Der Boden besteht aus schwarz gestrichenem Beton, die praktische Decke aus Wellblech, das bei Regen zum Perkussionsinstrument wird. Die glaslosen Fenster sind auf traditionelle Suaheli-Art mit Klappläden versehen.

Unten: Einer der Gründe, warum sich Gäste und Freunde hier so wohl fühlen, ist, dass Charlie – eigentlich Charlotte – und Philip Möbel bevorzugen, die großzügig und gemütlich sind.

Above: The sitting room is cool and calm, with locally made sisal rugs, and fat club chairs slip-covered in off-white linen. Some of the antiques came from local auctions, others are treasured family heirlooms. Charlie's father had been the district commissioner for Kilifi, further north, and Takaungu.
Right: The bedroom's most impressive occupant is a traditional Swahili Arab four-poster bed draped with romantic and necessary mosquito netting. The bed was found in Lamu, an archipelago further north.

Ci-dessus: Le salon est frais et calme, avec des tapis en sisal réalisés dans la région et de profonds fauteuils club houssés de lin blanc. Certaines des antiquités proviennent de ventes aux enchères locales, d'autres sont des trésors de famille. Le père de Charlie était administrateur régional pour Kilifi, un peu plus au nord, et Takaungu.
A droite: La pièce maîtresse de la chambre à coucher est le lit à baldaquin traditionnel, drapé d'une moustiquaire romantique mais néanmoins indispensable. Le lit vient de Lamu, un archipel plus au nord.

Oben: Dank der Sisalteppiche, die vor Ort gefertigt wurden, und der behäbigen, mit weißem Leinen bezogenen Clubsessel ist das Wohnzimmer kühl und strahlt Ruhe aus. Einige der Antiquitäten stammen von lokalen Auktionen, andere sind Familienschätze. Charlies Vater war District Commissioner für Takaungu und das weiter nördlich gelegene Kilifi.
Rechts: Das beeindruckendste Stück des Schlafzimmers ist dieses traditionelle suahelische Himmelbett, das äußerst romantisch und ebenso notwendig mit Moskitonetzen verhangen ist und aus Lamu stammt, einem weiter nördlich gelegenen Archipel.

Gerda and André Botha

Cape of Good Hope, South Africa

Kommetjie, à 30 kilomètres au sud-ouest de Cape Town, en Afrique du Sud, est sans doute la seule ville où l'on peut se réveiller sur la plage, visiter un élevage de serpents, se balader à dos de chameau, déjeuner dans un restaurant au doux nom de «La Grenouille qui Croasse», faire de la plongée sous-marine puis surfer le soir venu sur des vagues de renommée mondiale, tout ça dans la même journée. Lorsqu'elles atteignent la péninsule du Cap, les vagues de l'Atlantique ont eu amplement le temps de prendre de la puissance et de la hauteur. Par un bon jour et avec l'aide du vent, elles se hissent à des hauteurs vertigineuses, s'enroulent, se déroulent et viennent s'écraser dans les baies en rouleaux réguliers. Des montagnes escarpées se dressent au loin. Gerda Botha a découvert ce coin isolé et spectaculaire en accompagnant son fils André, devenu à 17 ans à Sunset Reef le plus jeune champion de bodyboard d'Afrique du Sud. Séduite par le paysage paisible et harmonieux, elle est tombée sur un panneau «à vendre» planté sur un terrain bordant la plage. Avec son mari, André senior, ils ont décidé d'y construire la maison de leurs rêves.

Kommetjie, 30 kilometers south-west of Cape Town, South Africa, is perhaps the only town where you can wake up at the beach, visit a snake farm, take a camel ride, enjoy lunch at a restaurant called "The Croaking Frog", go scuba-diving, and head for early evening surfing in world-class rollers, all in one day. There on the Cape Peninsula, Atlantic Ocean waves have had time to gather power and rise to full intensity. In bays there, on a good day with wind assistance, the surf towers, curls, unfurls, and crashes in even breaks. Jagged mountains rear up in the distance. It was this dramatic, remote place, and Sunset Reef in particular, that first drew Gerda Botha and her son, André, who was competing in the South African Bodyboarding Championships, becoming the youngest world champion at the age of 17. Gerda became enamored of the peace and harmony of the beaches, and happened to see a "For Sale" sign on a beach property. She and her husband, André senior, built their dream house there.

Kommetjie, 30 Kilometer südwestlich von Kapstadt gelegen, ist wahrscheinlich die einzige Stadt, in der man am Strand aufwachen, eine Schlangenfarm besichtigen, eine Runde auf einem Kamel drehen, im »Quakenden Frosch« zu Mittag essen, einen Tauchgang einlegen und am frühen Abend über Wellen surfen kann, die absolute Weltspitze sind – und das alles an einem Tag! Hier an der Kaphalbinsel hatten die Wellen des Atlantiks genug Zeit, um Kräfte zu sammeln und sich zu voller Größe zu erheben. Wenn der Wind etwas nachhilft, dann baut sich das Wasser an guten Tagen zu ebenmäßigen, perfekten Wellen auf. In der Ferne erheben sich gezackte Berge. Zu diesem entlegenen und dramatischen Ort, vor allem zu Sunset Reef, fühlten sich Gerda Botha und ihr Sohn André hingezogen. André kam damals, um an den südafrikanischen Bodyboarding-Meisterschaften teilzunehmen und wurde im Alter von 17 Jahren der jüngste Champion. Gerda verliebte sich in den Frieden und die Harmonie, den die Strände ausstrahlten und sah zufällig ein »For-Sale«-Schild an einem Strandgrundstück. Dort baute sie mit ihrem Mann, André senior, ihr Traumhaus.

Facing page: Sunset Beach Guest House on the southern reaches of the Cape Peninsula, near Cape Town. The dunes in front of the residence and guest house have been carefully restored and preserved with new plantings of native grasses. Interior designer Laureen Rossouw helped Gerda Botha to decorate the interiors, using white cottons, an international collection of antiques, and accents of Atlantic Ocean blue.

Above: Daughter Kayla rests in one of the bedrooms, with views over the dunes to the Atlantic Ocean.

Following page, clockwise from top left: The sideboard is from Bali; the elaborate mirror is from Indonesia; the architect of the guest house and residence was John Samuel: comfortable nooks and crannies were encouraged; in one cranny, a painting by André Botha senior.

Last page: Kayla Botha in her bedroom. The family lives in Durban, spends holidays in Kommetjie.

Page de gauche: la Sunset Beach Guest House, au sud de la péninsule du Cap, près de Cape Town. Les dunes devant la résidence et la maison d'hôte ont été soigneusement remodelées en y replantant des espèces locales. La décoratrice Laureen Rossouw a aidé Gerda Botha à décorer l'intérieur avec des cotonnades blanches, une collection internationale d'antiquités et des touches de bleu atlantique.

Ci-dessus: Kayla, la fille de Gerda, fait la sieste dans une des chambres, d'où l'on aperçoit l'océan par-dessus les dunes.

Page suivante, dans le sens des aiguilles d'une montre, du haut à gauche: La commode vient de Bali; le miroir est indonésien; la maison d'hôte et la résidence ont été conçues par l'architecte John Samuel. On lui avait donné carte blanche pour user et abuser des coins et recoins douillets; dans un de ces coins, une peinture d'André Botha senior.

Dernière page: Kayla Botha dans sa chambre. La famille vit à Durban et passe ses vacances à Kommetjie.

Linke Seite: Sunset Beach Guest House liegt am südlichen Ende der Kaphalbinsel nahe Kapstadt. Die Dünen vor dem Wohn- und Gästehaus sind sorgfältig wieder aufgebaut und zu ihrem Schutz mit Dünengras neu bepflanzt worden. Gerda Botha wurde von der Innenarchitektin Laureen Rossouw unterstützt. Stilmittel waren weiße Baumwollstoffe, Ozeanblau als Farbakzent und eine international ausgerichtete Antiquitätensammlung.

Oben: Töchterchen Kayla faulenzt in einem der Schlafzimmer mit Blick über die Dünen zum Atlantik.

Folgende Seite, im Uhrzeigersinn von oben links: Die Kommode stammt aus Bali; der kunstvolle Spiegel kommt aus Indonesien; Architekt des Gästehauses und des Haupthauses war John Samuel; in einer Ecke hängt ein Gemälde von André Botha senior.

Letzte Seite: Kayla Botha in ihrem Schlafzimmer. Die Familie lebt in Durban und verbringt die Ferien in Kommetjie.

Every New Year's Day, the usually colorful Cariocas – the inhabitants of Rio de Janeiro – dress all in white, and throng to Copacabana Beach. There they give thanks to the goddess of the sea, Iemanjá, for bestowing good fortune and happiness. Further up the coast, the golden shores of Salvador are alive with rhythmic dancers and musicians and the reverberations of drums and chanting. On the rough-and-tumble coast of Chile, the wild waves crash and roar, dashing against the rocks. Sun-worshippers lying like lizards around swimming pools overlooking the Pacific are oblivious to the surge and sway of the cool turquoise water. Summer at the shore on Long Island seems to last forever, and days may be spent, sunstruck and silly, watching fishing boats and lithe yachts, and slipping in and out of the gray-green sea. Lunches of freshly caught fish and garden-grown lettuces and tomatoes become hours of wine and wild honey and celebration. Florida and Mexico live in perpetual summer, fresh and energetic. Miami means music, and avant-garde design. The Costa Careyes coast promises softly dramatic sunsets. The sun flashes and hovers surrounded in red and gold gauze, then decides to disappear. Days on the coast of California are spent outdoors, sometimes doing nothing. The open book is unread. Silvery strands invite strolling on shell-spotted sands, and quiet contemplation. Hours go by, and the day's greatest accomplishment may simply be viewing the ocean fog as it approaches and swoops landwards, like a lonely ghost longing for human company.

Beach Life in the Americas

A Rio de Janeiro, chaque Nouvel An, les cariocas pourtant généralement bariolés s'habillent de blanc et se pressent sur la plage de Copacabana. Là, ils remercient la déesse de la mer, Iemanjá, de leur donner chance et bonheur. Plus au nord, les plages dorées de Salvador grouillent de danseurs et de musiciens et vibrent au son des tambours et des chants. Sur la côte déchiquetée du Chili, des vagues furieuses rugissent et s'écrasent contre les rochers. Les adorateurs du soleil qui se dorent au bord des piscines surplombant le Pacifique se moquent bien du tumulte de ses eaux froides couleur turquoise. Les étés sur la côte de Long Island semblent durer une éternité et l'on passe ses journées étourdis par le soleil à regarder des chalutiers et des yachts élancés aller et venir sur la mer vert-de-gris. Les déjeuners de poissons frais et de salades cueillies directement dans le potager s'éternisent en dégustations de vins et de miel sauvage. La Floride et le Mexique vivent un été perpétuel, frais et énergique. Miami est synonyme de musique et de design avant-gardiste. La Costa Careyes promet des couchers de soleil spectaculaires tout en douceur. Le soleil clignote et se nimbe d'une aura rouge et or, puis décide de disparaître. Sur la côte californienne, les jours se passent au grand air, parfois à ne rien faire. Le livre reste ouvert sans être lu. La grève argentée invite à la chasse aux coquillages enfouis dans le sable et à la contemplation. Les heures défilent et la seule activité du jour est parfois l'observation de la brume océane qui s'approche et étend ses volutes vers la terre, tel un fantôme à la recherche d'un peu de chaleur humaine.

Jedes Jahr am Neujahrsmorgen hüllen sich die sonst farbenprächtig gekleideten Cariocas – die Einwohner von Rio de Janeiro – ganz in Weiß. Sie wandern in Scharen zur Copacabana, um dort der Meeresgöttin Iemanjá dafür zu danken, dass sie ihnen Glück gebracht hat. Weiter nördlich beleben rhythmisch sich wiegende Tänzer und Musiker mit ihren Trommelklängen und Gesängen die goldenen Küsten von Salvador. An der wilden Küste von Chile brechen sich donnernd die Wellen und schwappen gegen die Felsen. Die Sonnenanbeter, die sich Eidechsen gleich am Rand der Pools mit Blick auf den Pazifik versammeln, nehmen das Anschwellen der kühlen türkisfarbenen Wogen allerdings kaum zur Kenntnis. Auf Long Island scheint der Sommer ewig zu dauern. Man verbringt sonnendurchflutete und ausgelassene Tage damit, Fischerboote und wendige Yachten zu beobachten und zwischendurch ins graugrüne Meer zu gleiten. Ein Lunch aus frisch gefangenem Fisch mit Blattsalaten und Tomaten aus dem Garten entwickelt sich schnell zu fröhlichen, weinseeligen Stunden, eingehüllt in den Duft von wildem Honig. In Florida und Mexiko ist der Sommer zu Hause. Hier ist alles frisch und voller Energie. Miami steht für Musik und Avantgarde-Design. Die Costa Careyes verspricht sanft-dramatische Sonnenuntergänge und tatsächlich blitzt die Sonne auf und verharrt wie in rotgoldene Gaze gehüllt, bis sie sich zum Verschwinden entschließt. Entlang der kalifornischen Küste verbringt man die Tage draußen. Manchmal mit süßem Nichtstun. Ein offenes Buch bleibt ungelesen. Silbrige Strände laden zum Schlendern auf Sand und Muscheln ein und zur Nachdenklichkeit. Die Stunden vergehen. Und vielleicht war das einzig Bemerkenswerte, was man an diesem Tag geschafft hat, den Nebel zu beobachten, wie er vom Meer landeinwärts zieht, wie ein einsamer Geist, der sich nach menschlicher Gesellschaft sehnt.

Judyth van Amringe

Coast of Maine

L'artiste Judyth van Amringe a trouvé le parfait antidote aux jours gris et brumeux de la légendaire côte du Maine. Elle a peint les escaliers de son cottage en jaune soleil et a badigeonné le plancher de généreuses couches de kaki. La vieille porte d'entrée est éblouissante d'éclats de verre ramassés sur la plage et crochetés avec du fil d'argent. Pourtant, le regard d'Amringe est constamment attiré vers la nature au-delà de ses murs en galets. «Comme je ne vois jamais personne, j'ai l'impression d'habiter sur une île», déclare cette ex-new-yorkaise. «J'observe les huards, les aigles et les phoques faisant des cabrioles; je fais du kayak le long de la grève...». Son cottage, construit en 1919, était à l'origine un pavillon d'agrément pour les thés du dimanche après-midi. «Les invités en grande tenue arrivaient par bateau au son d'un orchestre», dit Judyth van Amringe. Entourée de majestueux épicéas, elle s'endort en respirant des arômes de résine et d'iode.

Artist Judyth van Amringe found the perfect antidote for misty, gray days on the fabled Maine coast. She painted the stairs of her cottage sunshine yellow, and splashed the hardwood floor with generous coats of cheerful khaki green. The weathered front door is adazzle with shards of beach glass suspended on silver threads. But still her eye is drawn constantly to the natural world outside her shingled walls. "I see no one and I feel as if I'm on an island, surrounded by water," said the former New Yorker. "I watch the loons and eagles and cavorting seals, and go kayaking along the water's edge." Her cottage was built in 1919 as an ornamental pavilion for summer Sunday afternoon teas. "Glamorous guests would arrive by boat, and a band played," van Amringe noted. Surrounded by handsome spruce trees, she falls asleep with the fragrance of balsam and sea salt.

Die Künstlerin Judyth van Amringe hat das perfekte Mittel gegen die trüben, verhangenen Tage an der dafür bekannten Küste von Maine gefunden. In ihrem holzverkleideten Cottage leuchten die Treppen in Sonnengelb und die Fußböden glänzen in intensivem Khakigrün, an der wettergegerbten Eingangstür funkeln an zarten Silberfäden Glasscherben vom Strand. In der Natur sucht sie nach neuen Eindrücken. »Dann sehe ich niemanden. Ich fühle mich wie auf einer Insel, völlig von Wasser umschlossen«, sagt die Ex-New-Yorkerin. »Ich beobachte die Seetaucher, die Adler und die umhertollenden Seehunde und paddele mit dem Kajak an der Küste entlang.« Nachts schläft sie umhüllt vom Salzgeruch des Meeres und vom Duft der Fichtenbäume, die das Haus umstehen. Errichtet wurde ihr Cottage im Jahr 1919 als Zierpavillon für sommerliche Sonntagnachmittagstees. »Die ›glamourösen‹ Gäste wurden mit dem Boot hierhergebracht und dann von einer Kapelle unterhalten«, weiß sie zu berichten.

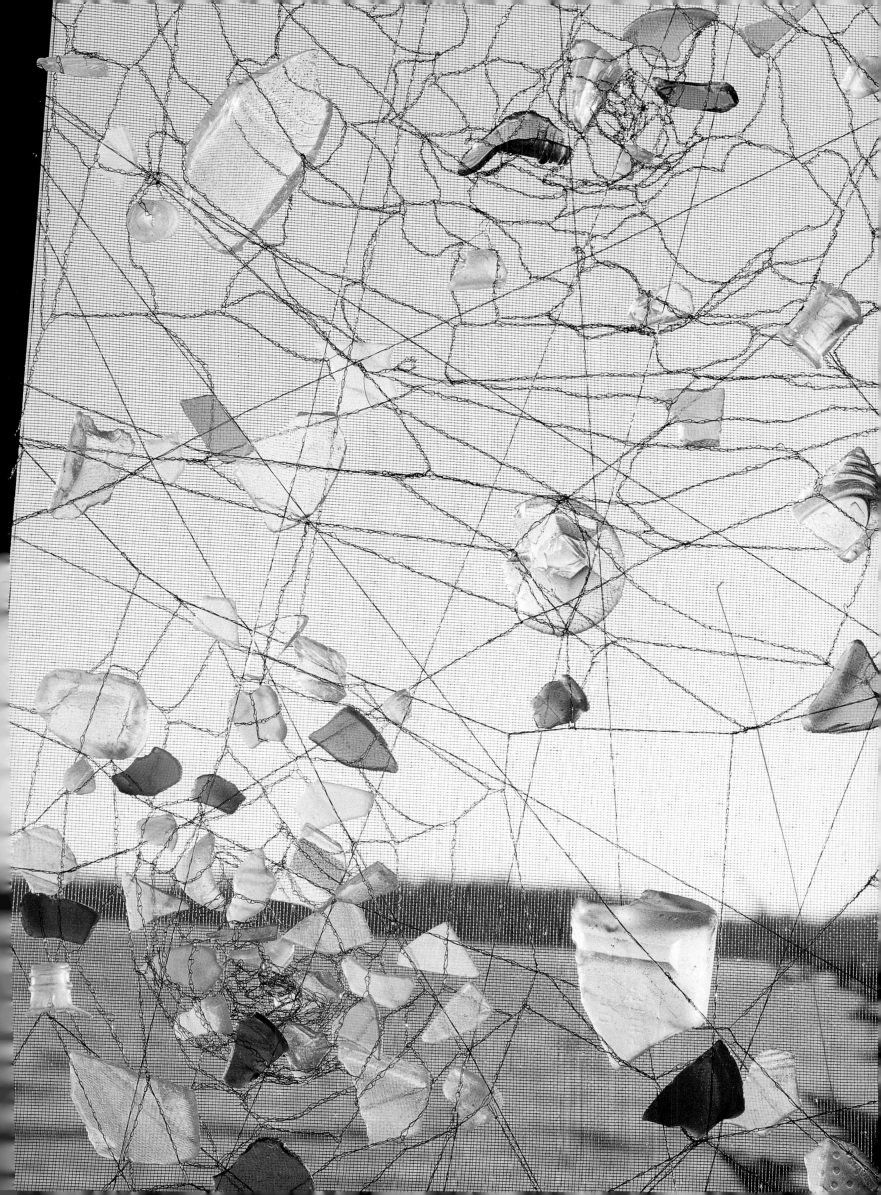

Previous pages: *Artist Judyth van Amringe's cottage fronts onto the Maine coast near Mount Desert and the Acadia National Park. The free-form door screen was hand-crocheted by van Amringe using beach glass washed up on her shore.*
Right: *For her corner "office", van Amringe improvised a desk from a salvaged saw horse and a slab of glass jeweled with gold and silver leaf.*
Below: *Old logs in the seating area are original to the house. Flea markets, antique shops, carnivals, and garage sales provided many of her decorating treasures, said the artist.*

Double page précédente: *Le cottage de Judyth van Amringe donne sur la côte du Maine, près de Mount Desert et du parc national d'Acadia. L'écran de la porte d'entrée est une œuvre originale d'Amringe réalisée avec des morceaux de verre échoués sur la plage.*
A droite: *Dans le coin «travail», van Amringe a improvisé un bureau avec de vieux tréteaux et un plateau en verre décoré de feuilles d'or et d'argent.*
Ci-dessous: *Les vieilles bûches, dans le coin salon, datent de l'époque de la construction. L'artiste a glané la plupart des trésors qui décorent sa maison dans des marchés aux puces, des kermesses ou des débarras de particuliers.*

Vorhergehende Doppelseite: *Vom Cottage der Künstlerin Judyth van Amringe fällt der Blick auf den Küstenstreifen zwischen Mount Desert und Acadia Nationalpark von Maine. Den frei gestalteten Türvorhang hat Judyth van Amringe selbst aus Glasscherben gearbeitet, die am Strand angeschwemmt wurden.*
Rechts: *Ihr »Eckbüro« hat die Künstlerin improvisiert – mit einem Schreibtisch aus einem alten Sägebock und einer Glasplatte, die mit Blättern aus Silber und Gold belegt ist.*
Unten: *Die alten Balken im Wohnzimmer sind original. Viele der Einrichtungsgegenstände fand die Künstlerin auf Flohmärkten, in Antiquitätenläden, auf Jahrmärkten oder privaten »garage sales«.*

Above: The cottage consists of two large, sunny rooms: the 6 x 12-meter living room, and the 3 x 3.70-meter bedroom. Her table was crafted from 18th-century forged-iron hearth pot supports and a scavenged top, silver-leafed and painted green. An old aquarium displays candles.

Right: Van Amringe found her painted porch swing at an antique shop in Pennsylvania. It's covered with old Maine camp blankets and cushions of vintage fabrics. The artist crafted a pair of hand-painted lamps with festive octagonal shades of hand-dyed silk.

Ci-dessus: Le cottage est constitué de deux grandes pièces ensoleillées, le salon de 6 mètres sur 12 et la chambre de 3 mètres sur 3,70 mètres. La table a été réalisée avec un support de chaudron en fer forgé du 18ᵉ siècle et un plateau recouvert de feuilles d'argent et peint en vert. Un vieil aquarium sert de présentoir à bougies.

A droite: Chinée chez un antiquaire de Pennsylvanie, la balancelle est recouverte de vieux plaids du Maine et de coussins en tissus anciens. Van Amringe a créé la paire de lampes qu'elle a surmontées de joyeux abat-jour octogonaux en soie teinte à la main.

Oben: Das Cottage besteht aus zwei großen, sonnendurchfluteten Räumen: dem 6 x 12 Meter großen Wohnzimmer und dem 3 x 3,70 Meter großen Schlafzimmer. An den eisernen Beinen des Tischs wurden im 18. Jahrhundert Töpfe über Feuerstellen gehängt. Die Platte ist ein Fundstück, das die Künstlerin grün gestrichen und mit silbernen Blätter verziert hat. In einem alten Aquarium stehen Kerzen.

Rechts: Die bemalte Verandaschaukel fand van Amringe in einem Antiquitätenladen in Pennsylvania. Die Kissen sind mit alten Stoffen bezogen, die Decken sind alte Campingdecken aus Maine. Die Künstlerin fertigte die festlichen achteckigen Lampenschirme aus handgefärbter Seide und bemalte die Ständer selbst.

Left: In the kitchen, van Amringe has corralled an international collection of vivid German ceramic lobsters, African metal plates, American pressed-glass candlesticks, and a lampshade adorned with vintage buttons.
Below: A salvaged, painted chimney cupboard was put to use as a pantry. Metal canisters, which formerly stored flour and lard in a farmhouse, now contain nourishment for her standard poodles.

A gauche: Dans sa cuisine, van Amringe a assemblé une collection internationale et colorée de homards allemands en céramique, d'assiettes africaines en métal, de bougeoirs américains en verre compressé et d'un abat-jour orné de boutons anciens.
Ci-dessous: Un placard de cheminée a été repeint et recyclé en garde-manger. Les boîtes en métal, qui viennent d'une ferme où elle servaient à stocker la farine et le lard, contiennent à présent la nourriture de ses caniches de concours.

Links: In ihrer Küche hat van Amringe eine internationale Sammlung ausgestellt: äußerst lebendig wirkende Keramiklangusten aus Deutschland, afrikanische Metallteller, amerikanische Kerzenständer aus Pressglas und einen mit alten Knöpfen geschmückten Lampenschirm.
Unten: Ein bemalter Kaminschrank, ein Fundstück, wurde zur Speisekammer umfunktioniert. In Metallkanistern, die früher auf einem Bauernhof zur Aufbewahrung von Mehl und Schmalz dienten, lagert nun das Futter für Judyths Rassepudel.

Facing page: In the bedroom, van Amringe festooned a mirror frame and lampshade with clusters of multicolored French velvet grapes. The 19th-century brass and painted tin headboard is Chinese.

Page de gauche: Dans la chambre à coucher, van Amringe a orné le cadre d'un miroir et un abat-jour de grappes de raisin multicolores en velours, réalisées en France. La tête de lit 19ᵉ, en laiton et en fer peint, est chinoise.

Linke Seite: In ihrem Schlafzimmer hat van Amringe einen Spiegelrahmen und einen Lampenschirm mit französischen Samttrauben in verschiedenen Farben geschmückt. Das Kopfteil des Betts aus bemaltem Messing und Blech kommt aus China.

Above: On the narrow balcony, where the local band used to perform for summer guests, is a cushy guest bed from a Maine summer house.
Right: "Maine can go foggy and grey, even in summer, so I brightened the stairs with yellow paint," noted the artist, who was known for her colorful antique store in Manhattan.
Facing page: The tiny bathroom was added to the house, but looks old thanks to van Amringe's artful selection of a turn-of-the-century English washbasin, an antique painted table, and vintage frosted-glass wall lamps.

Ci-dessus: Ce balcon étroit, où un orchestre local jouait autrefois pour les invités, accueille à présent un douillet lit provenant d'une maison de campagne du Maine.
A droite: «Dans le Maine, il peut faire brumeux et gris même l'été. C'est pourquoi j'ai égayé l'escalier avec du jaune», explique Amringe, qui était connue à Manhattan pour sa boutique colorée d'antiquités.
Page de droite: Bien qu'ajoutée ultérieurement, la minuscule salle de bains paraît ancienne grâce au choix astucieux d'un lavabo anglais du début du siècle, d'une table ancienne repeinte et de vieilles appliques en verre dépoli.

Oben: Auf dem schmalen Balkon spielten früher Kapellen aus der Nachbarschaft den Sommergästen auf. Heute steht hier ein äußerst bequemes Gästebett, das Judyth van Amringe in einem Sommerhaus, ebenfalls in Maine, gefunden hat.
Rechts: »In Maine kann es grau und neblig sein – auch im Sommer. Deshalb habe ich die Treppe in intensivem Gelb gestrichen«, sagt die Künstlerin, die früher in Manhattan für ihr ausgefallenes Antiquitätengeschäft bekannt war.
Rechte Seite: Das winzige Badezimmer ist ein nachträglicher Anbau. Bermerkenswert sind das englische Waschbecken aus der Jahrhundertwende und die alten Wandlampen aus mattiertem Glas.

Judyth van Amringe acquired her 1918 log cabin, which measures 2.5 x 6 meters, at auction. She had it moved to her 20 000-square-meter property on a flatbed truck – an escapade which made the front page of the local newspaper. Originally crafted as an ice-fishing cabin, it rolled on wheels to be moved onto a winter lake by a team of horses. "I gave it a new roof, but everything else, including the hand-carved bed and stone fireplace, is original," noted the artist. Fish prints, a woven fishing creel, a collection of wood burls, and twig frames adorn the piscatorial interior.

Judyth van Amringe a acheté cette cabane en rondins de 2,50 mètres sur 6, qui date de 1918, dans une vente aux enchères avant de la faire transporter sur son terrain de deux hectares sur un camion à fond plat, une expédition qui a fait la une de la presse locale. Conçue à l'origine pour la pêche dans les glaces, l'hiver venu, elle était montée sur roues et tirée par des chevaux jusqu'au bord d'un lac. «J'ai fait re-faire le toit, mais tout le reste, y compris le lit sculpté et la cheminée en pierre, est d'origine», observe l'artiste. Des gravures de poissons, un panier de pêche tressé, une collection d'objets en loupe d'arbres et des cadres en branchages complètent ce décor de pêcheur.

Die aus dem Jahr 1918 stammende Blockhütte erwarb Judyth van Amringe auf einer Auktion. Der Transport des 2,50 x 6 Meter großen Hauses auf einem Tieflader zu ihrem zwei Hektar umfassenden Anwesen landete sogar auf der Titelseite der Lokalzeitung. Ursprünglich diente die Hütte zum Eisfischen und wurde auf Rollen von Pferden über zugefrorene Seen gezogen. »Ich habe das Dach ersetzt, doch alles andere war bereits vorhanden, sogar das handgeschnitzte Bett und der steinerne Kamin«, erklärt die Künstlerin. Drucke mit Fischmotiven, ein geflochtetener Fischkorb, eine Sammlung von knorrigen Baumauswüchsen und Rahmen aus Zweigen erinnern an die ursprüngliche Verwendung der Hütte.

Olga Opsahl-Gee and Peter Gee

Provincetown, Cape Cod, Massachusetts

«Provincetown est le dernier bastion du style de vie traditionnel en bord de mer», affirme Olga Opsahl-Gee, artiste, décoratrice et professeur d'art. Elle s'est engagée à faire revivre la Hawthorne School of Art, créée il y a un siècle à Cap Code. La vieille grange, l'atelier, la maison et le quai qu'elle a soigneusement restaurés avec Peter Gee comptent parmi les derniers vestiges de l'architecture originale du Cap Code. «Lorsque nous avons acheté ces bâtiments, il y a 16 ans, nous avons retrouvé la couleur d'origine de leurs façades et de leurs meubles d'extérieur. L'atmosphère ici, au bord de l'eau, incite à la gaieté». Lorsque la marée se retire, le cliquetis des haubans métalliques des voiliers fait un contrepoint musical à la basse continue primordiale et profonde des vagues. «Les nuits de pleine lune, quand la marée se retire, on entend l'eau ruisseler entre les vieux piliers», observe Opsahl-Gee. Tennessee Williams a passé un été à écrire dans une de ces maisons.

"Provincetown is one of the last bastions of the old, traditional way of coastal life," avers Olga Opsahl-Gee, an artist, interior designer and art teacher who has committed herself to reviving the century-old Hawthorne School of Art on Cape Cod. The old barn and craft studio, residence, and wharf which she and Peter Gee carefully restored are some of the last vestiges of the original Cape Cod buildings. "When we acquired them 16 years ago, we brought the original colors back to the exterior of the buildings and the outdoor furniture," she said. "It's very conducive to fun, right here by the water." As the tide goes out, the clanging of metal halyards on sailing ships provides a musical counterpoint to the primeval basso profundo of ocean waves. "When there's a full moon and low tide, you can hear the water rushing out through the old pilings," noted Opsahl-Gee. Dramatist Tennessee Williams wrote in one of these dwellings one summer.

»Provincetown ist eine der letzten Bastionen des althergebrachten, traditionellen Lebens an der Küste«, versichert Olga Opsahl-Gee. Die Künstlerin, Innenarchitektin und Kunstdozentin hat sich der Aufgabe verschrieben, die ein Jahrhundert alte Hawthorne Art School auf Cape Cod wieder zu beleben. Die alte Scheune mit dem Atelier, das Wohnhaus und der Kai, die sie und Peter Gee sorgfältig restauriert haben, gehören zu den letzten ursprünglichen Bauten auf Cape Cod. »Als wir die Gebäude vor 16 Jahren erwarben, strichen wir sie wieder in den Originalfarben, die wir auch für die Outdoor-Möbel verwendeten«, sagt Olga Opsahl-Gee. »Hier am Wasser ist alles auf Spaß ausgerichtet.« Wenn bei Ebbe das Wasser langsam verschwindet, bildet der metallene Klang der Flaggleinen den musikalischen Kontrapunkt zum urzeitlichen Basso profundo. »Bei Vollmond und Ebbe hört man das Wasser durch die alten Pfähle rauschen«, weiß Olga Opsahl-Gee. Der Dramatiker Tennessee Williams schrieb einen Sommer lang in einem dieser Häuser.

Previous pages: brightly painted cottages, once used for drying cod, on Captain Jack's Wharf in Cape Cod. The dozen cottages, with names like "Venus", "Borealis", and "Neptune", are popular summer retreats for painters and writers. The century-old revived barn is now used by the Gee's Hawthorne School of Art. Two Gee siblings and a friend gather at the door of the barn, where the Hawthorne School of Art is held each summer.
Right: The hooked rug on the stairs of the main house depicts the history of Cape Cod in vivid colors.
Below: the kitchen in the main house.

Doubles pages précédentes: des maisons aux couleurs gaies, autrefois utilisées pour sécher la morue, sur le quai du capitaine Jack à Cap Code. Les dizaines de cottages, portant des noms tels que «Vénus», «Borealis» ou «Neptune», sont très prisés des peintres et des écrivains qui viennent s'y retirer l'été. La grange restaurée, vieille de cent ans, est devenue une annexe de l'école de Gee, la Hawthorne School of Art. Deux petits Gee et un ami se tiennent devant la porte de la grange où, chaque été, les cours ont lieu.
A droite: Le chemin d'escalier en crochet, dans la maison principale, raconte l'histoire de Cap Code en scènes vivement colorées.
Ci-dessous: la cuisine de la maison principale.

Vorhergehende Doppelseiten: An Captain Jack's Wharf auf Cape Cod steht ein Dutzend in lebhaften Farben gestrichene Cottages, die ursprünglich zum Trocknen von Kabeljau dienten. In den Häusern, die Namen wie »Venus«, »Borealis« oder »Neptun« tragen, verbringen gerne Maler und Schriftsteller den Sommer. In der 100 Jahre alten Scheune findet jeden Sommer die Hawthorne School of Art der Gees statt. Zwei ihrer Sprösslinge haben sich mit einem Spielkameraden am Scheunentor getroffen.
Rechts: Der abgelaufene Teppich auf den Treppenstufen zeigt Motive in lebhaften Farben aus der Geschichte von Cape Cod.
Unten: die Küche im Haupthaus.

Above: The kitchen has an old stove with shell handles. The shingled residence was built around 1850, and was dragged by mules from the center of Provincetown to its current windswept position on the Cape Cod dunes. Straw hats are for the use of students when they paint outdoors in the bright Atlantic Ocean light.
Right: The Gees expressed their love and appreciation of the old house by using old-fashioned blue and red milk paint on plaster walls. Olga collects antique American primitive furniture, old hooked rugs, hand-crafted kitchenware, and displays them throughout the residence.

Ci-dessus: Le vieux four de la cuisine a des poignées en nacre. La maison en bardeaux a été construite en 1850 et traînée par des mules depuis le cœur de Provincetown jusqu'à cet avant-poste balayé par le vent dans les dunes du Cap Code. Les chapeaux de paille servent aux étudiants lorsqu'ils vont peindre en extérieur dans la lumière vive.
A droite: Les Gee ont exprimé leur amour et leur respect de la vieille bâtisse en peignant ses murs enduits au plâtre d'un bleu et d'un rouge laiteux à l'ancienne. Olga collectionne les meubles primitifs américains, les vieux tapis au crochet, la vaisselle tournée à la main et les expose un peu partout dans sa maison.

Oben: In der Küche steht ein alter Herd mit Muschelgriffen. Das Holzhaus wurde um 1850 errichtet und mit Maultieren aus dem Ortskern von Provincetown an den windumtosten Platz auf den Dünen von Cape Cod gezogen. Die Strohhüte dienen den Studenten als Schutz vor der gleißenden Sonne, wenn sie draußen malen.
Rechts: Die Gees strichen die vergipsten Wände mit altmodischer blauer und roter Milchfarbe. Olga Opsahl-Gee sammelt schlichte amerikanische Möbel, alte Knüpfteppiche und handgearbeitetes Küchengeschirr.

Vicente Wolf

Montauk, Long Island

Ce sont la simplicité de sa vieille ville et le calme de ses plages donnant sur l'Atlantique qui ont attiré le décorateur new-yorkais Vicente Wolf à Montauk, à 160 kilomètres de Manhattan. Située à la pointe de Long Island, Montauk a toujours séduit un assortiment éclectique de citadins, dont Andy Warhol, Richard Avedon, Robert de Niro et Ralph Lauren. Wolf, qui est la discrétion même, s'y rend pour sa tranquillité, son jardin où il peut désherber et planter à loisir, et sa piscine. «Pour moi, l'océan est une force vitale», déclare ce natif de Cuba, décorateur à New York depuis 28 ans. «La mer régénère ma créativité. J'observe les vagues et tout le stress de la ville s'évanouit». Généralement, il n'invite qu'un ou deux amis à la fois. «Dans mon travail, je suis toujours en représentation. Ici, j'aime être en tête à tête avec la nature et quelques amis». A Montauk, dit-il, la vue est plus importante que sa décoration.

New York interior designer Vicente Wolf was drawn to Montauk, 160 kilometers from Manhattan, by the unpretentious old town and remote Atlantic beaches. At the furthest point of Long Island, Montauk has always attracted an eclectic group of city-dwellers, including Andy Warhol, Richard Avedon, Robert de Niro and Ralph Lauren. Wolf, no name-dropper, goes there for the isolation, a garden where he can lose himself in weeding and cultivating, and a lap pool. "The ocean is a life force for me," said Wolf, who was born in Cuba. He has worked as a designer in New York for 28 years. "The sea replenishes my creativity. I watch the waves and all the city stress falls away." He usually invites just one or two friends. "I have to be 'on' for business so there I relate one-on-one with nature and my friends." In Montauk, he said, the view is more important than his decorating.

Was den New Yorker Interior-Designer Vicente Wolf am 160 Kilometer entfernt gelegenen Montauk interessierte, waren die einsamen Strände des Atlantiks und ein Städtchen, dem jegliche Prätention abging. Montauk, an der Inselspitze von Long Island gelegen, hat schon immer eine bunte Mischung von Stadtmenschen angezogen, darunter Andy Warhol, Richard Avedon, Robert de Niro und Ralph Lauren. Vicente Wolf schätzt allerdings hier nicht die Anwesenheit berühmter Menschen, sondern die Ruhe, seinen Pool und den Garten, wo er zwischen Unkrautjäten und Anpflanzen völlig aufgeht. »Für mich birgt der Ozean Lebenskraft«, sagt der gebürtige Kubaner Vicente Wolf, der seit 28 Jahren als Designer in New York arbeitet. »Das Meer lädt meine Kreativität wieder auf. Ich beobachte die Wellen und dabei fällt der ganze Großstadtstress von mir ab.« Meist lädt er nur ein oder zwei Freunde ein. »Da ich in der Stadt nie ganz abschalte, will ich hier ganz persönliche Erfahrungen mit der Natur und einzelnen Freunden erleben.« In Montauk, so sagt er, sei die Aussicht wichtiger als das Interior-Design.

Previous page: *Cultivating contrasts in the decor, Wolf covered the floor with rough-quarried stone, and painted all woodwork smooth, creamy white. A white-framed mirror, leaning against the wall, amplifies the apparent space of the living room.*
Left: *When they purchased the beach house 16 years ago, Wolf and his former partner, Bob Patino, replaced small panes with ocean-grabbing acres of glass.*
Below: *Wolf's cadence of Degas pastels smudges the boundaries between indoors and wild nature outside. Sky-lit cotton canvas, natural linen, and raw silk are his chosen fabrics.*

Page précédente: *Cultivant les contrastes, Wolf a tapissé le sol de dalles en pierres brutes et peint les boiseries d'un blanc lisse et crémeux. Un miroir au cadre blanc, adossé au mur, amplifie l'espace du salon.*
A gauche: *Lorsqu'il a acheté cette maison sur la plage il y a 16 ans, Wolf et son ancien associé, Bob Patino, ont remplacé les petites fenêtres par de grandes baies vitrées embrassant la mer.*
Ci-dessous: *La palette de pastels à la Degas brouille les frontières entre l'intérieur et la nature sauvage à l'extérieur. Les toiles de coton lumineuses, le lin naturel et les soies grèges sont les étoffes de prédilection de Wolf.*

Vorhergehende Seite: *Vicente Wolf liebt Kontraste: Er kombiniert raue Steinplatten auf dem Fußboden mit Holzoberflächen in einem ebenmäßigen Eierschalenton. Der weiß gerahmte Spiegel an der Wand betont die – scheinbare – Größe des Wohnzimmers.*
Links: *Als sie vor 16 Jahren das Strandhaus erwarben, setzten Vicente Wolf und sein damaliger Partner Bob Patino große Fensterscheiben ein, die einen atemberaubenden Blick aufs Meer bieten.*
Unten: *Pastellfarben, die an die Palette von Degas erinnern, lassen die Grenzen zwischen Innenräumen und Natur verschwimmen. Feste Baumwollstoffe, naturbelassenes Leinen und Rohseide sind Vicente Wolfs Lieblingsstoffe.*

Above: Wolf plays with transparency by slipcovering metal patio chairs with a swirl of tissue-weight Irish linen. He plays up contrasts, with a yin/yang balance of antiques and yard-sale finds, luxurious silks and simple glass vases, and lustrous lacquered ceilings which shimmer above rough stone floors.

Right: Wolf has been collecting museum-quality photographs for decades. "Taking pictures is the opposite of designing," he noted. "Decorating is about order, and photography is about letting go, embracing the chaos."

Ci-dessus: Wolf joue avec les transparences en recouvrant ces chaises de jardin en métal de housses en lin irlandais ultra-léger et virevoltant. Il accentue les contrastes en créant un équilibre yin et yang entre les antiquités et les objets chinés dans des brocantes, les soieries luxueuses et de simples vases en verre, le plafond laqué et les dalles en pierres brutes du sol qui s'y reflètent.

A droite: Wolf collectionne des photographies dignes de musées depuis des décennies. «Prendre des photos, c'est le contraire de décorer», observe-t-il. «La décoration est une question d'ordre, la photographie demande qu'on se laisse aller, qu'on embrasse le chaos».

Oben: Vicente Wolf spielt mit durchsichtigen Stoffen: Die Hussen seiner Gartenstühle aus Metall sind aus hauchdünnem irischen Leinen. Er perfektioniert Kontraste und sucht nach einer Yin-Yang-Balance zwischen Antiquitäten und Zufallsfunden bei Privatverkäufen, zwischen luxuriösen Seidenstoffen und einfachen Glasvasen, zwischen glanzlackierter Decke und Böden aus unbehauenem Stein.

Rechts: Seit Jahrzehnten sammelt Vicente Wolf museale Fotografien. »Fotografie ist das Gegenteil von Design«, sagt er. »Beim Design geht es um Ordnung, bei der Fotografie um das Loslassen und darum, das Chaos willkommen zu heißen.«

Facing page: *Vicente Wolf displays his favorite framed photographs on new shelves on the bathroom wall. The shower, like the floor, is a mosaic of quarried stone.*
Above: *The upholstered bed is a Wolf design. The multi-drawered table is by Jean-Michel Frank. Still, Montauk is not about pretension, he insists. "I can go down to the local coffee shop unshaven, in old pyjama bottoms and no one would notice," he laughed.*
Right: *Immersed up to his neck in the restored copper tub, Wolf can relax or watch the shadows and sunlight on his sheltered terrace.*

Page de gauche: *Les photographies préférées de Wolf sont encadrées et alignées sur de minces étagères dans sa salle de bains. La douche, comme le sol, est une mosaïque de pierres brutes.*
Ci-dessus: *Le lit a été dessiné par Wolf. La table de chevet à plusieurs rallonges est signée Jean-Michel Frank. Toutefois, on ne fait pas de chichis à Montauk. «Si je me rends au café du coin mal rasé et en pantalon de pyjama, personne ne le remarquera», affirme Wolf en riant.*
A droite: *Plongé jusqu'au cou dans le tub en cuivre qu'il a restauré, Wolf peut se détendre ou contempler les ombres et la lumière qui dansent sur sa terrasse abritée.*

Linke Seite: *Im Bad hat Vicente Wolf seine gerahmten Lieblingsfotografien auf neuen Regalen aufgestellt. Wie der Boden ist auch die Dusche ein Mosaik aus behauenen Steinplatten.*
Oben: *Das gepolsterte Bett ist ein Eigenentwurf. Der mit vielen Ausziehladen versehene Tisch stammt von Jean-Michel Frank. Trotz dieser Perfektion steht das Leben in Montauk aber nicht für Prätention: »Ich könnte unrasiert und in alten Pyjamahosen in den ›coffee-shop‹ an der Ecke gehen und es würde keinem auffallen«, lacht Wolf.*
Rechts: *Bis zum Hals in die aufgearbeitete Badewanne aus Kupfer getaucht – so kann Vicente Wolf entspannen.*

Ellen O'Neill

Sag Harbor, Long Island

D'élégantes pièces de bois chantournées, que tous les amateurs d'antiquités victoriennes connaissent sous le nom de «gingerbread», ornent la ravissante maison en bois d'Ellen O'Neill à Sag Harbour. Ce vieux port de baleiniers de Long Island est depuis longtemps une retraite pittoresque pour les artistes, les écrivains et les New-yorkais exilés de l'été. O'Neill tomba un jour en arrêt devant cette maison de deux étages. Comme elle n'était pas à vendre, elle s'attela à créer un bon karma afin de pouvoir un jour en devenir la propriétaire. «Ma mère m'a conseillé d'enterrer dans le jardin une statue de saint Joseph, le saint patron de l'immobilier», raconte-t-elle. La foi inébranlable et les prières d'O'Neill finirent par porter leurs fruits. «La maison appartenait à la même famille depuis sa construction en 1895 et n'avait jamais été restaurée. Les plafonds recouverts de panneaux en fer blanc, les lambris, les parquets, les grandes vérandas, les pièces spacieuses... tout était intact».

Fanciful wooden fretwork, known to all lovers of Victoriana as "gingerbread", adorns Ellen O'Neill's graceful wooden house. Sag Harbor, an old whaling town on Long Island, has long been a picturesque haven for artists, writers and summer exiles from New York City. Almost as captivating is her story of how she fell in love with the two-story house at first sight one summer night, and then set out to create good karma so that she would one day own it. "The house was not for sale," recounted O'Neill. "My mother suggested that I should bury a statue of St Joseph, the patron saint of real estate, in the garden." O'Neill's good faith and prayers finally worked. "The house had been in one family since it was built in 1895 and had never been remodeled," she said. "The tin ceilings, wainscotting, hardwood floors, wide verandahs and large rooms were all intact."

Ausgefallene Holzverzierungen, die die Liebhaber der viktorianischen Zeit als »Knusperhäuschenstil« bezeichnen, schmücken das anmutige Holzhaus von Ellen O'Neill. Sag Harbor lebte früher vom Walfischfang, doch schon seit langem ist das auf Long Island gelegene, pittoreske Städtchen ein Zufluchtsort für Künstler, Schriftsteller und all diejenigen New Yorker, die der Hitze des Sommers entfliehen wollen. Ebenso faszinierend wie die Geschichte des Städtchens ist die Liebesgeschichte zwischen Ellen und ihrem zweigeschossigen Haus, das sie in einer Sommernacht zum ersten Mal sah. Sie setzte Himmel und Hölle in Bewegung, um es zu bekommen, denn es war damals nicht zu verkaufen. »Meine Mutter schlug vor, im Garten eine Statue des Heiligen Josef zu vergraben, des Schutzpatrons der Immobilienhändler«, schildert Ellen. Ihr Glaube und ihre Gebete wurden erhört. »Das Haus war seit seiner Erbauung im Jahr 1895 im Besitz einer einzigen Familie. Es waren keine Umbauarbeiten vorgenommen worden und die Vertäfelungen, blechverkleideten Decken, Hartholzböden, breiten Veranden und großen Zimmer waren alle noch im Originalzustand.«

Ellen O'Neill, vice-president of Home Furnishing and Design for Polo Ralph Lauren in New York, heads for the farthest reaches of Long Island every summer weekend. Before she found the home of her dreams, which stands on a 2000-square-meter triangular plot, she looked for six years for an old residence that had not been updated or "modernized". She sees all room arrangements as "fluid" and often moves furniture, paintings, and objects around. "I spend all my weekends there in summer, and I'm a restless re-arranger" she said.

Tous les week-ends d'été, Ellen O'Neill, vice-présidente du département d'ameublement et de design de Polo Ralph Lauren à New York, met le cap sur la pointe extrême de Long Island. Avant de trouver la maison de ses rêves, qui se dresse sur un petit terrain triangulaire de 2000 mètres carrés, elle a passé six ans à rechercher une vieille bâtisse n'ayant jamais été réaménagée ni «modernisée». Ellen aime les décors «fluides» et déplace souvent les meubles, les tableaux et les objets. «L'été, je passe ici tous mes week-ends et je n'arrête pas de tout réarranger».

Ellen O'Neill ist Vice-President für den Bereich Heimtextilien und Design im Imperium von Polo Ralph Lauren in New York. Im Sommer unternimmt sie an jedem Wochenende die Reise hierher an die äußerste Spitze von Long Island. Bevor sie ihr Traumhaus fand, das auf einem 2000 Quadratmeter großen, dreieckigen Grundstück steht, suchte sie sechs Jahre lang nach einem alten Anwesen, das weder modernisiert noch umgebaut worden war. Für Ellen O'Neill sind Zimmerarrangements stets »im Fluss«; entsprechend oft räumt sie Möbel, Bilder und Objekte um. »Ich verbringe alle Sommerwochenenden hier und bin eine rastlose Umräumerin«, sagt sie.

Sag Harbor, Long Island 41°00'N 72°18'W   Ellen O'Neill

Clockwise from top left: *On summer afternoons and evenings, the screened porch is a cool, quiet, mosquito-free haven; the kitchen remained unchanged; Ellen O'Neill decided to keep the old stove; she sponged down the dining room walls and applied a pale pearl-grey Fortuny-esque stencil.*

Du haut à gauche, dans le sens des aiguilles d'une montre: *Les après-midi et les soirs d'été, le porche protégé de moustiquaires offre un refuge frais et calme; la cuisine n'a pas été touchée; Ellen a décidé de garder le vieux poêle; elle a simplement lessivé les murs de la salle à manger et peint au pochoir un papier peint dans des tons gris perle à la Fortuny.*

Im Uhrzeigersinn von links oben: *An sommerlichen Nachmittagen und Abenden ist die geschützte Veranda ein kühler, ruhiger und mückenfreier Zufluchtsort; die Küche wurde nicht umgebaut; Ellen O'Neill behielt den alten Ofen; sie bearbeitete die Wände des Esszimmers einfach nur mit dem Schwamm und brachte eine blassgraue, perlmuttfarbene Wandverzierung im Fortuny-Stil an.*

Sag Harbor, Long Island 41°00'N 72°18'W

Ellen O'Neill

Vintage wood furniture was painted white (or left with interesting chips and nicks). "I wanted the walls to look as if I had simply stripped off the wallpaper and left the plaster exposed," said O'Neill. Still, it needs some expert art-direction to get it right, so she had an artist work in a little more white paint to get the desired chalky effect.

De vieux meubles en bois ont été peints en blanc – ou laissés tels quels avec quelques jolis gnons et la peinture écaillée juste ce qu'il faut. «Je voulais donner l'impression qu'on s'était contenté d'enlever le papier sur les murs, laissant le plâtre exposé», explique O'Neill.

Ceci dit, comme cela nécessite un doigté expert, c'est une artiste qui est venue donner les petites touches de blanc nécessaires pour obtenir l'effet crayeux voulu.

Alte Holzmöbel wurden weiß gestrichen, besonders interessante Patina wurde allerdings belassen. »Die Wände sollten so aussehen, als wären die Tapeten einfach nur abgezogen worden, um den nackten Putz sichtbar zu machen«, erklärt sie. Doch ein solcher Effekt lässt sich nur vom Experten erreichen und deshalb heuerte Ellen O'Neill einen Maler an, der etwas weiße Farbe in die Wände einarbeitete.

A Shingled Beach Cottage

Water Island, Fire Island

La ville de Water Island n'est qu'à un jet de pierre à l'est de Manhattan, au terme d'un relaxant trajet en ferry. Pourtant, on s'en croirait à des années-lumière. C'est dans ce petit coin assoupi de Fire Island, où les voitures sont bannies, que le publicitaire Donald Sterzin et son associé, Mark Campbell, ont acheté et décoré un étonnant cottage en bois d'un étage donnant sur la plage. Cette maison toute en coins et recoins, aujourd'hui un nid chic et douillet décoré de tissus Ralph Lauren, de photos de Bruce Weber et de lithographies de Matisse, fut construite sur le continent en 1875. Démontée, elle fut traînée sur les glaces jusqu'à son emplacement actuel pendant l'hiver 1906. D'après Campbell, ses propriétaires de l'époque avaient sans doute calculé que les chevaux de halage revenaient moins cher que de reconstruire un bâtiment sur l'île. Tels des Fitzcarraldo, ils transportèrent par ferry antiquités, rotins, tapis indiens et livres rares, avant de les acheminer à dos d'homme jusqu'à la plage.

The town of Water Island is just a hop and a skip – and finally a relaxing ferry ride – east of New York City, but it's time-zones away with its slow-motion living and barefoot style. It was on this sleepy corner of Fire Island – no cars allowed – that advertising executive, Donald Sterzin, and his associate, Mark Campbell, acquired and decorated a one-story shingled beach cottage with an intriguing history. The rambling house, now a chic haven with Ralph Lauren fabrics, Bruce Weber portraits, and Matisse prints, had originally been built on the mainland in 1875. Dismantled, it was slid across winter ice in 1906 to its present location. Campbell muses that perhaps the Edwardian-era owners found draught horse-haulage cheaper than new building materials and labor. Fitzcarraldo-like, antiques and wicker, Indian dhurries and rare books were also ferried over, then hand-carried down the beach.

Das Städtchen Water Island ist nur einen Katzensprung – und eine entspannende Fährenfahrt – östlich von New York gelegen. Doch hier spielt sich das Leben einfach und im Zeitlupentempo ab und scheint auf einem anderen Planeten stattzufinden. Auf der verschlafenen Insel Fire Island, wo Autos keinen Zutritt haben, fanden der Werbeboss Donald Sterzin und sein Partner Mark Campbell ein eingeschossiges, holzverkleidetes Strandcottage mit einer interessanten Vergangenheit. Das verwinkelte Haus, nun mit Stoffen von Ralph Lauren, Porträts von Bruce Weber und Drucken von Matisse perfekt durchgestylt, stammt aus dem Jahr 1875. Ursprünglich stand es auf dem Festland und wurde im Winter 1906 über das Eis an seine heutige Position gezogen. Wahrscheinlich, so glaubt Mark Campbell, war es für die damaligen Bewohner billiger, das Haus mit Pferdestärken versetzen zu lassen als Baumaterialien und Arbeitskräfte für einen Neubau zu bezahlen. Wie in einer Szene aus »Fitzcarraldo« wurden Antiquitäten und Gegenstände aus Korbgeflecht, indische handgewebte »Dhurries« und seltene Bücher per Fähre übergesetzt und dann von Hand den Strand entlang transportiert.

The sleepy verandah is cushioned with Ralph Lauren ticking-striped pillows on creaky old wicker chaises. Gloxinias and orchids are ferried over from Manhattan. From the airy upper porches, wraparound views invite lingering ... and malingering.

Une véranda où il fait bon s'assoupir dans de vieux fauteuils en rotin grinçants, tapissés de coussins en toile à matelas rayée de chez Ralph Lauren. Les gloxinies et les orchidées sont apportées de Manhattan par ferry. Depuis le balcon panoramique, la vue invite à la paresse et à l'indolence.

Auf der verträumten Veranda stehen alte knarrende Korbstühle, die mit Kissen in Ralph Laurens »ticking-stripe«-Muster ausgelegt sind. Die Gloxinien und Orchideen werden per Fähre von Manhattan hierher transportiert. Die luftige obere Veranda mit ihrem alles umspannenden Blick lädt zum Verweilen ein ... und dazu, sich vor der Arbeit zu drücken!

Denim-covered armchairs, vintage painted tables, auction-house prints and porcelain, a mahogany dining table, art pottery, and assorted armoires and chairs were purchased and arranged in one summer decorating blitz. "Thank goodness for flea markets, tag sales and antique dealer friends," praised Campbell. "Do it quick, do it well, was Donald's motto." Charting a fair-weather course with their favorite blue-and-white cottons and splashes of turquoise, the two friends created a place of delight and luxury for weekend guests.

Les fauteuils tapissés de jean, les vieilles tables peintes, les gravures, les objets en porcelaine dénichés dans des ventes aux enchères, la table en acajou, les poteries d'art, les armoires et les chaises ont tous été achetés et disposés lors d'un même été placé sous le signe de la décoration à gogo. «Dieu soit loué pour les marchés aux puces, les débarras et les amis antiquaires», déclare Campbell. Sa devise: «Vite fait, bien fait.» Optant pour une gamme de couleurs «beau fixe» et misant sur leurs cotonnades blanches et bleues favorites agrémentées de quelques touches de turquoise, les deux amis ont créé un petit coin de plaisir et de luxe pour les amis qui viennent passer le week-end.

Mit Jeansstoff bezogene Polstersessel, alte bemalte Tische, in Auktionshäusern erworbene Drucke und Porzellan, ein Esstisch aus Mahagoni, Keramik und verschiedenste Konsolen und Stühle wurden in einer nur einen Sommer dauernden Blitzaktion erworben. »Gott sei Dank gibt es Flohmärkte, ›garage sales‹ und Freunde, die mit Antiquitäten handeln«, sagt Campbell. »Es muss schnell gehen und es muss gut aussehen, das war Donalds Motto.« Die beiden Freunde bevorzugten blauweiß gestreifte Baumwolle und Farbtupfer in Türkis, die gute Laune verbreiten. Dieser Platz ist für ihre Wochenendgäste ein Ort des Luxus und der Freude geworden.

In Sterzin and Campbell's hands, a basic blue-and-white color scheme is anything but bland. Old tag-sale blue-and-white porcelain plates and platters add instant texture and patina to a simple white wall. Mundane white cabinetry is disguised behind inviting old chairs and armfuls of crimson and pink dahlias, roses, orchids and daisies. It's the kind of plank-floored, sand-dusted house that inspires summer memories and years of nostalgia. Summers there are May-to-September brief, and city friends wait impatiently for winter months to end, and for weekend invitations to go out.

Entre les mains de Sterzin et de Campbell, la gamme basique bleu-blanc prend des tons virulents. De vieilles assiettes et des plats en porcelaine bleue et blanche chinés dans des débarras ajoutent instantanément texture et patine à un simple mur blanc. Les placards blancs utilitaires sont déguisés derrière de vieilles chaises accueillantes et des brassées rouges et roses de dahlias, de roses, d'orchidées et de marguerites. Avec ses planchers et ses boiseries décapés, c'est le genre de maison qui suscite les souvenirs de vacances et des années de nostalgie. Ici, les étés durent de mai à septembre. Les copains de la ville trépignent d'impatience en attendant l'arrivée de la belle saison et les invitations à venir passer le week-end.

Unter den kundigen Händen von Donald Sterzin und Mark Campbell kann auch aus einer simplen blauweißen Farbpalette einfach nichts Langweiliges werden! Auf »garage sales« erstandene alte Porzellanteller und -platten in Blau und Weiß verleihen einer schlichten weißen Wand Patina und Struktur. Einfache Wandschränke sind hinter einladenden alten Sesseln und Unmengen von Dahlien in Purpur und Pink, Rosen, Orchideen und Gänseblümchen versteckt. Häuser dieser Art, mit einfachen Bohlen ausgelegt und überall knirschend vor Sand, bergen Sommererinnerungen. In der Stadt können es die Freunde kaum erwarten, eine der begehrten Wochenendeinladungen zu erhalten.

White-painted siding walls on the Water Island bedroom provide a crisp background for striped cotton canvas in traditional shades of sporty red and white. Vintage-look florals and a horde of old shells gave the interiors the look of age from day one. Sterzin's credos: Bring together all the things you love, don't fuss, and let the eye be seduced by serendipity. Bed linens and cotton slipcover fabrics are all from the Ralph Lauren Home Collection. Vintage wicker, framed prints, and rustic collections were all shipped over from New York City.

Les murs à bardeaux blancs de la chambre offrent un fond éclatant aux cotonnades rayées dans les tons pimpants et traditionnels rouges et blancs. Des bouquets à l'ancienne et une pléthore de vieux coquillages donnent au décor un air de vieille maison de famille. Sterzin a plusieurs credo: n'assembler que des objets que l'on aime, ne pas être maniaque et se laisser séduire par les assemblages fortuits et heureux. La literie en lin et les housses en coton viennent de la ligne de maison Ralph Lauren. Les vieux meubles en rotin, les gravures encadrées et les collections rustiques ont été acheminés depuis New York.

Im Schlafzimmer bilden die weiß gestrichenen Wände einen attraktiven Hintergrund für gestreifte Baumwollstoffe im traditionellen kräftigen Rot und Weiß. Konservativ gehaltene Blumensträuße und viele alte Muscheln verliehen dem Interieur gleich vom ersten Tag an eine nostalgische Atmosphäre. Sterzins Credo lautet denn auch: alle Dinge vereinen, an denen das Herz hängt, nicht zu viel Aufhebens darum machen und das Auge vom glücklichen Zufall verführen und leiten lassen. Bettwäsche und Baumwollbezüge stammen alle aus der Ralph Lauren Home Collection. Die alten Korbmöbel, gerahmten Drucke und rustikal wirkenden Sammlungen wurden aus New York hierher gebracht.

Carey and Andrew King

Grayton Beach, Emerald Coast, Florida

Grayton Beach, un croissant de sable blanc et fin de plus d'un kilo-mètre en bordure du golfe du Mexique, a été élue la plus belle plage du monde. Il est vrai que la nature ici s'est montrée généreuse. Gray-ton Beach est bordée d'une vaste réserve naturelle. Des dunes sculp-tées par le vent dessinent son relief. Pas le moindre hôtel à l'horizon. Des sapins et des magnolias, taillés par les bourrasques, sont profon-dément enfoncés dans le sable. L'été, les tortues viennent pondre sur la plage. Les monarques orange et jaunes volettent au-dessus du sable lors de leur migration automnale vers le Mexique. De l'autre côté des dunes, des marais salants, des pinèdes, des lagons à marées et des étangs d'eau douce attirent les randonneurs et les pêcheurs à la ligne. C'est ici que le chirurgien orthopédiste Andrew King et sa femme, Ca-rey, peintre, qui habitent à la Nouvelle-Orléans, ont demandé à l'ar-chitecte Carey McWorther de leur construire une maison de vacances.

Florida's Grayton Beach, a sunny, mile-long curve of talcum-pow-der white sand on the Gulf of Mexico, has been voted the most beautiful beach in the world. Nature is bountiful here. Grayton Beach is edged by a large nature preserve, and sculpted sand dunes – not hotels – paint the landscape. Slash pines and magno-lia trees, "pruned" by gusts and gales from the Gulf, stand knee-deep in the sand dunes. Turtles clamber and hatch their eggs on the beach during the humid summer months. Orange and yellow Monarch butterflies hover and swarm over the beach on their an-nual autumn migration to Mexico. Across the dunes, salt marshes, pine woods, tidal lagoons, and freshwater ponds attract hikers and anglers alike. It was here that New Orleans residents, orthopedic surgeon Andrew King and his wife, Carey, a painter, commissioned Carey McWhorter to build their getaway cottage.

Er wurde zum schönsten Strand der Welt gewählt: Floridas Grayton Beach am Golf von Mexiko, eine sonnige, kilometerlange Kurve aus Sand so weiß wie Talkumpuder. Hier ist die Natur großzügig und frei-gebig. Grayton Beach wird von einem großen Naturschutzgebiet ein-gefasst. In Sand gemeißelte Dünenformationen bestimmen die Land-schaft – und nicht Hotels. Pinien und Magnolienbäume, vom Wind geformt, stehen knietief in den Dünen. Während der feuchten Som-mermonate arbeiten sich Schildkröten den Strand hinauf und legen dort ihre Eier. Auf ihrem jährlichen Überwinterungsflug nach Mexiko schweben orange und gelb gezeichnete Monarchfalter in Schwärmen über dem Strand. Auf der anderen Seite der Dünen finden sich Salzwiesen, Pinienwälder, Tidenlagunen und kleine Süßwasserseen, die Wanderer und Angler gleichermaßen anziehen. Hier ließen sich der in New Orleans lebende Orthopäde und Chirurg Andrew King und seine Frau Carey, eine Malerin, von Carey McWhorter einen klei-nen Zufluchtsort errichten.

Carey and Andrew King – he's originally from New Zealand – and their three children have an unobstructed view of Gulf of Mexico sunsets from their beachfront deck and the windows of their living room. The house, which stands on a 30 x 30 meter lot, is elevated on a precast concrete foundation. "Hurricanes and fierce storms occasionally visit this region, so windows are reinforced with steel," said architect, Carey McWhorter. A children's playroom, a bunkroom, and a study stand on the ground level. The large living room, with a four-meter-high ceiling, is shaded by the wide eaves of the long front porch.

Depuis leur véranda et les fenêtres du salon, Carey et Andrew King – il est originaire de Nouvelle-Zélande – peuvent admirer les couchers de soleil sur le golfe. La maison, bâtie sur un terrain de 30 x 30 mètres, repose sur des fondations en béton précoulé. «La région essuyant parfois des ouragans et de violentes tempêtes, les fenêtres sont renforcées avec de l'acier», explique Carey McWorther. Le rez-de-chaussée accueille une salle de jeux pour les trois enfants, une chambre à coucher et un bureau. Le vaste salon, avec ses quatre mètres sous plafond, est protégé du soleil par les grands avant-toits du porche.

Von der zur Strandseite ausgerichteten Terrasse und vom Wohnzimmer aus haben Carey und Andrew King – er stammt ursprünglich aus Neuseeland – und ihre drei Kinder einen unverbauten Blick auf die Sonnenuntergänge am Golf von Mexiko. Das Haus, erbaut auf einem Grundstück von 30 x 30 Metern, steht erhöht auf einem Betonsockel. »Diese Gegend wird gelegentlich von Hurricanes und heftigen Stürmen heimgesucht. Deshalb wurden die Fenster mit Stahl verstärkt«, erklärt die Architektin Carey McWhorter. Im Erdgeschoss liegen ein Kinderspielzimmer, ein Schlafzimmer und ein Arbeitszimmer. Das große Wohnzimmer, das vier Meter hoch ist, erhält Schatten von dem breiten Verandadach.

Grayton Beach, Emerald Coast, Florida 30°20'N 86°10'W   Carey and Andrew King

A 50s Residence by Morris Lapidus

Biscayne Bay, Florida

L'architecte nonagénaire, Morris Lapidus, est une des idoles de Miami. Devenu célèbre dans les années 50 pour ses plans du très chic hôtel Fontainebleau, il a également construit de remarquables résidences privées. L'une des plus importantes, restée intacte depuis sa construction en 1958, tourne le dos à la baie de Biscayne. Les propriétaires, des collectionneurs passionnés de meubles des années 50 à notre fin de siècle, sont devenus des amis de l'architecte. Ils aiment leurs pièces spacieuses et claires, leurs plafonds hauts de trois mètres cinquante, leurs sols en marbre, même leurs interrupteurs et poignées de portes, dessinés pour la maison. «On adore le mobilier italien des années 50, 60 et 70. Il est si libre, expérimental et humoristique», déclare le mari. «Aujourd'hui, nous vivons dans un monde tellement conservateur!». De nombreuses pièces de leur collection ont été achetées pour une bouchée de pain il y a une quinzaine d'années, avant que les années 60 ne redeviennent à la mode.

Nonagenarian Florida architect Morris Lapidus is an icon of Miami architecture. Famous for his glamorous design of the Fontainebleau Hotel, which first towered over Miami Beach in the 50s, he also built notable residences. Among the most significant is a house which turns its back onto Biscayne Bay. It has remained unremodeled since it was built in 1958. The owners, passionate collectors of mid-century and end-of-century furniture, have become close friends of Lapidus. They appreciate the light-filled, spacious rooms, the three-meter ceilings, the marble-tile floors, even the original light switches and door knobs. "We love Italian furniture from the 50s to the 70s. It was so free, so playful and experimental," said the husband. "The world today has become so conservative!" Many pieces were acquired for a song 15 years ago, before the 60s were back in vogue.

Der Architekt Morris Lapidus ist schon in seinen 90ern und lebt in Florida. Und er ist eine Ikone der Architektur von Miami. Berühmt wurde er mit dem glanzvollen Design des Fontainebleau Hotel, das Miami Beach seit den 50er Jahren überragt. Er baute jedoch auch bemerkenswerte Privathäuser. Zu den bedeutendsten unter ihnen zählt ein Haus, dessen rückwärtige Seite einen Blick auf Biscayne Bay bietet. Seit seiner Erbauung im Jahr 1958 ist es nicht verändert worden. Seine Besitzer sammeln mit Leidenschaft Möbel aus der Zeit von den 50er bis zu den 90er Jahren und wurden enge Freunde des Architekten, denn sie schätzen seine lichtdurchfluteten, großzügig angelegten Räume mit Deckenhöhen von drei Metern, die Marmorböden und die originalen Lichtschalter und Türklinken. »Wir lieben italienische Möbel der 60er bis 70er Jahre. Sie sind verspielt, experimentierfreudig und frei gestaltet. Heute ist die Welt doch so konservativ geworden«, konstatiert der Ehemann. Viele Möbelstücke wurden für wenig Geld vor 15 Jahren erworben, als die 60er Jahre noch nicht wieder in Mode waren.

Previous pages: A "Bubble chair", designed in 1968 by Eero Aarnio, hangs in the study. Beside it is the "Triennale" lamp (1954).
Above: a happy trio of "Pastille" chairs (1967/68), of moulded fiberglass, by Eero Aarnio around the pool terrace.
Right: The back of the house faces the glossy, protected waters of Biscayne Bay. None of the walls, floors, or ceilings have cracked in 40 years, even though the house is built on sand.
Facing page: Highlights of the collection include a "Memphis" sofa by Marco Zanini, and a ceramic totem by Ettore Sottsass.

Double page précédente: Une «chaise bulle» (1968) de Eero Aarnio, est suspendue dans le bureau. A ses côtés, la lampe «Triennale» (1954).
Ci-dessus: un joli trio de chaises «Pastille» (1967/68) moulées en fibre de verre, signées Eero Aarnio.
A droite: La façade de la maison qui donne sur les eaux brillantes et abritées de la baie de Biscayne. Bien qu'elle ait été construite sur du sable il y a une quarantaine d'années, les murs, les sols et les plafonds n'ont pas une fissure.
Page de droite: Parmi les plus belles pièces de la collection, un sofa «Memphis» de Marco Zanini et un totem en céramique de Sottsass.

Vorhergehende Doppelseite: Ein »Bubble Chair« (1968) von Eero Aarnio hängt im Arbeitszimmer, daneben die »Triennale«-Lampe (1954).
Oben: ein fröhliches Trio am Außenpool: drei »Pastille«-Sessel (1967/68) von Eero Aarnio aus geformtem Fiberglas.
Rechts: Die Rückfront des Hauses geht direkt auf die geschützten Gewässer von Biscayne Bay. Auch 40 Jahre nach seiner Erbauung weist das Haus keine Risse auf, obwohl es auf Sandboden errichtet wurde.
Rechte Seite: Zu den Highlights der Sammlung gehören ein »Memphis«-Sofa von Marco Zanini und ein aus Keramik geformtes Totem von Ettore Sottsass.

Biscayne Bay, Florida 25°30'N 80°25'W   A 50s Residence by Morris Lapidus

Facing page: In the red breakfast room, a quartet of colorful "543 Broadway" chairs (1993) by Gaetano Pesce surround a "Sansone" table (1980) by Pesce. The lamp is by Michele de Lucchi.
Above: The remarkable 5.80-meter-long custom-crafted storage system by Pesce, "Miami Sound", has secret compartments and a framework that mirrors the shape of the Miami peninsula.
Right: A lamp by Gaetano Pesce glows in the bedroom above a bed designed by Gio Ponti. The tall lamp, left, by Aldo Rossi, is one of a collection of 90 in the house.

Page de gauche: Dans la salle à manger rouge qui donne sur le jardin, un quartette coloré de chaises «543 Broadway» (1993) de Gaetano Pesce entoure une table «Sansone» (1980), de Pesce également. La lampe est signée Michele de Lucchi.
Ci-dessus: Le superbe meuble de rangement long de près de 5,80 mètres de long, «Miami Sound» de Pesce, possède des compartiments secrets et une silhouette qui rappelle celle de la péninsule de Floride.
A droite: Dans une chambre, une lampe de Gaetano Pesce illumine un lit dessiné par Gio Ponti. Le lampadaire d'Aldo Rossi, à gauche, est l'un des 90 disséminés dans toute la maison.

Linke Seite: Im roten Frühstückszimmer steht das bunte Stuhl-Quartett »543 Broadway« (1993) von Gaetano Pesce um einen »Sansone«-Tisch (1980), ebenfalls von Pesce. Die Lampe entwarf Michele de Lucchi.
Oben: Das außergewöhnliche Aufbewahrungssystem »Miami Sound« von Pesce ist eine 5,80 Meter lange Spezialanfertigung mit Geheimfächern und einem Rahmenwerk, das an die Form der Halbinsel Miami erinnern soll.
Rechts: Im Schlafzimmer hängt über einem Gio-Ponti-Bett eine Lampe von Gaetano Pesce. Links steht eine von 90 Lampen im Haus; diese wurde von Aldo Rossi entworfen.

Above: The owner said this is his most comfortable chair. It's the "Ribbon" chair, designed in 1965 by Pierre Paulin.
Right: The dining table and chairs, among the first pieces collected by the owners, are the "Gazelle" series from 1958 in heavy cast bronze by Dan Johnson, a California designer. The Scandinavian-designed 60s bent-plywood storage and display system, chock-a-block with spun aluminum pieces by American industrial designer Russel Wright, is one of the few unidentified pieces in the house.

Ci-dessus: D'après son propriétaire, ce fauteuil «Ruban» (1965) de Pierre Paulin, est le plus confortable.
A droite: La table et les chaises en bronze massif de la salle à manger, parmi les premières pièces achetées par les propriétaires, appartiennent à la série «Gazelle» (1958) du designer californien Dan Johnson. Le meuble de rangement et d'exposition en contreplaqué plié, meuble scandinave des années 60, plein d'objets en fils d'aluminium du designer industriel américain Russel Wright, est l'une des rares pièces de la collection dont on ignore le nom du créateur.

Oben: Dies sei sein bequemster Sessel, so der Hausherr. Es handelt sich um dem 1965 von Pierre Paulin entworfenen »Ribbon«-Sessel.
Rechts: Der Esstisch und die Stühle gehörten zu den ersten Sammlerstücken der Hausbesitzer. Sie stammen aus der Serie »Gazelle«, die der kalifornische Designer Dan Johnson 1958 in schwerem Bronzeguss arbeitete. Das Regalsystem aus gebogenem Sperrholz wurde in den 60er Jahren in Skandinavien gefertigt und gehört zu den wenigen Möbelstücken des Hauses, die nicht genau bestimmt werden können. Die Aluminiumobjekte im Regal stammen von dem amerikanischen Industriedesigner Russel Wright.

Biscayne Bay, Florida 25°30'N 80°25'W   A 50s Residence by Morris Lapidus

Marguerite and Tony Staude

Big Sur, California Coast

La côte lointaine de Big Sur au centre de la Californie est un parfait perchoir d'où contempler et vivre les humeurs et les mystères de la nature. Les maisons perchées sur des affleurements de granit ou perdues dans des prés parsemés de fleurs sauvages sont exposées à la colère aveugle de l'hiver, aux délires de couleurs du printemps, aux déferlements psychédéliques des lupins bleus de l'été et aux brumes errantes de l'automne. En décembre, les baleines grises passent en batifolant en route vers le sud et la mer de Cortez. En mars, elles repassent avec leur progéniture en route vers l'Alaska et saluent les habitants de Big Sur en projetant d'extravagantes gerbes d'écume. Des otaries de mer se bousculent et chahutent sur les rochers noirs fouettés par les vagues. En 1965, Tony et Marguerite Staude ont acheté 54 hectares de terrain dans le Canyon Anderson. En 1969, ils ont engagé George Brook-Kothlow, un architecte de Carmel, pour dessiner leur maison rustique. La porte d'entrée n'est qu'à deux mètres du bord de la falaise. Tony n'est pas encore revenu de sa chance.

The remote coast of Big Sur in Central California presents a perfect perch from which to view and experience the moods and mysteries of nature. Houses on granite outcrops and wildflower-strewn meadows are exposed to winter's wild wrath, spring's hallucinatory hillsides of wild flowers, summer's psychedelic blue lupin fields, and the drifting mists of autumn. In December, gray whales spout and frolic as they head south to the Sea of Cortez. In March, the whales return to Alaska with their youngsters, and greet Big Sur's residents with exuberant showers of spume. Playful sea otters bask in kelp jungles among wave-wracked black rocks. Tony and Marguerite Staude acquired 54 hectares in Anderson Canyon in 1965. In 1969, they engaged Carmel architect George Brook-Kothlow to design their rugged residence. The front door is just two meters from the cliff edge. Earth, sky, and sea inspire epiphanies. Tony Staude still marvels at his luck.

Big Sur an der entlegenen Küste Zentralkaliforniens ist der ideale Ort, um die Geheimnisse der Natur zu entdecken und ihre Stimmungen zu erleben. Auf Felsnasen aus Granit und Wiesen voller Wildblumen sind die Häuser hier dem wilden Zorn des Winters ausgesetzt, den halluzinatorischen Farben der Frühlingswiesen, dem psychedelischen Blau der sommerlichen Lupinenfelder und im Herbst den vom Meer herüberziehenden Nebelschwaden. Im Dezember vergnügen sich hier prustend und schnaubend die Grauwale auf ihrem Weg gen Süden in die Sea of Cortez. Im März kommen sie mit ihrem Nachwuchs wieder vorbei, nun auf dem Weg nach Alaska, und grüßen die Bewohner von Big Sur mit überschwänglich versprühter Gischt. Verspielte Seeotter aalen sich in Seetangwäldern zwischen schwarzen Steinen, die die Wellen angespült haben. Im Anderson Canyon erwarben Tony und Marguerite Staude 1965 ein 54 Hektar großes zerklüftetes Grundstück. 1969 beauftragten sie den Architekten George Brook-Kothlow aus Carmel mit dem Bau ihres Hauses. Die Eingangstür ist nur zwei Meter von der Klippe entfernt. Darüber kann sich Tony Staude noch heute freuen.

Old weathered, clear-heart redwood timbers which originally supported the turn-of-the-century Buck Creek Bridge over the coastal highway, shape the curved, pavilion-like exterior of the house. From his terrace, 27 meters above the restless waves, Tony Staude can see 50 kilometers of coastline on a clear day. In the living room, fanlike redwood columns are arranged concentrically in homage to the dynamic coastal geography. Timber posts, with original rusty bolts, paint and sawn edges intact, were knee-braced to increase the support of the curved, laminate ceiling.

Des poutres anciennes patinées par le temps et taillées dans du cœur de séquoia donnent sa forme arrondie à l'extérieur de la maison, qui rappelle un pavillon. Au début du siècle, elles soutenaient le pont de Buck Creek qui enjambait la route longeant le bord de mer. Par temps clair, Tony peut contempler 50 kilomètres de côte depuis sa terrasse, perchée 27 mètres au-dessus des eaux bouillonnantes. Dans le salon, un éventail de colonnes en séquoia disposées de manière concentrique rendent hommage à la géographie dynamique du littoral. Les poutres, qui ont conservé leurs boulons rouillés, leurs vestiges de peintures et leurs arêtes sciées, ont été profondément enfoncées dans le sol pour pouvoir soutenir le plafond incurvé.

Verwittertes Redwood-Holz, aus dem Inneren des Baums geschnitten, wurde für den Außenbereich des Hauses verwendet. Die Planken stammen von der Buck Creek Bridge, die um die Jahrhundertwende den Küstenhighway überspannte. 27 Meter über den rastlosen Wellen liegt die Terrasse des Hauses, von der Tony Staude an klaren Tagen 50 Kilometer weit die Küste überblicken kann. Fächerartig angeordnete Redwood-Pfeiler im Wohnzimmer sind eine Hommage an die von Dynamik geprägte Küstengeografie. Die Holzpfähle sind mit ihren verrosteten Nägeln, dem originalen Farbanstrich und dem sichtbaren Schnitt belassen; sie erhielten allerdings Kopfbänder.

Gian Franco Brignone

Costa Careyes, Mexico

Imaginez des kilomètres de sable blanc s'étirant à perte de vue, sur lesquels les motifs abstraits dessinés par les algues échouées sur la plage constituent la seule trace des allées et venues de marées langoureuses. Ici et là, une ombre ou un petit trou gratté dans le sable chaud laisse deviner la présence d'oiseaux, de crabes et de tortues, mais on n'y voit jamais la moindre empreinte de pied humain. Pour accéder aux villes côtières les plus proches, Manzanillo et Puerto Vallarta, il faut parcourir une heure ou deux en quatre-quatre sur une route accidentée. Gian Franco Brignone, un ancien banquier qui a fui Turin et Paris, a aperçu ce paradis d'un avion, en 1968. Emerveillé, il est revenu l'explorer à pied et à cheval, se frayant un chemin dans la forêt à coups de machette, jusqu'à rejoindre une baie sauvage en forme d'aile d'ange. Des pélicans l'y ont accueilli. Fervents écologistes, les Brignone ont fini par acheter plus de 3 000 hectares de terrain le long de la Costa Careyes (Côte de la tortue). La plupart de ces terres sont aujourd'hui une réserve naturelle farouchement gardée.

Imagine miles of white beaches stretching into the hazy distance, with only abstract traceries of seaweed recording the languid coming and going of the tides. Shadowy, wind-buffed scratches in the hot sand offer evidence of birds, crabs, and turtles but no human footprints. The nearest coastal towns, Manzanillo and Puerto Vallarta, are a bumpy hour or two away via four-wheel drive. This is the dramatic Mexican domain of Italian visionary, Gian Franco Brignone, a former banker who fled Turin and Paris. He first spied his land from a plane in 1968. Brignone, transfixed, then explored the remote territory on foot and horseback, chopping through the forest with a machete, finally reaching an untouched bay in the shape of an angel's wing. Pelicans watched his arrival. Avid ecologists, Brignone and his family finally owned more than 3 000 hectares around Costa Careyes (Turtle Coast). Most of the land has been turned into a fiercely guarded nature preserve, and the turtles and pelicans live undisturbed.

Weißer Strand, kilometerweit, bis er sich in dunstiger Ferne verliert, Flechtwerk aus Seetang, einziges Zeichen des trägen Kommen und Gehens der Gezeiten. Im Schatten liegende und vom Wind zerrupfte Spuren auf dem heißen Sand verweisen auf Vögel, Krebse und Schildkröten. Menschliche Fußspuren finden sich nicht. Die nächstgelegenen Küstenstädtchen Manzanillo und Puerto Vallarta sind ein oder zwei holprige Stunden im Wagen mit Allradantrieb entfernt. Hier liegt der mexikanische Besitz des italienischen Visionärs und Exbankers Gian Franco Brignone, der Turin und Paris hinter sich ließ. Er entdeckte diesen Ort 1968 aus der Luft. Geradezu besessen erkundete er das entlegene Gebiet zu Pferd und zu Fuß und bahnte sich mit einer Machete den Weg durch den undurchdringlichen Wald, um schließlich an eine unberührte Bucht in der Form eines Engelsflügels zu kommen. Pelikane waren Zeugen seiner Ankunft. Brignone und seine Familie sind engagierte Umweltschützer. Heute gehören ihnen entlang der Costa Careyes, der Schildkrötenküste, über 3 000 Hektar Land, das größtenteils ein streng bewachtes Naturschutzgebiet ist.

Previous pages: *Gian Franco Brignone surveys his coastal domain. The blue-washed tower-building embraces guest bedrooms, studies, cool terraces, and a poetic lookout, all with views over miles of empty coastline. The open, palapa-style living room has a Tahiti-inspired palm-thatched roof supported by vine-twined tree trunks felled in the nearby forest.*
Left and below: *Guests and family climb the tower stairs to arrive at this viewing terrace above the tops of palm trees.*

Double page précédente: *Gian Franco Brignone contemple son domaine côtier. La tour badigeonnée de bleu accueille des chambres d'amis, des bureaux, des terrasses ombragées et un point de vue poétique d'où l'on peut contempler des kilomètres de côtes désertes. Le salon ouvert, dans un style inspiré des «palapas» tahitiennes, a un toit de chaume soutenu par des troncs d'arbres ceints de lianes recueillis dans la forêt voisine.*
A gauche et ci-dessous: *Les invités et les membres de la famille gravissent les marches de la tour pour rejoindre cette terrasse qui domine la cime des palmiers.*

Vorhergehende Doppelseite: *Gian Franco Brignone betrachtet »seine« Küste. Im blau gestrichenen Turm befinden sich Gästezimmer, Arbeitszimmer, Kühlung spendende Terrassen und ein Ausguck. Der Blick reicht meilenweit entlang der menschenleeren Küste. Das tahitianisch inspirierte Palmendach, das »palapa«, über dem offenen Wohnzimmer wird von lianenumrankten Baumstämmen gestützt, die im nahe gelegenen Wald geschlagen wurden.*
Links und unten: *Gäste und Familienmitglieder erklimmen diesen Turm, um den Blick von der eigens dafür eingerichteten Terrasse über die Kronen der Palmen zu genießen.*

Dazzled visitors to Tigre del Mar may spend hours watching the play of light as shadows stripe the concrete terrace floor or strobe a cushioned viewing platform. The effect of the heat on mind and body in this region cannot be overstated. At its most intense, the summer humidity causes a pleasant lethargy that keeps friends and family anchored to acres of convivial cotton-upholstered sofas. Ceiling fans freshen the air, and it is wise to remain in the shade until late afternoon. August rains, which can be torrential, are a welcome respite. Winters are mild, and ideal for swimming, hiking, and kayaking.

Les visiteurs émerveillés de Tigre del Mar passent des heures à observer l'ombre et la lumière zébrer le sol en ciment de la terrasse ou clignoter sur les coussins de la plate-forme panoramique. En plein été, l'humidité induit une plaisante torpeur qui cloue les amis et la famille sur des hectares de sofas tapissés de cotonnades. Les ventilateurs de plafond rafraîchissent l'air et il est plus prudent de rester à l'ombre jusqu'à la fin de l'après-midi. Les pluies d'août, souvent torrentielles, offrent un répit bienvenu. Les hivers sont doux, parfaits pour nager, faire des promenades ou du kayak.

Die Gäste in Tigre del Mar können Stunden damit zubringen, das Spiel des Lichts zu bewundern, das Schattenstreifen auf die Betonfußböden der Terrasse wirft oder über einen mit Kissen ausgestatteten Aussichtspunkt blitzt. In ihrer intensivsten Form bringt die Feuchtigkeit des Sommers eine angenehme Lethargie mit sich, die Freunde und Familienmitglieder auf riesigen, baumwollbezogenen Sitzlandschaften niedersinken lässt. Deckenventilatoren kühlen die Luft. Es empfiehlt sich, bis zum späten Nachmittag im Schatten zu bleiben. Da sind die oft sintflutartigen Regengüsse im August eine willkommene Verschnaufpause. Die Winter sind mild und ideal zum Schwimmen, Wandern und Kajakfahren.

Brignone is fond of dramatic and sometimes mysterious effects with hallucinogenic color, boldly sculptural walls, and an archetypal building vocabulary. Color in Tigre del Mar is as luxuriant as tropical flowers, and often seems to vibrate in the midday sun. Orange, indigo, white, chrome yellow and prettiest pink are layered with joy and abandon onto stucco walls, a lookout terrace, and stairs. Brignone, celebrating 30 years in Mexico, has full knowledge that hot sun unfiltered by air pollution will play games with the plastered walls and festive hues, refracting, muting and magnifying the colors.

Brignone a un faible pour les effets spectaculaires et parfois mystérieux des couleurs hallucinogènes, des murs sculpturaux aux lignes audacieuses et des archétypes de motifs d'architecture. A Tigre del Mar, les couleurs sont aussi luxuriantes que les fleurs tropicales et vibrent dans la lumière aveuglante. L'orange, l'indigo, le blanc, le chrome, le jaune et un rose ravissant revêtent avec une joie non dissimulée des murs stuqués, une terrasse panoramique et une cage d'escalier. Brignone, qui fête ses trente ans de Mexique, sait mieux que quiconque comment un soleil qu'aucune pollution ne vient filtrer joue sur les murs enduits au plâtre et les tons gais, réfractant, atténuant ou magnifiant les couleurs.

Brignone liebt die dramatischen, manchmal geheimnisvollen Effekte der halluzinogenen Farbflächen, kühnen skulpturartigen Wänden und archetypischen Baumustern. Die Farben in Tigre del Mar sind so üppig wie die tropischer Blüten. Orange, Indigo, Weiß, Parisergelb und die schönsten Pinktöne liegen auf- und übereinander auf gemörtelten Wänden, einer Ausguckterrasse und Treppen und strahlen Freude und Überschwang aus. Brignone, der schon seit 30 Jahren in Mexiko lebt, weiß, wie die heiße Sonne, die hier nicht durch Luftverschmutzung abgeschwächt ist, mit dem Wandputz und den festlichen Farben spielt und Töne bricht, abschwächt oder intensiviert.

A Rainforest Compound

Nevis, Lesser Antilles, Caribbean Sea

Lorsqu'Antonio Morello et Donato Savoie, deux architectes basés à New York, furent engagés par de fidèles clients pour concevoir un ensemble de trois maisons de vacances sur l'île de Nevis, ils décidèrent d'adopter une démarche innovatrice et audacieuse. Le Studio MORSA, leur bureau d'architecture créé il y a 25 ans, est connu pour son travail minutieusement contrôlé et plutôt intellectuel mais, pour ces refuges caraïbes, le duo de talent choisit une approche radicalement différente. «Notre briefing a été très bref», plaisante Savoie. «Nous ne voulions pas de vitre dans notre projet, de sorte que l'intérieur et l'extérieur s'interconnectent». Alors que la plupart des maisons de l'île sont au bord de la plage, celles-ci se dressent au milieu d'une forêt luxuriante à 365 mètres d'altitude. Elles résonnent des cris aigus des singes et baignent dans le parfum des orchidées sauvages et des palmiers qui filtre par les fenêtres.

When New York-based architects Antonio Morello and Donato Savoie were engaged by long-time clients to design a compound of three holiday houses on the island of Nevis, they decided to take a daring and creative approach to the design. Their 25-year-old New York architectural firm, Studio MORSA, is known for carefully controlled and quite intellectual work, but for these Caribbean hideaways a dramatically different tack appealed to the talented duo. "Our brief was very brief," quipped Savoie. "There would be no glass in the project, so that there would be an interlocking of interior and exterior," he said. The houses stand at an altitude of 365 meters. While most island houses are on the beach, these would be in the midst of a luscious rainforest, shrill with the calls of wild monkeys, and drenched with the fragrance of the wild orchids and palms which spill through the windows.

Als die New Yorker Architekten Antonio Morello und Donato Savoie von langjährigen Klienten damit beauftragt wurden, auf der Karibikinsel Nevis drei Ferienhäuser zu errichten, ließen sie sich auf das Wagnis ein, diese Aufgabe auf neue und kreative Weise zu lösen. Ihre seit einem Vierteljahrhundert bestehende New Yorker Architekturfirma Studio MORSA ist bekannt für ihren äußerst kontrollierten Stil und eine fast intellektuell zu nennende Herangehensweise. Doch für diese lauschigen kleinen Zufluchtsorte in der Karibik wollte das begabte Duo einen ganz anderen Weg einschlagen. »Es gab nur eine Anweisung«, erinnert sich Savoie, »kein Glas und damit keine klare Trennung von innen und außen.« Meist werden Inselhäuser am Strand gebaut – diese hingegen wurden auf 365 Meter Höhe mitten im üppigen Regenwald errichtet, der von den Schreien wild lebender Affen widerhallt, den der schwere Duft wilder Orchideen durchzieht und in dem Palmen ihre Wedel ins Fenster strecken.

Previous pages: *The three houses in the Nevis compound were colored red, yellow, and blue and look as colorful as the wild parrots that flock and squawk in the surrounding rainforest. Studio MORSA's dramatic Yellow House was inspired by the simple geometries of Nevis' vernacular style. "They are vivid but they blend in well with traditional houses and the ruins of sugar plantations on the island," said Savoie.*
Above and left: *"You don't spend much time inside," observed Savoie, who designed the interiors simply so that they could serve many holiday purposes with ease.*

Double page précédente: *Les trois maisons ont été peintes en rouge, jaune et bleu, dans des tons aussi vifs que ceux des perroquets qui volettent et crient dans la jungle environnante. La théâtrale Maison Jaune du Studio MORSA s'inspire de la géométrie simple de l'architecture de Nevis. «Nos maisons sont voyantes mais elles se fondent bien avec les maisons traditionnelles et les ruines des anciennes plantations de canne à sucre de l'île», déclare Savoie.*
Ci-dessus et à gauche: *«On ne passe pas beaucoup de temps à l'intérieur», observe Savoie qui a conçu les intérieurs simplement afin qu'ils s'adaptent facilement à toutes sortes de vacances.*

Vorhergehende Doppelseite: *Die drei Häuser der Siedlung auf Nevis wurden in Rot, Gelb und Blau gestrichen und sehen genauso farbenprächtig aus wie die wilden Papageien, die sich unter aufgeregtem Gekreische in Schwärmen im Regenwald ringsumher versammeln. Das dramatische Gelbe Haus von Studio MORSA wurde von der einfachen Geometrie der regionalen Bauweise von Nevis inspiriert. »Trotz ihrer Leuchtkraft passen sie sich den Häusern und den alten Ruinen auf den Zuckerplantagen der Insel an«, sagt Savoie.*
Oben und links: *Savoie hielt das Innere bewusst einfach, damit es für die unterschiedlichsten Urlaubszwecke adaptiert werden kann.*

Nevis, Lesser Antilles, Caribbean Sea 17°10'N 62°34'W   A Rainforest Compound

Furniture, shutters, doors and other woodwork in the three houses were all crafted using Brazilian tropical hardwoods, which are denser than mahogany. The houses, which range in size from 150 to 340 square meters, are all surrounded by outdoor terraces which open to the sea and the rainforest, and by covered open loggias. Roofs are painted red, a tropical sign of welcome.

Les meubles, les volets et les autres boiseries des trois maisons sont tous en bois tropicaux durs venant du Brésil, plus denses que l'acajou. Les maisons, qui font entre 150 et 340 mètres carrés, sont toutes ceintes de loggias couvertes et de terrasses qui donnent sur la mer et la forêt pluviale. Les toits sont peints en rouge, un signe de bienvenue sous les tropiques.

Für Möbel, Rollläden, Türen und andere Holzarbeiten wurde in allen drei Häusern brasilianisches Hartholz aus dem tropischen Regenwald verwendet, das eine höhere Härte aufweist als Mahagoni. Die Häuser mit einer Wohnfläche von knapp 150 bis 340 Quadratmetern sind von überdachten Loggien und von Terrassen umgeben, die sich zum Meer und zum Regenwald öffnen. Die Dächer sind in Rot gehalten – in den Tropen ein Willkommenssignal.

Previous pages: *Perhaps the most striking part of Studio MORSA's design is the infinity pool ... which has a dramatic cubist wall of blue stucco.*
Right and below: *The teaming jungle is ever-present in the Blue House, both with its damp and verdant foliage, just outside, and in the vivid green colors on the kitchen walls. The living room is furnished with an Indonesian teak bench, scattered with cushions covered with hand-woven folkloric Guatemalan fabrics.*

Double page précédente: *Un des aspects les plus remarquables du projet du Studio MORSA est sans doute la piscine qui semble s'étirer à l'infini, avec son pan de mur en stuc bleu qui ajoute une note cubiste.*
A droite et ci-dessous: *Dans la Maison Bleue, la jungle grouillante est omniprésente, tant par son feuillage luisant et luxuriant que l'on aperçoit au dehors que par ses verts intenses que l'on retrouve sur les murs de la cuisine. Dans le salon, le banc en teck indonésien est couvert de coussins en étoffes guatémaltèques tissées à la main.*

Vorhergehende Doppelseite: *Das auffälligste Designelement von Studio MORSA ist sicherlich der »Infinity Pool«, der sich bis in die Unendlichkeit zu erstrecken scheint. Die dramatische, kubistisch wirkende Wand ist mit blau gestrichenem Mörtel verputzt.*
Rechts und unten: *Die pralle Lebenswelt des Regenwalds ist überall im Blauen Haus zu spüren – das grüne Blattwerk der Pflanzen wiederholt sich in den leuchtend grünen Farben der Küche. Das Wohnzimmer ist mit einer Bank aus indonesischem Teakholz eingerichtet; die Kissen sind mit handgewebten Stoffen aus Guatemala bezogen.*

The walls of the Red House bedroom are uncompromising, fearless jungle green, in homage to the palms and philodendrons which seem to be clamoring to come inside and join the holiday fun. During daily downpours, the outer shutters may be drawn to keep out some of the rain, but concrete floors can take a drenching and rooms quickly dry out in the typical 28°C heat. Nevis, with some 10 000 inhabitants, was traditionally a sugar plantation island. The architects took the block shapes of the houses from the remnants of many of the original old buildings.

Les murs de la chambre de la Maison Rouge sont peints d'un intrépide vert jungle en hommage aux palmiers et aux philodendrons qui se pressent aux fenêtres comme pour goûter eux aussi aux loisirs des vacanciers. On peut se protéger des déluges quotidiens en fermant les volets extérieurs mais les sols en béton ne craignent pas la pluie et les pièces sèchent rapidement dans la chaleur ambiante qui ne décolle pas des 28°C. Nevis, qui compte quelque 10 000 habitants, se consacrait autrefois à la culture de la canne à sucre. Pour concevoir la forme des maisons, les architectes se sont inspirés des ruines pittoresques de nombreuses vieilles plantations.

Im Roten Haus sind die Wände des Schlafzimmers in einem kompromisslosen Dschungelgrün gestrichen – als Hommage an die Palmen und Philodendren, die sich am Ferienspaß beteiligen möchten. Die Fensterläden gewähren während der täglichen Regengüsse einen gewissen Schutz. Den Betonböden kann das Wasser aber nicht viel anhaben und auch die Innenräume trocknen bei tropischen Durchschnittstemperaturen von 28 °C schnell. Auf Nevis, wo früher im großen Stil Zuckerrohr angebaut wurde, leben heute ungefähr 10 000 Menschen. Die Blockformen der pittoresken Überreste vieler ursprünglichen Gebäude inspirierten die Architekten zu ihrem Entwurf.

Facing page: The bedroom verandah of the Blue House has been furnished with an all-purpose daybed so that it may be used day and
night as tropical heat demands. All the woodwork in the house was
custom-crafted from Brazilian ipe wood, which is naturally resistant
to insects, dry rot, and other rainforest dangers. The wood was given a
simple finish of varnish.
Above: The bathroom and shower in the Blue House – and in the
others of this compound – were a simple matter: floors throughout
are polished concrete, and the walls are bold and raw concrete.

Page de gauche: La chambre véranda de la Maison Bleue est meublée d'un lit de repos polyvalent afin de servir de jour comme de nuit
selon les exigences de la chaleur tropicale. Toutes les boiseries de la
maison ont été fabriquées sur mesure dans de l'ipéca brésilien, qui ré-
siste naturellement aux insectes, à la pourriture sèche et autres aléas
de la jungle. Le bois a été simplement verni.
Ci-dessus: La salle de bains et la douche de la Maison Bleue, comme
des autres maisons de l'ensemble, est d'une simplicité audacieuse et
agréable: tous les sols sont en béton poli et les murs en béton brut.

Linke Seite: Die Schlafzimmerveranda des Blauen Hauses wurde mit
einem vielseitig verwendbaren Tagesbett ausgestattet, das – je nach
Hitzegrad – tagsüber oder nachts verwendet werden kann. Alle Holzarbeiten wurden aus brasilianischem Ipecacuanha-Holz handgefer-
tigt, das einen natürlichen Schutz gegen Insekten, Holzfäule und andere Gefahren des Regenwalds besitzt. Das Holz wurde nur mit
einem einfachen Finish-Lack versiegelt.
Oben: Bad und Dusche des Blauen Hauses wurden wie auch bei den
anderen Häusern einfach gehalten: Die Böden sind alle aus poliertem
Beton, die Wände aus Rohbeton – eine kühne, aber gelungene Idee.

Frank Visser

Curaçao, Netherlands Antilles, Caribbean Sea

Flottant sur la mer des Caraïbes au large des côtes du Venezuela et de la Colombie, les îles Sous-le-Vent, Aruba, Bonaire et Curaçao, territoire autonome néerlandais, sont parmi les plus éloignées et les plus peuplées de la région. On y parle le «papiamento», mélange cadencé d'espagnol et de portugais, saupoudré d'expressions hollandaises, africaines et anglaises. Curaçao est particulièrement cosmopolite, avec son vieux port hollandais de carte postale, Willemstad, et ses lointaines raffineries de pétrole high-tech brillamment illuminées. C'est à Curaçao que le styliste hollandais Frank Visser, après y avoir passé une enfance idyllique, a choisi de retourner. «J'y aime le style de vie décontracté, la musique, la danse et surtout les gens», dit Visser, qui passe une grande partie de l'année à voyager pour des magazines et des agences de publicité. Il est tombé sur une vieille maison de domestiques qu'il s'est empressé de louer.

Floating in the Caribbean Sea off the coast of Venezuela and Colombia like three happy goldfish, the "ABC islands" of Aruba, Bonaire and Curaçao are among the most remote and affluent in the region. There, in the Lesser Antilles, an autonomous Dutch territory, the people speak "Papiamento", a lilting mixture of Spanish and Portuguese with expressive Dutch, African and English elements. Curaçao is especially cosmopolitan, with the picture-perfect old Dutch port of Willemstad, and distant, brightly lit high-tech oil refineries. It was on Curaçao that Dutch stylist Frank Visser spent an idyllic childhood, later returning. "I like the relaxed life, the music, the dancing, and certainly the people," noted Visser, who travels much of the year working for magazines and advertising agencies. On Curaçao he found a former servants' house, which he promptly rented.

Wie drei glückliche Goldfische lassen sich die »ABC-Inseln« Aruba, Bonaire und Curaçao vor der Küste Venezuelas und Kolumbiens im Meer der Karibik treiben. Sie gehören zu den entlegendsten und gleichzeitig wohlhabendsten Inseln der Region. Hier, auf den Inseln unter dem Wind, die zu den Niederlanden gehören, sprechen die Einwohner »Papiamento«, einen Singsang aus Spanisch und Portugiesisch mit unüberhörbaren niederländischen, afrikanischen und englischen Sprachelementen. Curaçao selbst wirkt kosmopolitisch mit seinem alten, holländisch anmutenden Bilderbuchhafen Willemstad und den grell beleuchteten Ölraffinerien unserer Zeit. Hier verbrachte der niederländische Stylist Frank Visser eine idyllische Kindheit und hierher kehrte er später zurück. »Ich liebe dieses entspannte Leben, die Musik, den Tanz und natürlich die Menschen«, sagt Visser, der allerdings die meiste Zeit des Jahres für Zeitschriften und Werbeagenturen unterwegs ist. Als er dieses ehemalige Dienstbotenhaus entdeckte, mietete er es auf der Stelle.

First pages: *To create an outdoor dining room, Visser first cleared the overgrown garden of his "Landhuis Siberië". For shade, he hung a tent-like "roof" of lightweight cotton among the branches of indigenous trees.*
Previous page: *Visser, who is also a painter, created the amulet-like wall decorations by pressing objects into wedges of painted foam board and adding thin layers of silver dust.*
Right and below: *Visser painted the plaster walls in muted tones of grey and silver. "The light is dazzlingly bright on the island, so I wanted to cool things down," noted Visser who acquired his antiques on the island.*

Première double page: *Pour créer une salle à manger en plein air, Visser a commencé par défricher le jardin de sa maison «Landhuis Siberië». Une grande tenture légère fait office de toit.*
Page précédente: *Visser, qui est également peintre, a créé ce mur d'amulettes en incrustant des objets dans des plaques de mousse qu'il a ensuite recouvertes de fines couches de poudre d'argent.*
A droite et ci-dessous: *Visser a peint les murs en plâtre avec des tons sourds gris et argent. «Sur l'île, la lumière est aveuglante, j'ai donc cherché à créer de la fraîcheur», explique-t-il. Visser a acheté ses antiquités sur l'île.*

Eingangsseiten: *Für sein Esszimmer unter freiem Himmel rodete Visser als Erstes den überwucherten Garten seines »Landhuis Siberië«. Als Schattenspender hing er dann an den Ästen der Bäume ein zeltähnliches »Dach« aus leichter Baumwolle auf.*
Vorhergehende Seite: *Visser ist auch Maler. Die amulettartigen Wanddekorationen fertigte er aus Objekten, die er in eingefärbten Schaumstoff drückte und dann hauchdünn mit Silberstaub überzog.*
Rechts und unten: *Die gipsverputzten Wände strich Visser in zurückhaltenden Grau- und Silbertönen. »Das helle Licht auf den Inseln kann einen schier blenden«, erklärt er, »deshalb wollte ich es im Haus etwas dämpfen.« Visser erwarb seine Antiquitäten auf Curaçao.*

Life is lived on the beach and outdoors under the trees. But often the heat on Curaçao is so intense that residents must slow their pace, escape the white-hot daylight, and find refuge indoors. In his cool, calm retreat, Visser paints, reads, and cooks with just the simplest ingredients. "All you need here is a stove, a bed, a fridge, one table and a chair," commented Visser. Hand-dyed muslin banners create the illusion of room separation, in what is basically a one-room hacienda. In the alcove-of-a-kitchen, Visser hordes his few tools on a steel counter, a wooden workbench, and an improvised wall hanger.

A Curaçao, on vit sur la plage ou sous les arbres mais la chaleur devient souvent si intense que les habitants doivent se réfugier à l'intérieur. Dans sa retraite calme et fraîche, Visser peint, lit, cuisine le plus simplement possible. «On n'a besoin que d'un réchaud, d'un lit, d'un frigo, d'une table et d'une chaise», commente-t-il. Des voiles de mousseline teints à la main créent l'illusion de cloisons dans ce qui est en fait une hacienda d'une seule pièce. Dans sa cuisine alcôve, Visser entasse ses quelques outils et ustensiles sur un comptoir en acier, un établi en bois et un accroche-vaisselle improvisé.

Hier verbringt man sein Leben am Strand und im Freien unter den Bäumen. Doch oft ist es auf Curaçao so heiß, dass man vor dem gleißend hellen Tageslicht in den Häusern Schutz suchen muss. An seinem kühlen, ruhigen Zufluchtsort verbringt Visser die Zeit mit Malen und Lesen und kocht mit einfachsten Zutaten. »Alles was man hier braucht, sind ein Herd, ein Bett, ein Kühlschrank, ein Tisch und ein Stuhl«, sagt er. Handgefärbte Musselinstoffe dienen als Raumteiler in dem einzigen Raum der Hacienda. In der Küche – eigentlich ein Alkoven – bewahrt Visser seine wenigen Utensilien und Küchengeräte auf einer Abstellfläche aus Stahl, einer hölzernen Arbeitsplatte und in einem improvisierten Hängeregal auf.

Pia and Andrès Ferreyra

Cabo Polonio, Uruguay

Cabo Polonio, sur la côte plane au nord-est de Montevideo, abrite les plages les plus jolies et les plus isolées d'Uruguay. Bien que ses lagons et ses forêts soient d'une beauté spectaculaire, ce petit coin de paradis presque à cheval sur la frontière brésilienne est trop éloigné de la capitale pour y venir passer le week-end. Protégé par un vaste parc national, il est également hors de portée des diktats du style et des boutiques chics. Les quelques habitations impromptues qu'on y trouve conviennent plutôt aux débrouillards plus résistants et aux âmes créatives qui se nourrissent des bruits solitaires de l'océan et du paysage monochrome. Un bel ensemble de vieilles maisons de pêcheurs s'est peu à peu enrichi d'un assortiment de cottages et de bungalows à la charmante esthétique «baba cool». C'est ici que Pia et Andrès Ferreyra ont construit leur maison d'été, avec esprit, imagination et ingéniosité.

Cabo Polonio, on the flat coastline north-east of Montevideo, is one of Uruguay's loveliest and loneliest stretches of beach. It's too far for an easy weekend sojourn from the capital. Although the nearby lagoons and forest are dramatically beautiful, few find their way here. Protected by a large national park, the area stands almost at the Brazilian border and is proudly independent of style-setters and chic boutiques. Rather, the cluster of impromptu dwellings here is for hardier, self-sufficient and creative souls, who feed on the solitary sounds of the sea, and the monochromatic landscape. An appealing mix of authentic fishermen's dwellings is now joined by an assortment of cottages and cabins with a charming post-hippie aesthetic. Here, Pia and Andrès Ferreyra's summer house was built, using wit and imagination and ingenuity.

Cabo Polonio, am flachen Küstenstreifen nordöstlich von Montevideo gelegen, gehört zu den schönsten und einsamsten Stränden von Uruguay. Für Wochenendausflüge liegt es zu weit von der Hauptstadt entfernt und obwohl die nahe gelegenen Lagunen und Wälder von dramatischer Schönheit sind, finden doch nur wenige den Weg hierher. Durch einen großen Nationalpark geschützt, liegt dieses Gebiet kurz vor der Grenze zu Brasilien. Hier gibt es weder elegante Boutiquen noch Trendsetter. Wer hier lebt, ist abgehärtet, autark und kreativ, schätzt die Einsamkeit, das Rauschen des Meeres und die monochrome Landschaft. Gerade wurde hier eine faszinierende Mischung von authentischen Fischerhütten mit Cottages und Hütten in liebenswerter Späthippie-Ästhetik zu einem neuen Ganzen gefügt. Und hier wurde auch das Sommerhaus von Pia und Andrès Ferreyra errichtet – mit Humor, Fantasie und Einfallsreichtum.

First pages: The image is a domestic scene on the coast of Uruguay, but its archetypal simplicity and gravity give it the universality of a dream. Who would not wish to escape civilization for this undeveloped patch of land, within a few steps of an endless beach?
Right and below: An old door was knocked together using driftwood battens, and the result is as interesting as any hand-carved portal. The simple three-burner kitchen has all the charm of a seagoing vessel. Vegetables and fruits, and cooking essentials like flour and sugar and salt, are strung and balanced on a series of driftwood logs to keep voracious insects and other predators at bay.

Première double page: Dans sa simplicité et sa solennité, cette scène domestique sur la côte uruguayenne revêt l'universalité d'un songe. Qui n'aimerait pas abandonner la civilisation pour ce petit coin sauvage, à quelques pas d'une plage sans fin?
A droite et ci-dessous: La porte a été assemblée avec des lattes rejetées par la mer, prenant l'aspect d'un vieux portail sculpté. La cuisine, avec son réchaud à trois brûleurs, a tout le charme d'une cambuse. Les fruits et les légumes, ainsi que les produits de base comme la farine, le sucre et le sel, sont suspendus sur des morceaux de bois ramassés sur la plage pour les protéger des insectes voraces et autres prédateurs.

Eingangsseiten: Diese Szene an der Küste Uruguays besitzt die archetypische Einfachheit und universelle Bedeutung eines Traums. Wer wünschte sich nicht, der Zivilisation zu entfliehen und nur wenige Schritte vom Meer entfernt auf unerschlossenem Boden zu leben?
Rechts und unten: Aus Treibholzlatten wurde eine Tür improvisiert, die sich mit jedem handgeschnitzten Portal messen kann. Die schlichte Küche mit drei Gasflammen besitzt den Charme eines seetauglichen Boots. Gemüse, Obst und Grundnahrungsmittel wie Mehl, Zucker und Salz balancieren auf einer Reihe von Treibholzstücken – außerhalb der Reichweite von hungrigen Insekten und anderen Jägern!

Above: With the hand-crafted bricks and mortar in place, Ferreyra and his helpers whitewashed the walls to create a calming canvas for the few selections of furniture. Curvy old rattan chairs, themselves pleasingly sun-faded, syncopate with a quiet rhythm around the tree-trunk table. The playful chandelier was improvised from an old cork floater from a fisherman's net, pierced with blue-painted wires and candle-holders.
Right: A sculpture of an old toy boat hangs on the wall above a shuttered window.

Ci-dessus: Une fois les briques façonnées à la main et le mortier en place, Ferreyra et ses aides ont blanchi les murs à la chaux, créant une apaisante toile de fond pour ses quelques meubles choisis. De vieilles chaises en rotin tout en courbes, délicieusement fonées au soleil, forment une ronde tranquille autour d'une table en tronc d'arbre. L'amusant lustre été fabriqué à partir d'une bouée en liège prise dans un filet de pêcheur, percée de fil de fer et de porte-bougies peints en bleu.
A droite: Une vieille maquette de bateau est suspendue au-dessus d'une fenêtre à volets.

Oben: Als Mörtel und handgearbeitete Backsteine verarbeitet waren, machte sich Ferreyra mit seinen Helfern an den Kalkanstrich der Wände, um für die wenigen auserwählten Möbel einen beruhigenden Hintergrund zu schaffen. Schön sonnengebleichte, geschwungene Rattanstühle ordnen sich rhythmisch um den Tisch, der aus einem Baumstumpf besteht. Der verspielte Kronleuchter wurde aus dem Korkschwimmer eines alten Fischernetzes sowie blau gestrichenen Drähten und Kerzenhaltern improvisiert.
Rechts: Ein altes Spielzeugboot hängt als Skulptur über einem Fensterladen.

Casa del Cabo, a collage of driftwood and weathered timbers, has the look of a dwelling which was itself washed up on the shore. It was built from bricks made locally from sand and sea shells. Flotsam and jetsam became the Ferreyra's furniture. Each offering from the sea – a Japanese sake barrel, a mast, an old craft – is adapted for their use. The three-meter-long canoe, plump with down cushions covered in natural cotton, becomes a bed.

Casa del Cabo, un collage de planches échouées sur la plage et de poutres rongées par le sel, semble elle-même avoir été rejetée par la mer. Elle a été construite en briques fabriquées dans la région avec du sable et des coquillages, puis meublée avec des épaves. Chaque offrande de la mer, un tonneau de saké japonais, un mât, une vieille barque, a été recyclée. Le canoë, long de trois mètres et confortablement tapissé de coussins en plumes, est devenu un lit.

Casa del Cabo, eine Collage aus Treibgut und wettergegerbtem Holz, wirkt, als sei es als Ganzes an Land geschwemmt worden. Errichtet wurde das Haus aus Backsteinen, die lokal aus Sand und Muschelkalk gefertigt wurden. Strandgut jeder Art übernahm die Rolle der Inneneinrichtung. Jedem Geschenk des Meeres – ein japanisches Sakefass, ein Mast, altes Kunsthandwerk – wird ein neuer Nutzen zugedacht. So wird aus einem drei Meter langen, mit weichen Kissen ausgepolsterten Kanu ein Bett.

Alan Faena

Punta del Este,
Uruguayan Riviera

Mais où courent donc tous les adorateurs du soleil habitant à Montevideo, Buenos Aires, ou même São Paulo, de novembre à février pour
leur dose d'U.V. et d'eau de mer? A Punta del Este, naturellement!
La station balnéaire chic de l'Uruguay, où soleil, sable, baies paisibles,
boîtes de nuit tonitruantes et même de petits coins tranquilles où
s'isoler cohabitent sur une même péninsule superbe. Au sud s'étend
l'Argentine, à l'est, le bleu de la mer s'étire à l'infini. Les noctambules
viennent y chercher les casinos, les gratte-ciel et les restaurants bran-
chés. Les adeptes de la nature et les surfeurs n'ont qu'à parcourir
quelques kilomètres pour laisser derrière eux les amourettes de plage.
Les aventuriers se régalent dans les montagnes en dents de scie, sur
les plages qui s'étalent sur des kilomètres et dans les rouleaux déchaî-
nés. A Punta del Este, que les habitués appellent simplement
«Punta», l'Argentin Alan Faena, décorateur d'hôtels et architecte
d'intérieur, s'est construit une maison d'été bleue et blanche, un
joyeux hommage à la joie de vivre et au plaisir de collectionner.

Just exactly where do sun-worshipping residents of Montevideo
and Buenos Aires – even Brazil's São Paulo – head from November to February for their salt water and sunshine refreshment? It's
Uruguay's fashionable Punta del Este, an ultra-violet ray of a
place, where sun and sand, placid bays and screaming discos,
and perhaps a place to be alone, all co-exist on one glorious
peninsula. To the south lies Argentina, and to the east the sea disappears into hazy blue infinity. Fun-seekers at Punta del Este are
attracted to the casinos, high-rises and happening restaurants,
while nature-worshippers and devoted surfers need travel only a
few miles to leave the beach flirtations behind. Adventurers find
blade-shaped mountains, miles of open Atlantic Ocean beaches,
and wild waves. In Punta del Este – habitués call it Punta – Argentinian hotel fashion and interior designer, Alan Faena, designed
himself a blue and white summer house, a happy tribute to the
joys of living and the pleasures of collecting.

Wo zieht es die sonnenhungrigen Einwohner von Montevideo, Buenos
Aires und sogar São Paulo zwischen November und Februar hin,
wenn sie Erfrischung in Salzwasser und Sonne suchen? Nach Punte
del Este, Uruguays angesagtem Badeort. Die wunderschöne Halbinsel, fast eher ein Sonnenstrahl aus ultraviolettem Licht, vereint Sonne
und Sand, friedliche Buchten und dröhnende Discos und trotzdem
kann man hier auch Ruhe und Einsamkeit finden. Südlich der Halbinsel liegt Argentinien, im Osten verliert sich das Meer in dunstig-
blauer Unendlichkeit. Wer Unterhaltung sucht, findet sie in Punta del
Este in den Casinos, den Wolkenkratzern, den In-Restaurants. Natur-
liebhaber und sportbesessene Wellenreiter müssen nur wenige Kilometer weit fahren, um den Flirts der belebten Strände zu entkommen.
Dann liegen scharfkantige Berge, kilometerlange offene Atlantik-
strände und wild hereinbrechende Wellen vor ihnen. In Punta del
Este – von Eingeweihten Punta genannt – hat der argentinische
Hoteldesigner und Innenarchitekt Alan Faena ein blau-weißes Sommerhaus für sich entworfen, eine fröhliche Hommage an Lebenslust
und Sammelfreuden.

Every weekend, Alan Faena, pictured opposite, makes the half-hour flight from Buenos Aires to Punta del Este in Uruguay. The magnet: his blue and white beach house with its fluttering draperies, broad verandahs, and fields of carefully cultivated cosmos. Faena then drives 20 kilometers north to José Ignacio, and heads for his own remote stretch of seaside, which he dubbed Tierra Santa. Faena's company, Cosmic Carrot, develops boutique hotels with French designer, Philippe Starck. From the verandahs, Faena gazes on nothing but white sand, wild ocean, fields of agapanthus and perhaps a figure or two in the misty distance.

Chaque week-end, Alan Faena, ci-contre, prend le vol Buenos Aires – Punta del Este, pressé de retrouver sa maison de plage, avec ses voilages volant au vent, ses larges vérandas et ses champs de cosmos soigneusement cultivés. Après une demi-heure d'avion, Faena parcourt vingt kilomètres en voiture vers le nord jusqu'à José Ignacio avant de rejoindre son propre lopin de côte isolée, qu'il a baptisé sa «terre sainte». Sa société, Cosmic Carrot, crée des boutiques d'hôtels avec le designer français, Philippe Starck. De ses vérandas, Faena ne voit que du sable blanc, l'océan et, parfois, une silhouette ou deux au loin.

Jedes Wochenende begibt sich Alan Faena (links) auf den halbstündigen Flug von Buenos Aires nach Punta del Este in Uruguay. Wie ein Magnet zieht ihn sein blau-weißes Strandhaus mit flatternden Vorhängen und breiten Veranden an, das Kosmeerfelder umgeben. Von dort fährt Alan Faena noch 20 Kilometer nach Norden bis nach José Ignacio, wo ihm ein entlegener Strand gehört, den er Tierra Santa getauft hat. Faenas Firma Cosmic Carrot entwirft in Zusammenarbeit mit dem französischen Designer Philippe Starck Hotelboutiquen. Von seinen Veranden aus sieht Faena nur weißen Sand und den ungezähmten Ozean.

Previous pages: Alan Faena's seven-year-old beach cottage makes life colorful and simple. Just one large room with adjacent kitchen and bathroom, it entertains and embraces Faena and guests with bursts of colorful international antiques and crafts and comfortable sofas. The 28 x 8 meter living room is also furnished with folk art collections from Guatemala, Bali, Mexico, and remote regions of South America.
Facing page: The cheerful kitchen, with antique furniture from old Argentinian estates, is where Faena prepares his superb Argentinian "asado" (barbecue).
Above and right: the bath, which overlooks the beach.

Double page précédente: La maison de plage d'Alan Faena, construite il y a sept ans, rend la vie gaie et simple. Ne comportant qu'une vaste pièce, avec cuisine et salle de bains adjacentes, elle accueille Faena et ses amis parmi des antiquités colorées, des objets artisanaux et de confortables canapés. Le salon de 28 mètres sur 8 abrite également des collections d'art folklorique du Guatemala, de Bali, du Mexique et de régions lointaines d'Amérique du Sud.
Page de gauche: La cuisine joyeuse, avec des meubles anciens provenant de vieilles estancias argentines, où Faena prépare de succulents «asados» (le barbecue argentin).
Ci-dessus et à droite: la salle de bains, qui domine la plage.

Vorhergehende Doppelseite: Es gibt nur einen großen Raum mit angeschlossener Küche und Bad und dieser umfängt Faena und seine Gäste mit einer wahren Farbexplosion aus Kunsthandwerk und gemütlichen Sofas. Das Wohnzimmer von 28 x 8 Meter ist mit Volkskunst aus Guatemala, Bali, Mexiko und entlegenen Teilen Südamerikas ausgestattet.
Linke Seite: Die fröhliche Küche ist mit antiken Möbeln aus alten argentinischen Herrschaftshäusern bestückt.
Oben und rechts: das Bad mit Strandblick.

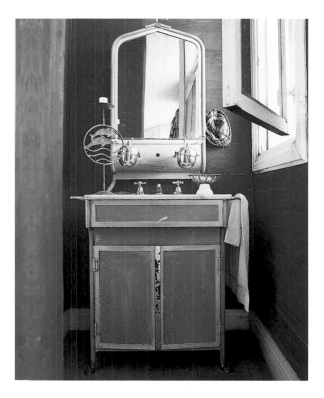

Toti and João Calazans

Espelho da Maravilha, Southern Bahia, Brazil

La côte du Brésil pointe un nez dans l'océan Atlantique, bombe le torse vers l'est et le sud, puis, à partir de Natal et Recife, rentre le ventre jusqu'à Salvador de Bahia. A cet endroit se produit quelque chose de mystérieux et de magique. Une déesse marine se met à danser la samba sur le sable en sucre glace d'une plage isolée, toute drapée de blanc, majestueuse avec sa couronne d'or et ses colliers scintillants. D'un geste langoureux, elle adresse une bénédiction. A moins que ce ne soit les reflets du soleil sur les vagues de l'après-midi, la chaleur moite ou l'effet de plusieurs caipirinhas généreusement arrosés de rhum? Il n'est pas rare qu'un orchestre ou qu'une troupe de danseurs de samba surgissent hors de nulle part sur une plage de Bahia. La beauté de la côte incite à remercier cette déesse, qui aime la musique et la fête, pour ses somptueux présents. C'est dans ce coin inspiré du Brésil que le sculpteur João Calazans et sa femme Toti ont choisi de s'installer. Ils ont trouvé un lopin de terre à l'ombre des palmiers, au sud de la province, entre Trancoso et Caraíva, dans une région baptisée Espelho da Maravilha (Miroir des merveilles).

The coast of Brazil noses out into the Atlantic Ocean, curving eastwards and then south. From Natal and Recife, the land scoops sharply down to Salvador, Bahia. At this junction, something magical and mysterious seems to happen. A goddess of the seas sambas along the sugary sand of a remote beach, garbed all in white, majestic in her golden crown and glittering necklaces. She languidly waves a blessing. Or is it the sunlight glinting on the late afternoon waves, or the molten heat, and the effect of several rum-heavy caipirinhas? It's not unusual for a samba band or a troupe of dancers to appear out of nowhere on Bahia's beaches. The waterside, the edge of the ocean, is a place to give thanks to this lavish sea goddess for her magnificent gifts. It was to this spirit-infused corner of Brazil that sculptor João Calazans came with his wife, Toti. They found a piece of palm-shaded land in south Bahia, between Trancoso and Caraíva, in a region named Espelho da Maravilha (Mirror of Wonder).

Brasiliens Küste ragt wie eine Stupsnase in den Atlantik, indem sie erst nach Osten und dann gen Süden und hinter Natal und Recife steil bis hinunter nach Salvador verläuft. An diesem Punkt scheint etwas geheimnisvoll Magisches zu passieren. Eine Göttin der Meere tanzt Samba entlang des zuckrigen Sands eines einsam gelegenen Strands. Ganz in Weiß ist sie gekleidet, mit goldener Krone und glitzernden Halsketten. Mit einem lässigen Winken segnet sie den Beobachter. Oder täuscht die bleierne Hitze, kombiniert mit der rumschweren Wirkung mehrerer Caipirinhas? Dass eine Sambaband oder eine Tanztruppe scheinbar aus dem Nichts plötzlich am Strand von Bahia auftaucht, ist nicht ungewöhnlich. Das Ufer, die Grenze zum Ozean, ist der Ort, an dem man der großzügigen Göttin des Meeres für ihre wunderbaren Geschenke dankt. An diesen spirituellen Ort in Brasilien kamen der Bildhauer João Calazans und seine Frau Toti und fanden ein palmenbestandenes Stück Land im südlichen Bahia zwischen Trancoso und Caraíva in der Region Espelho da Maravilha (Spiegel der Wunder).

Previous pages: *The Calazans' house is an oasis, a retreat from the rhythms and bold color palette of Bahia. Stucco walls are painted crisp white, with the graphic punch of indigo window and door frames.*
Left and below: *The concrete floors, scored in stripes to add texture, are perfectly practical for the tropics. Arched doorways allow seasonal winds to sweep in and out. Furniture is kept to a Robinson Crusoe minimum. Sofas and sleeping platforms were improvised using local timbers and woven grass matting, all plumped up with down cushions. Mosquito nets are essential.*

Double page précédente: *La maison des Calazans est un refuge contre les rythmes et les couleurs vives de Bahia. Les murs enduits au stuc sont peints dans un blanc éclatant, auquel le bleu indigo des fenêtres et des portes ajoute une touche graphique revigorante.*
A gauche et ci-dessous: *Les sols en béton, creusés de sillons imitant des lattes, sont très pratiques sous les tropiques. Les portes en arche permettent aux vents saisonniers de traverser la maison de part en part. Le mobilier est d'un minimalisme à la Robinson Crusoé. Les sofas et les plates-formes de repos, fabriqués avec des bois locaux et des paillasses en herbes tissées, sont rendus plus douillets par des oreillers en plumes d'oie. Les moustiquaires sont indispensables.*

Vorhergehende Doppelseite: *Das Haus der Calazans ist eine Oase, in der man die lauten Rhythmen und kühnen Farben Bahias hinter sich lassen kann. Die Wände sind in klarem Weiß gestrichen. Kontrastreich: indigoblaue Tür- und Fensterrahmen.*
Rechts und unten: *Die Betonböden erhielten Rillen als zusätzliches Strukturelement. Für tropische Gebiete sind solche Böden praktisch. Türen mit Bögen sorgen für Belüftung durch den Wind. Das Mobiliar ist – nach der Art Robinson Crusoes – auf das Notwendigste begrenzt. Sofas und Schlafemporen wurden mit vor Ort gefälltem Holz und Grasmatten improvisiert und mit Daunenkissen kuschelig gemacht. Unverzichtbar sind die Moskitonetze.*

Above and right: Toti and João Calazans have kept the interior of the getaway house as unpretentious and appealing as the exterior. With one quick swipe the table top and seating benches are ready for lunch and dinner. Tableware and some staple foods are kept in wall closets, which are concealed behind hand-embroidered cotton panels.
Following pages: When Toti and João leave, all they have to do is turn off the lights! This is a minimal-care house, with open closets, no fussing, and no heavy-lifting. The shower is a basic bucket ...

A droite et ci-dessus: Toti et João Calazans ont voulu l'intérieur de leur refuge aussi simple et accueillant que l'extérieur. Un simple coup de torchon sur la table et les bancs et on est prêt pour déjeuner ou dîner. La vaisselle et les denrées de base sont gardées dans des placards sans porte encastrés, dissimulés derrière des pans de coton brodés à la main.
Double page suivante: Lorsque les Calazans s'en vont, il leur suffit d'éteindre la lumière! La maison sans chichis ne nécessite qu'un entretien minimum, avec des placards sans portes et aucun meuble lourd à déplacer. Un simple seau fait office de douche ...

Oben und rechts: Das Innere ihres kleinen Zufluchtsorts gestalteten Toti und João Calazans ebenso unprätentiös und ansprechend wie das Äußere. Die Oberflächen des Esstischs und der Sitzbänke werden einfach nur schnell abgewischt und können dann für Mittag- oder Abendessen eingedeckt werden. Besteck und einige Grundnahrungsmittel werden in Regalen aufbewahrt, die hinter handbestickten Baumwollbehängen versteckt sind.
Folgende Doppelseite: Beim Verlassen des Hauses müssen Toti und João nur einen Handgriff tätigen, nämlich das Licht ausschalten. Ihr Haus ist ganz bewusst äußerst einfach und pflegeleicht gehalten. So besteht die Dusche beispielsweise nur aus einem simplen Eimer.

Carla and Tuca Reinés

Trancoso, Southern Bahia, Brazil

Le photographe et architecte brésilien Tuca Reinés mène une existence enviable. Il vit dans la clameur et le tohu-bohu de São Paulo, sa ville natale, mais fait le va-et-vient entre New York, Rio de Janeiro, les montagnes du Brésil, les îles caraïbes et l'Europe. Reinés a étudié l'architecture et l'urbanisme, mais il concentre désormais toute son attention sur d'élégantes demeures, réalisant des reportages de décoration et d'architecture pour le «Vogue» brésilien, «Casa Vogue» et «Architectural Digest». Il s'intéresse également aux portraits et a photographié Mike Tyson à Atlantic City, les visages burinés de vénérables écrivains brésiliens, ceux de danseurs et de navigateurs. Selon sa femme Carla, Reinés est un homme passionné, entièrement dévoué à son art et à sa famille. Lorsqu'ils se retirent du monde, c'est pour se réfugier dans leur humble maison sur la plage, qui les repose du glamour et des projecteurs de la ville.

Many would envy the career and day-to-day life of Brazilian photographer and architect Tuca Reinés. He lives amid the clamor and bustle of São Paulo, where he was born, but travels constantly to New York, Rio de Janeiro, the hinterlands of Brazil, the Caribbean islands, and to Europe. Reinés studied architecture and urban design, but now his cameras are in and out of elegant houses constantly, as he photographs interiors and architecture and fashions for Brazilian "Vogue", "Casa Vogue", and "Architectural Digest". For his studies of people, he has focused his lenses on boxer Mike Tyson in Atlantic City, craggy faces of venerable Brazilian artists, along with dancers, and yachtsmen. Reinés, says his wife, Carla, is a passionate man, devoted to his craft and his family. And when they retreat from the world, they head for a remote beach house in southern Bahia, its white-washed walls the perfect anodyne for his gilded city life.

Viele beneiden den brasilianischen Fotografen und Architekten Tuca Reinés um seine Karriere und seinen Tagesablauf. Er lebt im hektischen geschäftigen São Paulo, seiner Geburtsstadt, ist aber ständig auf Reisen nach New York, Rio de Janeiro, in das brasilianische Hinterland, in die Karibik und nach Europa. Eigentlich hat Reinés Architektur und Städtebau studiert; heute jedoch richtet er seine Kameras auf elegante Häuser, die er für Interior-Design-, Architektur- und Modezeitschriften wie die brasilianische »Vogue«, die »Casa Vogue« und »Architectural Digest« fotografiert. Für seine Studien am menschlichen Objekt fing er den Boxer Mike Tyson in Atlantic City mit der Kamera ein, fotografierte die herben kantigen Gesichter berühmter brasilianischer Künstler und Schriftsteller und porträtierte Tänzer, Farmer und Segler. Reinés, so seine Frau Carla, ist ein leidenschaftlicher Mensch, der sich seiner Arbeit und seiner Familie mit Haut und Haaren verschrieben hat. Wenn sie die Einsamkeit suchen, dann ziehen sie sich ins südliche Bahia in ein entlegenes Strandhaus mit weiß getünchten Wänden zurück – dem perfekten Gegenpol zur glitzernden Großstadtwelt.

Previous pages: photographer Tuca Reinés, his daughter, Georgia, and wife, Carla, on the beach. If you head south down the coast from Salvador de Bahia, or north up the coast from Rio de Janeiro, midway between these two vivid cities you would find the slumbering, palmy town of Trancoso.

Facing page and following pages: "This place is a like a dream," said Carla. Tuca designed the house, and Carla designed the furniture. Their friend, Narciso, who lives in Trancoso, made the beds, art boxes, chairs and benches using indigenous woods. All the rooms are open, and windows have no glass, so that northeasterly winds can cool off the whole house.

Double page précédente: le photographe Tuca Reinés, sa fille, Georgia, et sa femme, Carla, sur la plage. Si vous descendez la côte vers le sud à partir de Salvador de Bahia, ou remontez vers le nord à partir de Rio de Janeiro, vous trouverez la paisible et délicieuse ville de Transcoso, à mi-chemin entre ces deux grandes villes animées.

Page de droite et double page suivante: «Cet endroit est comme un rêve», déclare Carla. Tuca a dessiné les plans et Carla le mobilier. Leur ami Narciso, qui vit à Transcoso, a réalisé les lits, les boîtes d'art, les chaises et les bancs dans des bois locaux. Toutes les pièces sont ouvertes aux éléments, les fenêtres n'ayant pas de vitres, de sorte que les vents du nord-est rafraîchissent toute la maison.

Vorhergehende Doppelseite: Fotograf Tuca Reinés, Töchterchen Georgia und seine Frau Carla am Strand. Wenn man von Salvador de Bahia aus an der Küste gen Süden oder von Rio de Janeiro nach Norden fährt, trifft man genau in der Mitte auf das verschlafene und palmenbestandene Städtchen Trancoso.

Rechte Seite und folgende Doppelseite: »Dieser Ort ist wie ein Traum«, sagt Carla. Entworfen hat das Haus Tuca; Carla übernahm den Entwurf der Möbel. Ihr Freund Narciso aus Trancoso baute die Betten, Stühle, Bänke und Setzkästen aus heimischem Holz. Alle Räume stehen offen und die Fenster haben keine Verglasung, damit der aus dem Nordosten kommende Wind für Abkühlung sorgen kann.

Above and right: Signs of happy days on the Brazilian coast include fresh fish captured by Tuca, vintage oars and paddles, and simple decor with no maintenance required. Tuca's favorite activities in Bahia: surfing, scuba-diving, playing with his children, Eric and Georgia, and grilling the fish he catches. The simple structure faces right onto the beach, not far from the Monte Pascoal National Park, and 60 kilometers from the tiny airport of Porto Seguro. Despite the distance from São Paulo, the Reinés family visits at least eight times a year, glorying in the simple, Edenic life.

Ci-dessus et à droite: Symboles de jours heureux sur la côte: les poissons pêchés par Tuca, les vieilles rames, les palmes, un décor simple qui ne nécessite aucun entretien. Les activités favorites de Tuca à Bahia: le surf, la plongée, jouer avec ses enfants, Eric et Georgia, faire griller le poisson. La structure simple donne directement sur la mer, non loin du parc national de Monte Pascoal, à 60 kilomètres du minuscule aéroport de Porto Seguro. Malgré la distance de São Paulo, la famille Reinés vient ici au moins huit fois par an.

Oben und rechts: Glückliche Tage an einem brasilianischen Strand – dazu gehören auch Tucas fangfrischer Fisch, alte Ruder und Paddel sowie einfaches Dekor, das wenig Pflege und Aufmerksamkeit benötigt. Zu seinen Lieblingsbeschäftigungen in Bahia zählt Tuca das Wellenreiten, Tauchen, mit seinen Kindern Eric und Georgia spielen und seinen Tagesfang grillen. Das einfach strukturierte Haus ist direkt auf den Strand ausgerichtet und liegt in der Nähe des Parque Nacional de Monte Pascoal, 60 Kilometer vom winzigen Flughafen Porto Seguro entfernt. Trotz der Entfernung zu São Paulo kommt die Familie mindestens achtmal im Jahr hierher.

Trancoso, Southern Bahia, Brazil 16°48'S 39°08'W

Cristián Boza

Los Vilos, Coquimbo Region, Chile

Prochain arrêt, Patagonie! La côte chilienne invite les aventuriers. Le pays tout entier n'est qu'un ruban de terre coincé entre la Cordillère des Andes et le Pacifique. Long de 4300 kilomètres, il fait par endroits à peine 90 kilomètres de large. Il commence dans le nord humide à Arica et Punta Lobos, descend vers Valparaíso et Concepción puis, après des marécages et des affleurements rocheux balayés par les vents, se désagrège à Puerto Montt. Là commence une chute vertigineuse vers l'Antarctique en une myriade de rochers gris et de fragments d'îles glacés. Après Isla Desolación, ce pays en pièces de puzzle s'interrompt parmi les icebergs aigue-marine du Cap Horn. Près de Los Vilos, à 150 kilomètres au nord de Valparaíso, l'architecte Cristián Boza, avec l'aide de son associée Paola Durruty, a bâti sa propre maison sur un promontoire rocheux.

Next stop Patagonia! Chile's coast invites adventurers. This attentuated 4300 kilometer sliver of a country, mostly coastal and a mere 90 kilometers of land in places, is squeezed between the high Andes Mountains and the Pacific Ocean. It starts in the humid north at Arica and Punta Lobos, slips down past Valparaíso and Concepción, and then, beyond swamps and wind-buffeted outcrops, the coast breaks apart at Puerto Montt. Crashing down vertiginously toward the Antarctic, Chile fractures into gray rocks and gelid fragments of islands. On past Isla Desolación, this puzzle of a country comes to a halt among aquamarine ice floes at Cape Horn. Situated close to Los Vilos, 150 kilometers north of Valparaíso, the house designed for himself by architect Cristián Boza, together with associate architect Paola Durruty, stands on a rocky stretch of coastline.

Nächster Halt: Patagonien! Chiles Küste ist etwas für Abenteurer. Lanzettförmig windet sich das Land an 4300 Kilometer Küstenlinie entlang, manchmal nur 90 Kilometer breit und eingeklemmt zwischen dem hohen Gebirgszug der Anden und dem Pazifik. Chile beginnt im feuchten Norden bei Arica und Punta Lobos, schlängelt sich hinunter, vorbei an Valparaíso und Concepción, Sümpfen und vom Wind umtosten Felsen. Dann erreicht man Puerto Montt, wo die Küste auseinanderbricht. Erst hinter Isla Desolación kommt das Puzzle aus grauen Felsen und eiskalten Inselfragmenten zur Ruhe, zwischen den aquamarinfarbenen, träge fließenden Eisschollen bei Kap Horn. Ganz in der Nähe von Los Vilos, 150 Kilometer nördlich von Valparaíso, errichtete der Architekt Cristián Boza mit Unterstützung der Architektin Paola Durruty für sich ein Haus am Meeresrand.

Boza confidently set his stone house right on the rocks. This is no ego-trip, however. The architect established an easy dialogue with the sea and the wave-lashed rocks. With its natural progression from indoors to outdoors, hand-sculpted rock walls, and a living room that measures 83 square meters and has a maximal height of 7.90 meters, it's an all-weather outpost. A yellow stucco wall, sail-shaped, shelters the sunset-viewing terrace. There's an island out front and a sandy fishing village nearby.

Boza a fermement planté sa maison en pierres directement sur les rochers. Ce n'est pas pour satisfaire son ego: l'architecte entretient une longue conversation avec la mer et les rochers fouettés par les vagues. Avec sa progression naturelle de l'intérieur vers l'extérieur, ses murs en pierres sculptées à la main et son salon de 83 mètres carrés et de 7,90 mètres sous plafond, c'est un avant-poste capable d'essuyer tous les temps. Un mur en stuc jaune en forme de voile protège la terrasse d'où l'on contemple les couchers de soleil, une île qui pointe juste devant et un village de pêcheurs enfoncé dans le sable non loin.

Mutig setzte Boza das Haus direkt auf den Fels. Trotzdem tut das Gebäude der Umgebung keine Gewalt an, sondern führt einen harmonischen Dialog mit dem Meer und den wellengeformten Klippen. Innen und Außen bilden eine natürliche Einheit. Die von Hand behauenen Steine und das Wohnzimmer von 83 Quadratmetern, das an der höchsten Stelle 7,90 Meter hoch ist, machen aus diesem Ort ein Refugium, das jedem Wetter trotzt. Gelbe Gipswände in Segelform beschatten die Terrasse, von der aus man einen fantastischen Blick auf den Sonnenuntergang, die gegenübergelegene Insel und das nahe Fischerdorf hat.

Trip to Asia, Australia, Oceania

Imagine the adventurous early Polynesians setting out across the Pacific Ocean with just the stars and fish and currents to guide them. They float for months using clouds as compasses, trusting the fates. And then a tuft of palm trees, a jagged peak, and a tangle of mangroves sprout on the distant horizon. They land their outriggers on these green and pleasant islands, feast on the luscious landscape, and stay forever. Mythological Tahiti, Raiatea, Rangiroa, Huahine, and Bora-Bora drift in the placid sea. Today, they appear as they did when the first seafarers set foot there, just as they looked when Gauguin painted his lolling maidens, white crowns of frangipani, and writhing sea-monsters. The sensual pleasures of swimming there may include watching reflections of clouds over the surface of a lagoon, or startling an octopus that looks you in the eye then shoots off in a cloud of sand. In the distant Indian Ocean, the mystical allure of the coast relaxes the mind. On the coast south of Colombo, hazy afternoons slide into evening, and a slight breeze ruffles sun-faded curtains. Music from a far-off time echoes across the sea. Summer is a time of rare beauty in Australia and New Zealand, as the retreating tides leave shells and shadows on powdery beaches. High above the sea, a Japanese glass house stands like a mirage. Is it an illusion? As the sea and sky change color, the house appears and disappears. The glass is seemingly lambent and liquid, reflecting light and water, the ultimate tribute to the mysterious beauty of the coast.

Imaginez les premiers aventuriers polynésiens traversant le Pacifique avec les étoiles, les poissons et les courants marins pour seuls guides. Des mois durant, ils se laissent ballotter par les vagues, utilisant les nuages comme boussole, se fiant à leur destin. Puis, une touffe de palmiers, un sommet escarpé et un enchevêtrement de mangroves se dessinent au loin. Ils accostent sur ces îles vertes et accueillantes, se repaissent de leur paysage luxuriant et ne repartent plus jamais. Tahiti, Raïatea, Rangiroa, Huahine et Bora-Bora baignent dans la mythologie et flottent sur une mer d'huile. Elles n'ont pas changé depuis l'époque où les premiers marins y ont accosté ou depuis que Gauguin y a peint ses belles langoureuses, ses couronnes de fleurs de frangipanier et ses tortueux monstres marins. Les plaisirs sensuels de la baignade incluent, entre autres, la contemplation du reflet des nuages dans les lagons, ou la rencontre inopinée d'une pieuvre qui vous regarde droit dans les yeux avant de s'enfuir dans un nuage de sable. Sur le lointain océan Indien, l'allure mystique de la côte détend l'esprit. Sur la côte au sud de Colombo, la chaleur de l'après-midi se dissipe en douces soirées quand une brise vient agiter les rideaux décolorés par le soleil. Une musique semblant venir des temps anciens se répercute sur la mer. En Australie et en Nouvelle-Zélande, l'été est une saison d'une beauté rare et les marées qui se retirent laissent derrière elles des coquillages et des ombres sur des plages poudreuses. Haut perchée au-dessus de la mer, une maison de verre japonaise se dresse tel un mirage. Est-ce une illusion? A mesure que la mer et le ciel changent de couleur, elle apparaît et disparaît. Le verre devient chatoyant et fluide, reflétant l'eau et la lumière, le plus bel hommage à la mystérieuse beauté de la côte.

Man denke für einen Moment an die frühen Polynesier, die abenteuerlustig den Pazifik überquerten und sich nur an den Gestirnen, den Fischschwärmen und den Meeresströmungen orientieren konnten. Monatelang ließen sie sich treiben, nahmen die Wolken als Kompass und vertrauten auf ihr Schicksal. Und plötzlich wurden ein Palmenbüschel, eine gezackte Bergspitze, ein Mangrovenknoten am entfernten Horizont sichtbar. Dann landeten sie die Auslegerboote an den grünen, paradiesischen Inseln, genossen die prächtige Landschaft und blieben – für immer. Tahiti, Raiatea, Rangiroa, Huahine und Bora-Bora – mythische Orte, die durch das ruhige Wasser zu gleiten scheinen. Heute wirken sie noch immer so wie damals, als die ersten Seefahrer hier landeten oder als Gauguin seine sich räkelnden Jungfrauen, weiße Kronen aus Frangipaniblüten, sich windende Meeresungeheuer malte. Schwimmen ist hier ein ganz sinnliches Erlebnis. Vielleicht beobachtet man dabei die Reflexionen der Wolken auf der Oberfläche einer Lagune oder schreckt einen Kraken auf, der einem erst ins Auge blickt und sich dann in einer Sandwolke davonmacht. Im weit entfernten Indischen Ozean ist es der schon mystische Reiz der Küste, der Entspannung bringt. Südlich von Colombo gleiten verhangene Nachmittage in den Abend hinüber und ein leichter Windhauch bewegt sonnengebleichte Vorhänge. In Australien und Neuseeland ist der Sommer eine Zeit von unvergleichlicher Schönheit. Wenn das Meer sich zurückzieht, hinterlässt es an puderzuckrigen Stränden Muscheln und Schatten. Hoch über dem Meer steht ein japanisches Glashaus ... eine Illusion? Das glänzende Glas wirkt, als sei es flüssig, denn es reflektiert Licht und Wasser – der wahre Tribut an die geheimnisvolle Schönheit der Küste.

Tom Kurth

Hana Iti, Huahine, Tahiti

Le premier Européen à poser le pied sur les îles de Tahiti fut un capitaine britannique, Samuel Wallis, à bord du vaisseau Dolphin, en 1767. Il fut bientôt suivi par des aventuriers français, espagnols, hollandais et britanniques et leurs équipages bigarrés qui traversaient le Pacifique en quête de plantes exotiques, de nouveaux territoires et du paradis terrestre. Au cours des siècles précédents et ceux qui ont suivi, les habitants polynésiens des 120 îles de l'archipel y ont vécu en parfaite harmonie. Quand ils ont faim, il leur suffit de patauger dans la mer protégée de récifs pour y pêcher du poisson ou de secouer le papayer, l'arbre à pain ou le manguier le plus proche pour recueillir les succulents ingrédients d'un repas sensuel. C'est sur l'île sous le vent de Huahine que Tom Kurth, inventeur et biologiste marin, originaire du Wisconsin, a jeté son dévolu. Il a acheté 23 hectares de terrain au bord d'un lagon tranquille pour créer un hôtel tropical à Hana Iti.

The earliest European to set foot on the islands of Tahiti was a British captain, Samuel Wallis, aboard the good ship Dolphin in 1767. He was followed soon after by a series of French, Spanish, Dutch, and British adventurers and their motley crews, who traversed the Pacific Ocean in search of exotic plants, new territory, and earthly paradise. For centuries before, and since, the Polynesian inhabitants of the 120 islands in the group have lived in perfect harmony, secure in the knowledge that they can wade into the reef-protected sea to catch fish when they are hungry, and have only to shake the nearest papaya, breadfruit, or mango tree to catch delectable ingredients for a sensual repast. It was the leeward island of Huahine that Wisconsin-born inventor and marine biologist Tom Kurth discovered for himself. He acquired 23 hectares on a quiet lagoon, and proceeded to create a tropical resort at Hana Iti.

Der erste Europäer, der seinen Fuß auf Tahiti setzte, war der britische Kapitän Samuel Wallis mit seiner tüchtigen »Dolphin«. Man schrieb das Jahr 1767. Ihm folgten schon kurz danach Abenteurer aus Frankreich, Spanien, Holland und England, die mit bunt zusammengewürfelten Mannschaften den Pazifik auf der Suche nach exotischen Pflanzen, neuen Ländern und dem Paradies auf Erden überquerten. Jahrhunderte vorher – und nachher – lebten die polynesischen Ureinwohner der 120 Inseln in perfekter Harmonie. Sie mussten nur in das riffgeschützte Meer waten, um Fisch zu fangen, oder den nächsten Papaya-, Brotfrucht- oder Mangobaum schütteln, um die köstlichsten Zutaten für eine sinnliche Mahlzeit zu erhalten. Die leeseits gelegene Insel Huahine wurde von einem modernen Eroberer entdeckt, dem aus dem US-Bundesstaat Wisconsin stammenden Erfinder und Meeresbiologen Tom Kurth. Er erwarb 23 Hektar Land an einer ruhigen Lagune und machte sich daran, bei Hana Iti ein tropisches Urlaubsparadies zu schaffen.

Facing page: the marine-theme beachfront Dolphin Bar of the Hana Iti resort, created by Tom Kurth. Decorative tree trunks and branches are of sustainable native ito trees. "This wood is so hard that you can't drive nails into it," noted Kurth, who worked with sculptor and builder Jean-Claude Michel and local craftsmen on the interiors.
Above and right: Kurth and his talented building crews used fallen logs to create natural supports for the salon. "We peeled and polished hardwood logs, and shaped them to show them in all their glory," said Kurth.

Page de gauche: Le Bar du Dauphin de l'hôtel Hana Iti, créé par Tom Kurth, est sous le signe de la mer. Les troncs et les branches décoratifs proviennent d'arbres locaux. «Le bois est si dur qu'on ne peut même pas y enfoncer un clou», raconte Kurth qui a travaillé avec le sculpteur et bâtisseur Jean-Claude Michel et des artisans locaux pour décorer les pièces.
Ci-dessus et à droite: Kurth et ses talentueux ouvriers ont recyclé des troncs d'arbres tombés pour soutenir le toit du salon. «On a poncé et poli les troncs en bois durs, puis on les a assemblés de manière à les montrer dans toute leur splendeur», explique Kurth.

Linke Seite: Die am Strand gelegene Dolphin Bar im Urlaubsparadies Hana Iti hat Tom Kurth ganz im Zeichen des Meeres eingerichtet. Die dekorativen Stämme und Äste stammen von den hier heimischen Ito-Bäumen. »Das Holz ist so hart, dass man es nicht schafft, einen Nagel hineinzuschlagen«, so Kurth, der bei der Gestaltung mit dem Bildhauer Jean-Claude Michel und hier ansässigen Handwerkern zusammenarbeitete.
Oben und rechts: Mit seiner findigen Crew baute Kurth aus umgestürzten Stämmen natürlich wirkende Stützen für den Salon. »Wir haben Hartholzstämme abgezogen und so lange poliert und in Form gebracht, bis sie sich in ihrer ganzen Pracht zeigten.«

Above: Sunrise peers into the bedroom, with its hand-crafted, canoe-like bed. The room has no glass windows and opens directly onto the lagoon.
Right: Outrigger canoes are the traditional watercraft in the Tahitian islands. The atoll-protected lagoon is teaming with fish, and fresh lobsters, grouper, snapper, and jackfish are generally on the menu for lunch or dinner.
Facing page: In this bathroom, sculpted from local woods, a poetic spout was improvised with a decorative mother-of-pearl nautilus shell. The handbasin is a handsome tridachne shell.

Ci-dessus: Les premiers rayons s'infiltrent dans une chambre dont le lit en forme de pirogue a été réalisé à la main. Les fenêtres n'ont pas de vitres et donnent directement sur le lagon.
A droite: une embarcation traditionnelle des îles tahitiennes. Le lagon, protégé par un atoll, regorge de poissons. Langoustes, mérous et daurades frais sont régulièrement au menu du déjeuner et du dîner.
Page de droite: Dans cette salle de bains, on a improvisé une fontaine poétique avec un nautile décoratif. Un superbe tridacne fait office de bassin.

Oben: Das Sonnenlicht blinzelt in das Schlafzimmer, in dem ein handgezimmertes Bett steht, dessen Form an ein Kanu erinnert. Das Zimmer hat keine Glasfenster, sondern öffnet sich direkt auf die Lagune.
Rechts: Die »outrigger« sind die traditionellen Boote auf Tahiti. Die von Atollen geschützten Lagunen sind sehr fischreich: Hummer, Zackenbarsch, Schnapper und Ritterfisch stehen täglich auf dem Speiseplan.
Rechte Seite: In diesem Badezimmer, das aus heimischen Hölzern gefertigt wurde, kommt das Wasser aus einer perlmutternen Nautilus-muschel. Als Waschbecken dient eine prächtige Riesenmuschel.

Hana Iti, Huahine, Tahiti 23°23'S 149°28'W

Tom Kurth

Living on a
Tidal Lagoon

Hana Iti, Huahine, Tahiti

Les Tahitiens ont un goût prononcé pour les légendes pittoresques et les mythes à l'érotisme torride. Pour expliquer l'existence de l'île lointaine de Huahine, ils racontent que Ta'aroa, le grand créateur de la mer et de la terre, a répandu son souffle de vie dans la mer, faisant surgir des eaux deux îles verdoyantes ceintes d'un collier de corail et étreignant un paisible lagon bleu. On dit aussi que Hutu-Hiva, une princesse de l'île voisine de Raïatea, s'enferma dans un tambour sacré en bois sculpté et se laissa doucement ballotter par les vagues à la recherche de l'amour. Poussée vers les rives de Huahine, elle fut découverte par un prince guerrier et, ensemble, ils eurent dix fils, de puissants guerriers qui donnèrent leur nom aux dix districts de l'île. L'air, les eaux nacrées et les hauts acacias — dont les graines sont portées par les courants marins — conspirent pour plonger les visiteurs dans une béatitude enchantée et les retenir à jamais dans un ravissement sans cesse renouvelé. Avec l'aide du sculpteur local Jean-Claude Michel, Tom Kurth a donc construit une maison romantique au bord du lagon à marées.

Tahitians have a particular fondness for wildly erotic myths and lavishly pictorial legends. To explain the existence of their distant island of Huahine, they tell of Ta'aroa, the great creator of sea and land, who breathed life into the sea, and thus arose dual verdant islands surrounded by a necklace of coral and embraced by a calm blue lagoon. It is said that Hutu-Hiva, a princess from the neighboring island of Raiatea, enclosed herself inside a sacred carved drum and floated on the gentle tides in search of love. She was washed ashore on Huahine, discovered by a warrior prince, and together they produced ten sons, mighty warriors who gave their names to the ten districts of Huahine. The air, the pearlescent waters, and the hovering acacia trees — their seeds borne by ocean currents — conspire to enfold the visitor in blissful enchantment, and a wild passion to stay there, forever enraptured. And so Tom Kurth, together with local sculptor Jean-Claude Michel, built a romantic pole house on a tidal lagoon.

Die Tahitianer haben eine besondere Vorliebe für wilderotische Mythen und fantastisch bildhafte Legenden. So erklärt man die Existenz der entlegenen Insel Huahine durch einen Akt von Ta'aroa, dem großen Schöpfer von Land und Meer, der dem Meer Leben einblies. Dabei erhob sich die grüne Doppelinsel aus dem Meer, umgeben von einer Kette von Korallen und in der Umarmung einer ruhigen blauen Lagune. Der Legende nach kam Hutu-Hiva, eine Prinzessin von den nahe gelegenen Insel Raiatea, auf der Suche nach der Liebe hierher: Sie hatte sich in einer heiligen Trommel aus geschnitztem Holz über die Wellen treiben lassen. Am Strand von Huahine wurde sie von einem Krieger entdeckt, der glücklicherweise auch noch ein Prinz war. Sie gebar ihm zehn Söhne, die nach dem Vater schlugen und den zehn Bezirken der Insel ihre Namen gaben. Das Zusammenspiel der Luft, des perlmuttern schimmernden Wassers und der wie schwebend wirkenden Akazienbäume, deren Samen von den Wellen des Meers angespült wurden, weckt in dem faszinierten Besucher den zutiefst leidenschaftlichen Wunsch, für immer hier bleiben zu dürfen. Und so baute Tom Kurth mit Hilfe des hier lebenden Bildhauers Jean-Claude Michel ein romantisches Pfahlhaus an der Tidenseite der Lagune.

Facing page and right: idylls of Tahiti. This beachfront villa, built inside a living banyan tree, offers enchanted life, à la Paul Gauguin. The pole house structure, like others built by Tom Kurth at Hana Iti, began with four large Douglas fir poles, onto which were bolted the basic roof skeleton and beams to support the floor.
Above: Roofs were made out of reed and pandanus panels. Jean-Claude Michel crafted these buildings with a great appreciation of the beauty of nature. The banyan tree grows around the bed. Nature is so profligate there, Kurth said, that often when he placed a branch in the ground to mark out floorplans, it would rapidly start growing.

Page de gauche et à droite: idylles de Tahiti. La villa en bordure de plage, construite à l'intérieur d'un banian vivant, offre une vie de rêve à la Paul Gauguin. Comme d'autres maisons construites par Tom Kurth à Hana Iti, la structure repose sur quatre gros sapirs de Douglas sur lesquels ont été montés une charpente rudimentaire et des poutres pour soutenir le plancher.
Ci-dessus: Les toits ont été réalisés en panneaux de joncs et de pandanus. Jean-Claude Michel a créé ces bâtisses avec un grand respect pour la beauté de la nature. Un banian pousse au bord du lit. Ici, la nature est si prolixe que, lorsque Kurth plaçait une branche pour marquer le plan de la maison au sol, celle-ci prenait racine.

Linke Seite und rechts: Idylle auf Tahiti. Diese Strandvilla im Innern eines lebenden Banyanbaums ist – wie die anderen Häuser von Tom Kurth in Hana Iti – eine Pfahlkonstruktion aus vier großen Fichtenstämmen, in die die Balken für Dach und Boden eingelassen wurden.
Oben: Das Dach besteht aus Weiden und Pandanus-Paneelen. Jean-Claude Michel errichtete die Gebäude mit großem Respekt vor der Schönheit der Natur. Der Banyanbaum wächst um das Bett herum. Die Natur ist hier so fruchtbar, dass sogar die Zweige ausschlugen, die Kurth als Markierung in den Boden gesteckt hatte.

Alice and Ponciano Saldaña

Isla Naburot,
Guimaras Island, Philippines

Mindanao, Luzon, Maltatayoc, Boracay, Cebu, Samar, Mindoro … Les noms des îles des Philippines sont comme des mots doux qu'on se chuchote à l'oreille sous les palmiers de la plage à minuit. Les 7 000 îles du groupe, dont la plupart ne sont qu'une touffe de feuillage luisant, un bouquet de fleurs tropicales, une traînée de sable ivoire, sont éparpillées entre la Mer de Chine Méridionale et la Mer de Célèbes. Beaucoup sont inhabitées et peu de voyageurs s'aventurent dans leurs collines ou sur les plus lointaines. Ils ont tort car ils passent à côté de la qualité particulièrement atemporelle des côtes philippines les plus isolées. Un nouveau jour se lève, l'océan scintille et miroite comme une nappe de mercure. Le ciel n'a pas encore décidé de quelle couleur il sera aujourd'hui. Il joue avec la lumière et la pénombre, hésite entre un gris pâle et un rose, essaie un bleu pervenche parsemé de blanc, puis opte enfin pour un joyeux bleu sans nuances. Le monde entier semble rayonner. Il n'y a pas encore de vent à cette heure matinale et la mer est d'huile. Les frangipaniers embaument l'air chaud et humide.

Mindanao. Luzon. Maltatayoc. Boracay. Cebu. Samar. Mindoro. The names of the islands of the Philippines sound alluring, like seductive whispering beneath the palms on a midnight beach. The 7 000 islands in the group, many of them just a plume of glossy foliage, ebullient tropical blooms, and a smudge of ivory-colored sand, are scattered between the South China Sea and the Celebes Sea. Most of the islands are uninhabited, and relatively few travelers venture into the hills or the furthermost islands. And so they miss the special timeless quality of the faraway Philippine coastline. The new day awakes, and the ocean shimmers and shines like mercury. The sky has not yet decided what color it wants to be, so it plays with light and shadow and tries out pale gray and pink, then periwinkle blue flashed with white, then finally a resolute and cheerful blue. The whole world seems to glow. There is no wind at this early hour so the water stays flat. The damp, warm air smells of frangipani.

Mindanao. Luzon. Maltatayoc. Boracay. Cebu. Samar. Mindoro. Schon die Namen der philippinischen Inseln klingen verführerisch wie ein gehauchtes Flüstern unter Palmen an einem mitternächtlichen Strand. 7 000 von ihnen liegen verstreut zwischen der Celebessee und dem Südchinesischen Meer, viele davon nicht mehr als ein paar Pflanzenwedel, einige farb- und lebenssprudelnde tropische Blüten und ein Klecks elfenbeinfarbener Sand. Die meisten Inseln sind unbewohnt und nur wenige Reisende finden den Weg in die Berge oder auf entfernter gelegene Inseln. Doch dadurch entgeht ihnen das ganz besondere, zeitlose Flair der philippinischen Küste. Ein neuer Tag erwacht und der Ozean glänzt und schimmert wie Quecksilber. Der Himmel hat sich noch nicht entschieden, welche Farbe er heute tragen wird, spielt mit Licht und Schatten, probiert es mit blassem Grau und Zartrosa, dann mit bläulichem Grün, durchsetzt mit Weiß, und entscheidet sich dann für ein eindeutiges und fröhliches Blau. Die ganze Welt scheint zu glänzen. Zu dieser frühen Stunde gibt es noch keinen Wind. Das Wasser ist glatt. Der Duft von Frangipani hängt in der feuchtwarmen Luft.

Ponciano – known as Pons – and Alice Saldaña and their six children
love to escape to their family house on Isla Naburot in Guimaras
Province, just across the Iloilo Strait from their house on the island of
Panay. Their retreat, which has no electricity, offers complete seclu-
sion and a respite from modern times in Iloilo City. The house and
cottages, now 18 years old, were built using terracotta tiles, massive
timbers, sculpted stone, indigenous shells, and antique tiles rescued
from demolished Spanish churches and former grand mansions built
for the old Spanish regime.

Ponciano Saldaña – qu'on appelle simplement Pons –, sa femme
Alice, et leurs six enfants adorent se réfugier à Isla Naburot, dans la
province de Guimaras, juste en face de leur maison principale et de
leurs cottages sur l'île de Panay, de l'autre côté du détroit de Iloilo.
Leur retraite, sans électricité, offre un isolement complet et un répit
des temps modernes à Iloilo City. La maison, qui a maintenant dix-
huit ans, a été construite avec des tuiles en terre cuite, des poutres
massives, de la pierre sculptée, des coquillages locaux et des carreaux
anciens récupérés dans des églises espagnoles en démolition ou d'anciennes grandes demeures coloniales.

Ponciano – als Pons bekannt – und Alice Saldaña und ihre sechs Kinder lieben es, wenn sie sich in ihr Familienhaus auf Isla Naburot in
der philippinischen Provinz Guimaras zurückziehen können. Das
Haus liegt gegenüber von ihrem Hauptwohnsitz, einem Haus und
mehreren Hütten auf der Insel Panay – auf der anderen Seite der
Iloilo Street. Hier gibt es keine Elektrizität, dafür aber kann man sich
völlig der modernen Hektik von Iloilo City entziehen. Das mittlerweile
18 Jahre alte Haus wurde aus Terrakottafliesen, Massivholz, behauenen Steinen, am Strand gefundenen Muscheln und alten Fliesen errichtet, die man aus zerstörten alten Kirchen und einstigen Herren-
häusern aus der Zeit der spanischen Herrschaft hatte retten können.

"If" House

Bay of Galle, Sri Lanka

Sri Lanka, une île verdoyante aux parfums musqués, est suspendue telle une larme près de la côte de l'Inde du sud. Le patrimoine architectural de l'île, étonnamment intact, inclut de vieux forts hollandais, des stûpas bouddhistes, des peintures rupestres, des Bouddhas géants debout ou couchés taillés dans les rochers, des lignes de chemin de fer de style colonial et de grandes demeures guindées, vestiges de l'empire britannique. Les visiteurs en quête d'une tasse du légendaire thé Broken Orange Pekoe prennent le train qui se hisse lentement vers le sommet brumeux du mont Nuwara Eliya. Là, ils séjournent dans de vieux hôtels de style Tudor ou Georgian tapissés de chintz défraîchis, hantés par des domestiques en livrée et débordants d'argenterie ciselée. Les aventuriers en mal de bains de mer optent pour les plages du sud-ouest où ils s'adonnent au surf et à la plongée. Dans la torpeur de l'après-midi, les vacanciers découvrent vite que l'humidité, le bruissement des palmiers et les brises parfumées induisent une léthargie tropicale qui les cloue dans leurs transats avec une limonade glacée et, peut-être, un bon vieux roman de gare.

Sri Lanka, an island of lavish verdure and musky perfumes, is suspended like a teardrop off the coast of southern India. The island's surprisingly intact architectural legacy includes old Dutch forts, Buddhist stupas, centuries-old painted caves, giant reclining and standing Buddhas carved from living rock, colonial-style railways, and fusty, stiff-upper-lip British colonial residences. Visitors to the island in search of a fragrant cup of Sri Lanka's legendary broken orange pekoe tea take a slow train to the misty hill station of Nuwara Eliya. There they stay in Tudor and Georgian-style high-country hotels decked out with faded floral chintzes, uniformed retainers, and ornate silver. Adventurers in need of salt-water therapy head for beaches on the south-west coast for surfing, snorkelling, scuba-diving. Beaches snooze in the midday sun. Humidity, whispering palms, and balmy breezes induce an equatorial lethargy that keeps visitors anchored to a beach chair with an iced lemonade and – perhaps – a trashy paperback novel.

Sri Lanka ist eine Insel mit verschwenderisch reicher Flora, eingehüllt in den intensiven Duft von Moschus. Wie eine zarte Träne hängt sie vor der Küste Südindiens. Ihr architektonisches Erbe ist überraschend intakt: Alte holländische Forts, buddhistische Stupas, jahrhundetealte Höhlenmalereien, riesige Buddhas, liegend oder stehend aus dem Fels gemeißelt, Eisenbahnen und Häuser, die noch die »stiff-upper-lip«-Atmosphäre der Kolonialzeit ausstrahlen. Wer die Insel auf der Suche nach dem legendären duftenden Broken-Orange-Pekoe-Tee bereist, der zuckelt per Zug zur dunstverhangenen Bergstation Nuwara Eliya und residiert dort in Hochland-Hotels im georgianischen oder Tudor-Stil, zwischen verblichenem Chintz mit Blumenmuster, Bediensteten in Uniform und reich zieseliertem Silber. Abenteurer riskieren eine Salzwassertherapie an den Stränden der Südwestküste, wo man surfen, schnorcheln und tauchen kann. In der Mittagsglut dösen selbst die Strände vor sich hin. Die hohe Luftfeuchtigkeit, das Flüstern der Palmen und die sanften Brisen verführen zu äquatorialer Lethargie. Man bleibt wie fest verankert im Liegestuhl am Strand sitzen, genießt eine geeiste Limonade und ein unterhaltsames Taschenbuch.

The "If" House – named after a classic Rudyard Kipling poem – stands at the edge of the Indian Ocean on a quiet beach protected by a coral reef. The house is situated just south of the historic town of Galle, a former Dutch and Portuguese fort. Shady verandahs furnished with traditional Anglo-Colonial furniture surround the spacious house, which is circled with cool pools and lush gardens: the haunt of kingfishers, snakes, and occasionally scorpions and curious monkeys. "The serenity here is wonderful," said Barbara Gall, one of the owners. "Time means little. We do not wear watches."

La maison «Si», baptisée d'après un poème de Rudyard Kipling, se dresse au bord de l'océan Indien, sur une plage tranquille protégée par un récif de corail. La maison se trouve juste au sud de la ville historique de Galle, un ancien fort hollandais et portugais. Des vérandas ombragées aménagées avec des meubles traditionnels anglo-coloniaux ceignent la maison. La maison spacieuse est entourée de bassins frais et de jardins luxuriants qui attirent les martins-pêcheurs, les serpents et parfois, des scorpions ou des singes curieux. «Ici, on jouit d'une sérénité merveilleuse», confie Barbara Gall, l'une des propriétaires. «Le temps ne compte plus. Personne ne porte de montre».

Das »Wenn«-Haus – benannt nach einem Gedicht von Rudyard Kipling – steht direkt am Indischen Ozean, an einem ruhigen Strand, der durch ein Korallenriff geschützt wird. Das Haus liegt direkt südlich von Galle, einem Fort aus portugiesisch-holländischen Tagen. Schattige Veranden mit traditionellen Möbeln im englischen Kolonialstil umgeben das geräumige Haus. Es ist von kühlenden Wasserbassins und üppigen Gärten umgeben, die Eisvögel, Schlangen und manchmal auch Skorpione und neugierige Affen anziehen. »Hier hat alles eine wunderbare Gelassenheit«, sagt Barbara Gall, eine der Besitzerinnen. »Zeit bedeutet nicht viel. Niemand trägt eine Uhr.«

Left: *Beyond the fountain, a pair of concrete sofas were placed to enable the residents to view the last rays of the sunset.*
Below: *The living room, which opens directly onto verandahs, was furnished boldly with overscale teak sofas and an upholstered bench. Two custom-made triangular teak tables can be moved into many configurations. "We can spend hours there watching the wind in the frangipani trees and the sunlight flickering in the palm trees," said Barbara Gall. She and her husband, Thomas, share the house with David and Jan Gerard. "We observe the wildlife and enjoy the fragrant air, and usually dine outdoors in a new dining pavilion."*

A gauche: *derrière la fontaine, une paire de canapés placés stratégiquement pour que les résidents puissent jouir des derniers rayons du soleil couchant.*
Ci-dessous: *Le salon, qui donne sur les vérandas, a été meublé avec d'immenses sofas douillets et un banc matelassé. Les deux tables basses triangulaires en teck, faites sur mesure, peuvent être disposées de multiples manières. «On peut passer des heures ici à regarder le vent dans les frangipaniers et le soleil se coucher entre les palmiers», dit Barbara Gall. Elle et son mari, Thomas, partagent la maison avec David et Jan Gerard. «On contemple la nature et on profite de l'air parfumé. On dîne généralement dehors sous un nouveau pavillon».*

Links: *Die beiden Betonsofas hinter dem Brunnen wurden so ausgerichtet, dass man noch die untergehende Sonne betrachten kann.*
Unten: *Das Wohnzimmer, das auf die Veranden hinausgeht, wurde mit riesigen Teaksofas und einer gepolsterten Bank eingerichtet. Zwei maßgefertigte dreieckige Teaktische lassen sich auf unterschiedlichste Weise kombinieren. »Wir können Stunden nur damit verbringen zu beobachten, wie der Wind in den Frangipani-Bäumen spielt und das Sonnenlicht in den Palmen blitzt«, sagt Barbara Gall. Sie und ihr Mann Thomas sowie David und Jan Gerard teilen sich dieses Haus. »Wir beobachten die Tiere, genießen die duftgeschwängerte Luft und nehmen unsere Mahlzeiten meist in unserem neuen Pavillon ein.«*

Above: One guest bedroom is graced with an antique Anglo-Colonial-style bed, simply dressed with a white cotton coverlet. Summer heat can be intense, even beside Sri Lanka's south-west coast, so floors throughout the house are cool tiles, walls are soothing white.
Right: In the shade adjacent to the kitchen, lunch can be prepared even on the hottest January days. Bougainvillea, frangipani, and tropical lilies are in their element here, and often the main focus of the gardener is to prune and trim and tame so that the garden will not engulf walls and pathways.

Ci-dessus: une chambre d'amis, avec un lit ancien de style anglo-colonial. En été, la chaleur est parfois intense, même sur la côte sud-ouest du Sri Lanka, aussi les sols sont en carrelage frais et les murs d'un blanc apaisant.
A droite: Sous le treillis adjacent à la cuisine, on peut déjeuner dehors même pendant les journées les plus chaudes de janvier. Les bougainvilliers, les frangipaniers et les lys tropicaux sont ici dans leur élément et le jardinier doit sans cesse les tailler pour qu'ils n'engloutissent pas les allées et les murs du jardin.

Oben: Ein Gästezimmer wird durch ein antikes Bett im englischen Kolonialstil verschönert. Die Sommer können selbst hier an Sri Lankas Südwestküste sehr heiß werden; deshalb sind die Böden im ganzen Haus mit kühlen Fliesen ausgelegt und die Wände in einem beruhigenden Weiß gestrichen.
Rechts: Im Schattenplatz neben der Küche lässt sich selbst an heißesten Januartagen das Mittagessen zubereiten. Bougainvillea, Frangipani und tropische Lilien sind hier in ihrem Element und die Hauptaufgabe des Gärtners ist oft das Zurückschneiden, Stutzen und Zähmen der Flora, damit der Garten nicht Wände und Wege überwuchert.

A House with a View

Rottnest Island, Australia

Perth, en Australie occidentale, est sans doute le point le plus extrême où l'on puisse aller avant de tomber dans l'Antarctique. Séparée de Sydney et de Melbourne par un continent, la ville jouit d'une saine nonchalance et d'un tempérament ensoleillé bien à elle. A vingt minutes de ferry se trouve Rottnest Island, Mecque des plongeurs qui raffolent de ses lagons protégés et de ses récifs peu profonds. Sur la côte ouest de Rottnest Island, l'océan Indien façonne de ces vagues vertigineuses dont rêvent les surfeurs. Les nageurs et les plongeurs sont attirés par les baies sablonneuses et les criques tranquilles de cette île calcaire de onze kilomètres de long. C'est également un paradis pour les écologistes. La faune et la flore y sont protégées, les voitures y sont proscrites et la bicyclette y est le principal mode de transport. Rottnest, «nid de rats» en néerlandais, doit son nom à un marin hollandais, Willem Vlamingh, qui, en 1696, prit ses habitants marsupiaux, les quokkas, pour de gros rats.

Perth, Western Australia, is about as far as you can wander without stubbing your toe on Antarctica. A continent away from Sydney and Melbourne, Perth has its own casual vibe and sunny attitude. Just a quick 20-minute ferry ride away lies Rottnest Island, a mecca for the world's skin-divers, who prize its protected lagoons and shallow reefs. On the western shores of Rottnest Island, Indian Ocean swells create the powerful waves surfers dream about. Swimmers and snorkelers are drawn to the sandy bays and quiet coves of the eleven-kilometer-long limestone island. It's heaven for ecologists, too. The native flora and wildlife are protected, so the island is completely free of cars, and bicycles are the transportation mode of choice. Rottnest – Dutch for rat's nest – got its name in 1696 when Dutch mariner Willem Vlamingh mistook the marsupial inhabitants, quokkas, for large rats.

Perth, Westaustralien. Viel weiter kommt man nicht, ohne dass man mit dem großen Zeh bereits an die Antarktis stößt. Diese Stadt liegt auf einem anderen Kontinent als Sydney und Melbourne, hat ihren eigenen lässigen Stil und ein sonniges Gemüt. Nur 20 Minuten dauert die Überfahrt per Fähre von Perth nach Rottnest Island, einem Mekka für Taucher aus der ganzen Welt, die die geschützten Lagunen und niedrigen Riffe dieser Insel schätzen. An der Westküste von Rottnest Island bildet der Indische Ozean die riesigen Wellen, von denen Surfer träumen. Wer lieber schwimmt oder schnorchelt, findet Gefallen an den Sandbuchten und ruhigen Strandnischen der elf Kilometer langen Insel aus Kalkstein. Auch für Umweltschützer ist die Insel ein wahres Paradies. Flora und Fauna stehen unter Naturschutz, die Insel ist autofreie Zone und man bewegt sich am besten mit dem Fahrrad vorwärts. Der Inselname stammt aus dem Holländischen und bedeutet »Rattennest«, denn 1696 hatte der holländische Seefahrer Willem Vlamingh die heimischen Beuteltiere, die Quokkas, irrtümlich für große Ratten gehalten.

First pages: A beach house on Rottnest Island, designed by film production designer Larry Eastwood, stands like a beach pavilion on the edge of the Indian Ocean. Locals say the reef fish on view rival the Technicolor aquatic ballets of the Great Barrier Reef.
Previous pages and right: Pivoting shutters protect the interior from sunlight and summer breezes. A series of Matisse-influenced, seaweed-inspired cut-outs are both decorative and functional, allowing breezes to cool the air.
Below: the open-plan living room.

Première double page: La maison conçue par le décorateur de cinéma Larry Eastwood, se dresse tel un pavillon de plage au bord de l'océan Indien. Les gens du coin affirment que les ébats des poissons du récif rivalisent avec les ballets aquatiques en Technicolor de la Grande Barrière de Corail.
Double page précédente et à droite: Des volets pivotants protègent l'intérieur du soleil et des brises de l'été. La frise découpée de formes d'algues, inspirée des collages de Matisse, est à la fois décorative et fonctionnelle: les jours laissent filtrer les brises fraîches qui aèrent la maison.
Ci-dessous: la salle de séjour ouverte aux éléments.

Eingangsseiten: ein Strandhaus auf Rottnest Island, entworfen von dem Filmproduktionsdesigner Larry Eastwood. Wie ein Strandpavillon steht es am Rand des Indischen Ozeans. Die Einheimischen behaupten, das die Rifffische, die man hier zu sehen bekommt, dem Technicolor-Wasserballett des Great Barrier Reef in nichts nachstehen.
Vorhergehende Doppelseite und rechts: Schwingflügelläden schützen das Hausinnere vor Sonnenlicht und Sommerbrisen. Das Schnitzwerk, das an Matisse und an Meeresalgen erinnert, ist gleichzeitig dekorativ und funktionell: So wird die Luft durch den Windzug abgekühlt.
Unten: das offen konzipierte Wohnzimmer.

Above: This mirage-of-a-residence was used in 1997 as a set for the feature film "Under the Lighthouse Dancing". Airy and bright, this corner of the house feels as if it had cast off and floated away on the waves. Eastwood set a perforated metal-and-teak counter between the kitchen and the dining area and designed a ceiling-mounted open-shelf system for essential storage. The chairs and the dining table were painted to look as if the sun had faded the indigo coloring.
Right: Just a few light-diffusing shutters lie between the bathroom and the beach beyond.

Ci-dessus: Cette maison mirage a servi en 1997 de décor au film «Under the Lighthouse Dancing» du réalisateur australien Graeme Rattigan. Aéré et clair, cet endroit de la maison semble avoir flotté sur la mer avant d'échouer sur le sable. Eastwood a installé un comptoir en métal perforé et en teck entre la cuisine et le coin repas. Il a aussi dessiné les étagères suspendues pour ranger les ustensiles de cuisine. Les chaises dépareillées et la table étaient peintes dans un ton indigo qui semble avoir été décoloré par le soleil.
A droite: Seuls quelques volets laissant filtrer la lumière séparent la salle de bains de la plage.

Oben: Dieser Wohnsitz, der 1997 als Kulisse für den Spielfilm »Under the Lighthouse Dancing« diente, gleicht fast einer Fata Morgana. In dieser hellen, luftigen Ecke des Hauses hat man das Gefühl, als gleite das Haus auf den Wellen dahin. Mit einer Theke aus perforiertem Metall und Teakholz trennte Eastwood Koch- und Essbereich. Auch das an der Decke verankerte Regalsystem zum Verstauen der wichtigsten Dinge stammt von Eastwood. Das Indigoblau der Stühle und des Esstischs wirkt ganz bewusst wie ausgebleicht.
Rechts: Nur einige Fensterläden, die das Sonnenlicht abfangen, trennen das Badezimmer vom Meer.

Shoei Yoh

Kyushu Island, Japan, Korea Strait

Seul un visionnaire n'ayant pas froid aux yeux tel que l'architecte néo-moderniste Shoei Yoh pouvait oser construire sa maison dans un tel lieu. Celle-ci semble avoir été simplement déposée là, à une quarantaine de kilomètres au sud de la ville de Fukuoka, sur l'île de Kyushu. Cette propriété spectaculaire, qui faisait autrefois partie d'une exploitation agricole, s'étend au bord de falaises qui dominent le détroit accidenté de Corée et, au loin, la mer du Japon. Rocheuse et isolée, elle est exposée aux tempêtes et aux vents tonitruants de l'hiver, ce qui n'a pas dissuadé Yoh, professeur d'architecture et d'urbanisme, d'opter pour l'acier et le verre. Les baies vitrées, dont la plupart vont du sol au plafond, sont unies par des joints invisibles en silicone. La maison semble flotter entre ciel et terre, tel un voilier. Deux dalles en béton verticales soutiennent deux dalles en acier horizontales, ce qui permet à la structure de saillir au-dessus du vide. Yoh a accentué la transparence de la façade qui donne sur la mer en tapissant les sols et les terrasses de marbre blanc. Le mobilier datant du milieu du siècle met en valeur la géométrie précise de cette architecture hors du temps.

Perhaps only a visionary and fearless architect designing for himself could place his house so boldly and yet so lightly on the land. Neomodernist Japanese architect Shoei Yoh chose to build his own residence 40 kilometers from the southern Japanese city of Fukuoka on the island of Kyushu. His dramatic property, formerly part of a farm, stands high on cliffs overlooking the rugged Korea Strait and the distant Sea of Japan. The location was challenging. Rocky and remote, it is subject to winter storms and buffeting winds. Yoh, a professor of architecture and urban design, nonetheless chose to build in glass and steel. The panels of glass, many of them reaching from floor to ceiling, are joined together seamlessly by silicone. And so this house seems to float between land and sea, like a sailboat. A pair of vertical concrete slabs were used to suspend two horizontal steel slabs, allowing the house to project out over the cliff. Yoh emphasized the gleaming transparency of the ocean-facing side of the house, by covering the floors and an open-air terrace with polished white marble.

Wohl nur ein ganz und gar furchtloser und visionärer Architekt, der für sich selbst baut, könnte sein Haus auf so kühne und gleichzeitig leichtfüßige Art errichten. Der neomoderne japanische Architekt Shoei Yoh suchte sich die Insel Kyushu aus, 40 Kilometer von der südjapanischen Stadt Fukuoka gelegen. Das spektakuläre Grundstück, früher Teil eines Bauernhofs, liegt hoch auf einer Klippe über der wilden Korea-straße mit Blick auf das dahinter liegende Japanische Meer. Das felsige, abgelegene Gebiet ist Winterstürmen und starken Windstößen ausgesetzt. Dennoch wählte Yoh, Professor für Architektur und Städtebau, Glas und Stahl als Baumaterialien. Die Glasscheiben, die vom Boden bis zur Decke reichen, wurden mit Silikon nahtlos aneinander gesetzt. Dadurch wirkt das Haus, als würde es zwischen Land und Wasser schweben wie ein Segelboot. Zwei horizontale Stahlplatten werden von zwei vertikalen Betonplatten getragen, so dass das Haus über die Klippe hinausragt. Die schimmernde Transparenz der dem Ozean zugewandten Hausseite betonte Yoh durch polierten weißen Marmor, mit dem die Böden und die Terrasse ausgelegt sind.

Kyushu Island, Japan, Korea Strait 33°45'N 130°30'E

Shoei Yoh

Previous pages: On the island of Kyushu, Japan, Professor Yoh's week-end house is suspended on a steep hill, 140 meters above sea level.
Above: Furniture in the west-facing rooms is pared-down and low-profile. Colors are subdued and secondary to the views. In severe winter weather, sea breezes spatter the windows with sea salt, which Yoh insists only makes the views more spectacular and immediate.
Right: The south side has a swimming pool, enclosed between concrete walls. Pierced walls offer glimpses of trees and hillsides.

Double page précédente: Sur l'île de Kyushu, au Japon, la maison de week-end du professeur Yoh est suspendue au sommet d'une colline escarpée, 140 mètres au-dessus du niveau de la mer.
Ci-dessus: Le mobilier des pièces orientées à l'ouest est simple et discret. Les couleurs sont étouffées, s'effaçant devant le panorama. Lors des tempêtes hivernales, les vents projettent des cristaux de sel sur les vitres, ce qui, selon Yoh, rend la vue encore plus spectaculaire et immédiate.
A droite: Côté sud, la piscine est abritée derrière des murs de béton. A travers les ouvertures dans les murs, on aperçoit les arbres et les collines.

Vorhergehende Doppelseite: Das Wochenendhaus von Professor Yoh hängt an einem steil abfallenden Berg, 140 Meter über dem Meeresspiegel, auf der japanischen Insel Kyushu.
Oben: In den gen Westen ausgerichteten Zimmern ist die Einrichtung sparsam und unauffällig. Auch die Farben ordnen sich dem Ausblick unter. In besonders stürmischen Wintern spritzt das Meerwasser gegen die Fenster – das macht den Ausblick für Yoh nur noch atemberaubender und unmittelbarer.
Rechts: Auf der Südseite liegt, eingeschlossen zwischen Betonmauern, ein Pool. Durchbrüche geben den Blick auf Bäume und Hügel frei.